Who Didn't See This Coming?

THE CONTINUING CONSEQUENCES OF THE SEXUAL REVOLUTION OF THE 1960s

JERRY D. LOCKE

Who Didn't See This Coming?

THE CONTINUING CONSEQUENCES OF THE SEXUAL REVOLUTION OF THE 1960s

JERRY D. LOCKE

All Scriptures are taken from the King James Bible.

Cover Design
Sarah Coats
www.belovedpaper.com

ISBN# 978-1-61119-230-8

Printed in the United States of America.

Printed by Calvary Publishing
A Ministry of Parker Memorial Baptist Church
1902 East Cavanaugh Road
Lansing, Michigan 48910
www.CalvaryPublishing.org

Contents

Dedication....................7

Prologue....................9

Introduction....................15

1960s Timleine....................22

Part I: Looking Back

1. The Sexual Revolution of the 1960s *29*

Part II: Looking Around

2. The Hippies of the 1960s are Today's Grandparents and They and Their Children are the Politicians Now Shaping America *53*

3. Satan is Alive and Well in America *79*

4. The Insanity of the Modern Non-Thinking "Reprobate Mind" *117*

5. The Mystery of Morality.................... *143*

6. The Shameless Super-Sexualization of Children *167*

7. The Civil Rights vs. Gay Rights Debate.................... *201*

8. The Bible Had Human Sexuality Right All Along ..239

9. Reclaiming Biblical Manhood in an Age of Radical Feminism 265

10. Living a "G" Rated Life in an "X" Rated World ...295

Part III: Looking Ahead

11. Coming to a Church Near You 323

12. Things Aren't Coming Apart, They're Coming Together 349

Bibliography 369

Other Books Available 385

Dedication

To my beloved grandchildren who are called to live boldly for Christ in this new America

QUINTON RYAN LOCKE
Graduating from University of Texas Tyler 2021

ANNA GRACE "GRACIE" JOHNSON
Graduating from Oklahoma University Norman 2022

JAMES GATLIN JOHNSON
Graduating from Aledo High School 2021

Prologue

Born in the 1940s, Grew up in the 1950s, Became an Adult in the 1960s

I was born in 1945, grew up in the 1950s and graduated from high school, married, graduated from Bible college, pastored my first full-time church and had our first child in the 1960s, and am now living in my ninth decade. It is a shock to me, too.

As a child, both of my biological parents were always present – even when I didn't want them to be. My dad was a pastor and was up early each day at his church office devoting his mornings to studying the Bible for the three sermons he preached each week for 37 years. My mom was a full-time homemaker – cooking, cleaning, sewing, ironing, etc. (and there were a lot of "etcs"). We lived in a neighborhood that was safe. We roamed the nearby open fields, fished the lake around the corner, rode our bikes, walked to school when necessary, played sandlot baseball and football – all generally unsupervised. When it came to meals at our house we didn't have "Take Out," we only had "Take it or Leave it" (really, we were not allowed to leave it). We lived in a house without air-conditioning. The windows were left open at night with nothing but a screen between us and the world outside. We eventually moved up in the world when we got water-cooled window fans. I had two older brothers – enough said. No, seriously, we did things together without our parents smothering us – fishing, hunting (starting with

Daisy Ryder BB guns which we occasionally used against each other) and working on and loving cars. My brothers and I shared a bedroom until we were older. None of us were exceptional in school, so I didn't have high expectations to live up to other than perfect attendance. The iPad I took to elementary school was a Big Chief tablet that worked well with a #2 pencil. To brighten things up, we had a 16 pack of Crayola Crayons. At public school every morning we would be led in the Pledge of Allegiance to the flag over the speakers from the principal's office, followed by a prayer, usually read by a student. The prayer wasn't deeply spiritual or theological, but it did say something, didn't it?

We didn't have two moms or two dads, or a mom and no dad or a dad and no mom. As I wrote earlier, we only had our biological parents for all our lives. I saw real masculinity and real femininity on display 24-7-365. My mom didn't bring a parade of boyfriends through our house. My dad didn't fool around with other women behind my mom's back. I never had to hear, "Jerry, your mother and I still love you; we just don't love each other anymore." I am certain that my parents had major disagreements about "stuff," but to my memory (and it's still pretty good) there was not a single open blow-up in front of us boys – ever. This alone gave us reason to never doubt that they were going to be married for life. We were never dragged to family court to appear before a judge to determine who got who, or who stayed with whom. There was no family violence other than an occasional brotherly fight or dad or mom applying "the board of education to the seat of knowledge." Were we ever in trouble? Plenty! But our parents never gave up on us – although we gave them plenty of reasons to do so.

Our family pictures included our entire family – Al, Mary, Al Jr., David and me. We also cherish the photos that included my grandparents. As I think about it, dad's family and mom's family were all very similar.

We spent vacations and holidays together as a family.

We went to church every week for every service. My dad was the preacher and my mom played the piano or organ. My two brothers and I made up "the Locke Trio" and were pretty exceptional in our day. We travelled with our parents on regular summer revival meetings – dad preaching, mom playing the piano and us boys singing. What amazes some is it did not make us hate church.

There was limited exposure to television because there were only three stations – NBC, ABC, and CBS. There was no color, no cable, no remote control, and no cussing.

My brother, David, once reminded me that *I* am the reason he doesn't have a sister. I quickly reminded him that *he* is the reason mom and dad had me!

As boys we had minimal chores – make up our bed each day, keep our room reasonably clean and wash the dishes after supper for mom. It's one of the reasons I know I am wanted. Mom had Al to wash the dishes and

David to rinse; they needed me to finish the process to dry. Eventually, us boys saved enough money to buy mom a portable dishwasher that hooked up to the kitchen faucet. There is no denying it was a very self-serving gift, but it got us out of the kitchen.

Dad never bought any of us a car, nor a gallon of gas (at 19 cents), or liability insurance. We were taught to work, save and buy what we had enough money to buy.

My, how things have changed in the last sixty years.

The days of our youth were so different.

None of my family or extended family ever had any sexual identity issues or gender dysphoria. None of us ever came out of the closet, except after a tornado threat. None of us have or are considering transitioning to another sexual identity. None of us ever remember a homosexual-lesbian club in high school. None of us had gender-neutral bathrooms or locker rooms. None of us remember someone imposing their minority sexual preferences upon the majority. None of us doubted the obvious difference between males and females. None of us were assaulted by the relentless LGBTQ propaganda. None of us could imagine men having sex with men or women having sex with women; it didn't make sense to us biologically. None of us remember teenage pregnancies as the norm, but as the exception. None of us remember women in military combat or female police officers. None of us remember legal abortions. None of us remember teachers or coaches sexually assaulting students. None of us remember same-sex marriages. None of us remember many people "shacking up." None of us remember "no-fault" divorces. None of us remember day-cares. None of us remember technology manufacturing babies. None of us remember Child Protective services. None of us remember family or child psychologists. None of us remember families looking like they do today.

Thankfully, I was not a victim of the Sexual Revolution of the 1960s. That's not to say that I have been unaffected by it. The fallout of the "liberation" came slowly and deliberately in the decades that have followed. I have lived to see the sad moral decay of the America in which my grandchildren must live, marry and raise their children. It is for them, Quinton, Gracie and Gatlin, and the countless Gen Xs (1965-1976), Millennials (Gen Y 1977-1995), and Centennials (Gen Z 1996 to present) that I offer this book.

I am aware that in writing this book there may be some price to pay. I will likely be warned that I will end up being on "the wrong side of history." My greater concern is that when I stand before my Lord and Savior I will have been on "the right side of the Bible."

Jerry D. Locke
Fort Worth, Texas
July 2020

Introduction

You may have heard the story of a woman who was involved in a bad accident. It looked for certain that she would die. Suddenly an angel appeared and promised that regardless of how bad things looked she would live another 25 years. She was in the hospital for weeks but made a full recovery. During her last days in the hospital she decided to take advantage of her promised new life, so she stayed a little longer having a face lift, tummy tuck, and liposuction-shaped hips. On the day of her release she had on a beautiful new dress to show-off her new figure, a stunning make-up job on her new face, and a spring in her step as she walked out of the hospital feeling great about her future. She stepped off the curb onto the street just outside the hospital and was hit by a huge truck and killed on the spot. She immediately arrived at the Pearly Gates and angrily asked her guardian angel how this could have happened since she had been promised another twenty-five years. The embarrassed angel said, "Well, the truth is, I didn't recognize you."

Most of us can hardly recognize the America we once knew or the one of which we have heard. What has happened to her? Some of us have lived to see a complete make-over of America and it is a totally botched job. In my youthful day there was a national *Christian consensus*, call it a general *Christendom* if you like. In the decades that followed, it quickly moved to a *post-Christian* era. Now in the second decade of the twenty-first century, America is trying to survive against a full-blown *anti-Christian* assault.

The Sexual Revolution did not begin at once like a Tsunami overpowering everything in its path but was more like the daily tide that eventually causes significant erosion. At first, the revolution was not a raging fire; it was more like termites silently, but strategically, eating away destroying the structure of the American culture.

Christian Theologian-Philosopher Francis Schaeffer (1912-1984) wrote thirty-five years ago, "Having turned away from the knowledge given by God, the Christian influence on the whole culture has been lost. In Europe, including England, it took many years – in the United States only a few decades. In the United State, in the short span from the twenties to the sixties, we have seen a complete shift. Ours is a post-Christian world in which Christianity, not only in the number of Christians but in cultural emphasis and cultural results, is no longer the consensus or ethos of our society." Then he warned, "Do not take this lightly! It is a horrible thing for a man like myself to look back and see my country and my culture go down the drain in my own lifetime."[1]

Southern Seminary President Albert Mohler, Jr. (1959-) has concluded, "I would argue that no moral revolution on this scale has ever been experienced by a society that remained intact."[2]

---

[1] Francis A. Schaeffer, *The Great Evangelical Disaster*, pp. 28-29.

[2] Albert Mohler, *Southern Seminary Winter 2014*, Vol. 82, No. 1.

Richard Land (1946-), former Ethics and Religious Liberty Commission of the Southern Baptist Convention, now President of Southern Evangelical Seminary believes, "The number one battle line now, and for the next decade, for the soul and conscience of America is the struggle over sexuality. The issues are clear and compelling. We must either reassert Judeo-Christian values or be submerged in a polluted sea of pagan sexuality."[3] He would later insist, "Frankly, the sexual revolution has done more damage to the country than anything ever has."[4]

R. C. Sproul (1939-2017) observed, "The most far-reaching, epochal revolution in American history began about fifty years ago and is now reaching its zenith. No war has been fought in terms of military conflict, but this revolution has killed millions of unborn people. Approximately three thousand lives, in fact, will be lost to this revolution before midnight tonight. And this number does not include the revolution's other casualties. Bodies will be mutilated in the name of 'changing' one's gender. Sexually transmitted diseases will sterilize, leave lasting physical and emotional scars, and even pronounce death sentences on men and women. Young women will get pregnant and be abandoned, leaving them to raise children in fatherless homes. Pornography will warp people's views of sex and relationships. I'm talking about the sexual revolution, which has wrought far more changes to the

---

[3] Richard Land, Brochure for a conference on *The Family and Human Sexuality,* Ethics and Religious Liberty Commission, 1998.

[4] Billy Graham Evangelistic Association, *The High Cost of "Free Love,"* Feb. 2, 2017.

cultural behavior of America than the War of Independence fought against England in the eighteenth century. This sexual revolution is a war that's been fought not against any earthly king but against the King of the cosmos, the Lord Himself. It's a war with roots that stretch much further back than the sixties—to Eden, when Adam and Eve joined Satan's cosmic revolt."[5]

Syndicated Columnist Cal Thomas (1942-), wrote about the 1960s, "In any revolution—political, or the sexual one championed by those like Hefner and Brown—there are casualties. No one wants to talk about the casualties of the sexual revolution because that wouldn't sell magazines or seduce a new generation of young people. Sex sells, but it also brings misery when it's misused."[6]

Dr. Jennifer R. Morse (1953-) reminds us, "The way we think about sex and childbearing and the decisions we choose to make constitute the genuine revolution."[7]

A & E's, History Channel proclaimed in their book, *1960s -The Decade that Changed a Nation,* "Just as the events of the 60s couldn't have been forecast, neither could the duration of its aftershocks have been predicted. The progress of the decade is a nagging

---

[5] R. C. Sproul, www.ligonier.org/learn/articles/revolution-enslaves/ January 1, 2017.

[6] www.billygraham.org/decision-magazine/february-2015/the-high-cost-of-free-love.

[7] Jennifer R. Morris, *The Sexual State*, p. 34

reminder of work unfinished."[8] One wonders what "progress" was made in the 1960s in their view. It probably doesn't match the "aftershocks" which began changing America.

Jim Daly (1961-), head of Focus on the Family, affirms, "Human sexuality is a beautiful and powerful thing, but it was designed to be practiced within the confines of a monogamous marital relationship. The belief is considered outdated in much of society today. Yet, in light of the cultural destruction and dysfunction we currently see, can a fair-minded person disagree that we are reaping the whirlwind sown by the Sexual Revolution and the abandonment of basic values."[9]

Seminary ethics professor Daniel R. Heimbach (1951-) warns, "Evangelicals must understand that total sexual revolution in America is not coincidental but is a carefully planned strategy called 'deconstruction' that is being developed by those wanting to redefine, redesign, and reconstruct every institution in America (marriage, family, law, politics, business, defense, entertainment, education and religion) from top to bottom. They know and understand that once sexual morality changes, the whole social system has to be completely redefined." [10]

The recent book by Stephen Baskerville (1957-), *The New Politics of Sex,* asserts, "The Sexual Revolution, it is now apparent, has been about much more than simply

---

[8] A & E History Channel, *The 1960s, The Decade That Changed a Nation,* p. 94.

[9] Jim Daly, *The Sexual Assault Scandals are a Consequence of the Sexual Revolution,* Daly Focus, Dec. 6, 2017.

[10] Daniel R. Heimbach, *True Sexual Morality,* 2004, p. 40.

discarding sexual inhibitions and restrictions. Like all revolutions, it has been driven from the start by revolutionaries seeking power. Feminists and more recently homosexual political activities have now positioned themselves at the vanguard of left-wing politics, shifting the political discourse from the economic and racial to the social and increasingly the sexual."[11]

The former Solicitor General of the United States and United States Court of Appeals judge Robert H. Bork (1927-) connected the "then" with the "now." "It is important to understand what the Sixties turmoil was about, for the youth culture that became manifest then is the modern liberal culture of today. Where that culture will take us next may be impossible to say, but it is also impossible even to make an informed guess without understanding the forces let loose by that decade that changed America."[12]

The sexual revolution of the 1960s "succeeded wildly" and "failed miserably." In the decades that have followed we have seen the high cost of low living. There is always a payday for every heyday!

Is anyone paying attention?

Where are we presently in this supposed liberation of the American culture from the old ways that have presumably held us captive for too long? The litmus test for those who desire to be among the "in" and "elite"

---

[11] Stephen Baskerville, *The New Politics of Sex*, p. 13.
[12] Robert H. Bork, *Sloughing Toward Gomorrah*, p. 17.

crowd is the demand that there are no "off limits" when it comes to sexuality and that everyone must join in the open celebration of deviant sexuality – all without discussion or debate. End of conversation.

The purpose of this book is to engage the conversation, not rail against those who are captured by their sinful misbehavior. All Americans can choose to live as unlawfully as they wish, but a sexually deviant minority should not be free to redefine life, marriage and behavior for everyone else. My goal is to sound an alarm that will challenge Christians and conservative churches to awake to the new norm in which younger generations must now live.

It is pointless to attempt to reclaim America. We are living in an anti-Christian culture. We should not spend our time and efforts on moral reform. All that would do is send good people to Hell. The compassionate proclaiming of the sinfulness of mankind and the saving message of Jesus Christ alone is what is needed. I agree with Peter R. Jones (1940-) who believes "nothing short of a spiritual revival can stop the rot."[13]

Join me in this historical and biblical journey by first *looking back* at the 1960s, then by *looking around* at modern America, and finishing by *looking ahead* to see how all history will end.

---

[13] Peter R. Jones, *Biblical Foundations for Manhood and Womanhood*, p. 271.

1960s Timeline

1960

- The Greensboro, North Carolina sit in by young black Americans at a segregated Woolworth's lunch counter and refused to leave after being denied service.
- The Pill, a contraceptive preventing pregnancy that in just two years 1.8 million women were using.
- The United States sent 3,500 U.S. troops to Vietnam.
- The first Playboy Club opened by Hugh Hefner (1926-2017).
- The television was introduced to the American home in the 50's, by the 1960s were in 52 to 60 million American homes.

1962

- *Sex and the Single Girl,* authored by Helen Gurley Brown was released.
- Rachel Carson's (1907-1964) *The Silent Spring* made her case for the urgent need to protect the environment.
- The Cuban Missile Crises occurred in October.
- Sam Walton (1918-1982) opened his first Wal-Mart located in Arkansas.
- Marilyn Monroe (1926-1962) died at age 36.

1963

- Betty Friedan (1921-2006) wrote *The Feminine Mystique,* a critique of the role of women in society.
- CBS and NBC expanded their evening news programs from 15 to 30 minutes.
- June 17, the Supreme Court of the United States ruled in Abington School District vs. Schempp that laws requiring the recitation of the Lord's Prayer or Bible verses in public schools was unconstitutional in a vote of 8 to 1.
- The first artificial heart transplant was performed by Dr. Michael E. DeBakey (1908-2008).
- The U.S. began using Zip Codes for mail.
- The March on Washington for jobs and freedom had 250,000 people participating.
- November 22, the assassination of President John F. Kennedy (1917-1963) was widely covered on television.
- The murder of presumed presidential assassin Lee Harvey Oswald (1939-1963) was covered live of television.

1964

- The Beatles appeared on the Ed Sullivan Show in February.
- July 2, the Civil Rights Act outlawed discrimination based on race, color, religion, sex, or national origin.
- Martin Luther King Jr. (1929-1968) was awarded the Nobel Prize.

1965

- March 8, 1965, President Lyndon Johnson (1908-1973) sought congressional approval for direct U.S. involvement in Vietnam, resulting in the deaths of more than 58,000 American soldiers.
- August 11, race riot erupted in the Watts section of Las Angeles, leaving 34 people dead and property destruction exceeding $200 million.
- The Voters Rights Act outlawed discriminatory voting practices, including literacy tests as a prerequisite to vote.
- Mary Quant (1934-) designed the mini-skirt in London and it became a fashion craze.
- The car culture explosion led to suburban flight and urban decay.
- Medicare for the elderly and Medicaid for the poor became law.
- The 8-track tape, developed by Learjet Corporation, housed in its plastic cartridge a continuous loop of magnetic tape that held a total of — you guessed it — 8 tracks.

1966

- January 1, by law all US cigarette packs began carrying the warning: "Caution! Cigarette smoking may be hazardous to your health."
- NOW (National Organization for Women) began, whose stated purpose was to "bring women into full participation in the mainstream of American society."

1967

- Rolling Stone published its first magazine issue.
- Dr. Timothy Leary (1920-1996), Harvard psychologist, advocated the use of LSD - "Tune in, turn on, drop out."
- Cassius Clay (aka Muhmmad Ali) (1942-2016) refused his draft notice as a "conscientious objector."
- In July, black riots in Newark, New Jersey resulted in 26 killed, 1,500 injured and 1,000 arrested; in Detroit, 40 killed, 2,000 injured, and 5,000 left homeless. The riots were eventually stopped by over 12,500 Federal troopers and National Guardsmen.

1968

- The television news program, *60 Minutes*, began.
- April 4, was the assassination of Martin Luther King Jr. (1929-1968) in Memphis, Tennessee, by James Earl Ray.
- June 6, was the assassination of Robert F. Kennedy (1925-1968) in Los Angeles, California, by Sirhan Sirhan

1969

- Andy Warhol's (1928-1987) *Blue Movie,* an adult film depicting explicit sex debuted.
- The police raided Stonewall Inn in Greenwich Village, galvanizing homosexual activism.
- On July 24, Apollo 11 landed on the Moon with three U.S. astronauts.

- August 15-18, Woodstock Music Festival, held at a dairy farm in Bethel, New York, hosted 400,000 hippies at what was billed as "an Aquarian Exposition: 3 Days of Peace & *Music*" and featured such acts as Janis Joplin, Jimi Hendrix, Jefferson Airplane, and The Who.
- President Richard Nixon (1913-1994) was the first to use the term "silent majority."
- The internet, called Arpanet, was invented by Advanced Research Projects Agency at the U.S. Department of Defense.
- The popular children's television show "Sesame Street" debuted.
- Native Americans occupied Alcatraz, though failing to gain title to the former prison, and inspired the native American movement.

Part I: Looking Back

- 1 -

The Sexual Revolution of the 1960s

Come gather 'round people wherever you roam
And admit that the waters around you have grown
And accept it that soon you'll be drenched to the bone
If your time to you is worth savin'
Then you better start swimmin' or you'll sink like a stone
For the times they are a-changin'

Come writers and critics, prophesize with your pen
And keep your eyes wide, the chance won't come again
And don't speak too soon for the wheel's still in spin
And there's no tellin' who that it's namin'
For the loser now will be later to win
For the times, they are a-changin'

Come senators, congressmen, please heed the call
Don't stand in the doorway, don't block up the hall
For he that gets hurt will be he who has stalled
There's a battle outside and it's ragin'
It will soon shake your windows and rattle your walls
For the times they are a-changin'

Come mothers and fathers throughout the land
And don't criticize what you can't understand
Your sons and your daughters are beyond your command
Your old road is rapidly agin'

So get out of the new one if you can't lend your hand
For the times they are a-changin'

The line it is drawn, the curse it is cast
The slow one now will later be fast
As the present now will later be past
The order is rapidly fadin'
And the first one now will later be last
For the times they are a-changin'

Bob Dylan
October 24, 1963

The 1960s

To quote the famed author Charles Dickens, who wrote a century before about France, the 1960s in America were in many ways "... it was the best of times, it was the worst of times, it was the age of wisdom, it was the age of foolishness, it was the epoch of belief, it was the epoch of incredulity, it was the season of light, it was the season of darkness, it was the spring of hope, it was the winter of despair, we had everything before us, we had nothing before us, we were all going direct to Heaven, we were all going direct the other way."[1]

The 1960s were about long hair and short skirts, polyester bell-bottomed pants, psychedelic clothes, and go-go boots. It was a decade when little girls had Barbie dolls and the little boys had G.I. Joe action figures. It was a decade of assassinations and anti-authority protests. It was the decade we kicked God out of public

---

[1] Charles Dickens, *A Tale of Two Cities,* 1859.

schools – no more prayer, no more Bible reading. It was the decade of segregation and desegregation. It was the decade of wars and rumors of wars – Vietnam and the Cuba Missile Crises. It was a decade of shag carpet and avocado green and harvest gold kitchen appliances. It was the decade of the Polaroid instant camera and mimeograph machines. It was the decade of the first Playboy Club and the first Walmart. It was the decade of Elvis Presley, the Beatles, and Woodstock. It was the decade of muscle cars and eight-track tapes. It was the decade of race riots in Watts California, Newark New Jersey, and Detroit Michigan. It was the decade of drugs – "tune in, turn on, drop out." It was the decade of suburban flight and blight. It was the decade of "the pill" and the first artificial heart transplant. It was the decade when the television was on the way into every American home and conversation was on the way out. It was the decade of the start of Medicare and "Moon landings." It was the decade that forever changed America.

The Beatnik

The beatniks were a media stereotype prevalent throughout the late 1940s, 1950s to mid-1960s that displayed the more superficial aspects of the Beat Generation literary movement of the late 1940s and early to mid-1950s. "The Many Lives of Dobie Gillis" featuring Bob Denver depicted that era.

"Beatnik" was a term coined by *San Francisco Chronicle* columnist Herb Caen in April 1958. It was a play on "Sputnik," Earth's first space satellite which had gone up in October 1957. Caen used the term to refer to "over 250 bearded cats and kits" "slopping up" free booze at a party sponsored by *Look* magazine. Like the more popular *Life* magazine, *Look* was obsessed with photographic spreads of beatniks.

The years between 1957 and 1960 marked the "the acceptance of the beatnik dissent and the emergence of a fad: a cultural protest transformed into a commodity," writes historian Stephen Petrus. There was fashion: loose sweaters, leotards, tight black pants, berets, and sunglasses were all the rage. There were spaces: coffee houses, cellar nightclubs, and espresso shops opened to meet the new demand. New York City even had a "Rent-A-Beatnik" service, where you could order up a poetry-reading/music-playing cool cat or cool chick for your event; sandals and bongos were available options.

The popular cultural responses to the beatniks ran from denunciation to tolerance to imitation. The 1960 Republican Convention featured J. Edgar Hoover proclaiming that "Communists, Eggheads, and Beatniks" were the country's great enemies. Some Americans associated beatniks with drugs, delinquency, and un-Americanism.

Then again, as Petrus writes, "the original beatniks themselves became a tourist attraction" in San Francisco's North Beach. There was even a political American Beat Party, which nominated a Presidential candidate in 1960. Words like "cool," "crazy," "dig," and "like," entered the general American lexicon.[2]

The Hippies

Michael Fallon started a series of stories for the *San Francisco Examiner* in 1965, introducing the word "hippie" to its readers. Fallon's articles describe the migration from North Beach to Haight-Ashbury to search for cheaper rent. Some popular hippie hangouts were like the notorious Blue Unicorn. While Fallon's articles were widely read, the term "hippie" would not be mainstream until 1967.

A teenage participant in the 1960s hippie movement gave his firsthand appraisal. "I was there. It was an amazing place to be as a teenager. Hippie Hill, The Fillmore, I and Thou Coffee House, The Straight Theater, Pacific Ocean Trading Poster Gallery, The Family Dog, good acid and thousands and thousands of young people shaking off the armor of the sexual repression slapped on them by their parents, priests and preachers."

A "hippy" was someone who was "hip." Someone who was "mod" was "modern."

The "Flower Children," a synonym for hippies, were the idealistic young people who gathered in San Francisco and the surrounding area during the Summer of Love in 1967. It was the custom of "flower children" to wear and

---

[2] Stephen Petrus, *Rumblings of Discontent: American Popular Culture and its Response to the Beat Generation, 1957-1960,* Studies in Popular Culture, Vol. 20, No. 1, October 1997, pp. 1-17. https://daily.jstor.org/how-the-beat-generation-became-beatniks/)

distribute flowers or floral-themed decorations to symbolize ideals of universal belonging, peace, and love. The mass media picked up on the term and used it to refer in a broad sense to any hippie. Flower children were also associated with the flower power political movement, which originated in ideas written by Allen Ginsberg in 1965.

The Parents of the Hippies

With the end of World War II, most American families were enjoying personal prosperity like they had never known. Theirs was not to compare with the way of life of the 2020s, but for that time it was like nothing they ever had known. One of the intentions of the survivors of WWII, the Greatest Generation as they came to be known, and its subsequent prosperity, was that their children would have it better than them. Without anyone trying, there was a remarkable shift away from their previous values. What was ushered in was a less hard-working and a more-permissive society. There was more money, more leisure, more entertainment, more choices, more fun...and with it...less demands, less values, less responsibilities, less reasoning.

In the 1950s, less than 25 percent of Americans thought premarital sex was acceptable; by the late 1970s, more than 75 percent thought it was okay. Did that mean a large percentage of Americans were personally engaged in immoral sex? No, but it did mean that their values were changing. "Between 1960 and 1980, the marriage rate dropped by about 25 percent; the average age of marriage for both men and women rose steadily; and the number of divorced men and women jumped by 200 percent. All told, according to a study by *Adweek* magazine, single people as a percentage of the total American population rose from 28 percent in 1970 to 41 percent in 1993. Young people had a voice and they were using it. The sexual revolution was in full swing."[3]

The Revolution

What is a revolution? A revolution is "a turn around."[4] The attempt of any revolution is "to change the environment in order to change the individual."

The 1960s were a decade of massive change. *Newsweek* magazine, November 1967, had a picture of a back view of the nude Jane Fonda with the title "Anything Goes," subtitled, "The Permissive Society." The magazine documented the sweeping change that marked that time. "The old taboos are dying. A new, more permissive society is taking shape... And, behind this expanding permissiveness is ... a society that has lost its consensus on such crucial issues as premarital sex... marriage, birth control and sex education... "[5]

Revolution or Evolution?

Were the 1960s a revolution or an evolution? Yes. It was both a revolution for the time and an evolution from the time and for the time to come. These were head-turning, ground-breaking, years of slow-moving changes until it was too late to change.

---

[3] Scott Stossel, *The Sexual Counterrevolution*, The American Project, Dec. 19, 2001.

[4] Latin: revolution, "a turn around."

[5] *Newsweek* Magazine, November 13, 1967, p. 74.

The Focus of the Revolution

While the battleground of the sexual revolution has many physical aspects, its conflict began and continues in the mind – how we think. It is literally a battle for the mind. "As believers in and followers of Jesus Christ, we need to consider how our commitment to Him affects not only our political and ethical convictions, but also the way we think and act about theology, philosophy, ethics, biology, psychology, sociology, law, politics, economics, and history. This collection of convictions is what we call a worldview. And it is in the arena of worldviews that one of the greatest battles of our time is now being waged 24/7 ..."[6]

The seemingly innocent scenes of naive hippies doing their thing – dropping out, doing drugs, being defiant, dancing to Rock and Roll music - when studied more closely was an all out assault on authority. It was the age that was anti-establishment. Many of them were openly asking, "Who has the right to determine for me what is right or wrong?" And they were loudly answering, "Not my parents, not the government, and not God!"

Social and military revolution has always been about "authority" – who's in charge. In the Bible of the days of the judges of the Old Testament it says, **"In those days there was no king in Israel: every man did that which was right in his own eyes."** (Judges 21:25; see also 17:6, 18:1, 19:1) There are three aspects of revolution then and now:

---

[6] David A. Noebel, *Understand the Times,* p. 2.

- Individualism – *"... every man..."*
- Amoralism – *"... did that which was right..."*
- Relativism – *"... in his own eyes."*

Please understand. God's existence or sovereignty is not threatened by those who say there is no ultimate "King." **"The fool hath said in his heart, there is no God."** (Psalm 14:1, 53:1). God is God with or without our permission. God doesn't exist because we believe in Him, nor does God cease to exist because we do not submit to Him.

The Fathers (and Mothers) of the Revolution

It was when I was a freshman in college in 1963 that I was introduced for the first time to some of the men who had shaped the thinking for the sexual revolution. One of the required courses for freshmen at state universities in the first semester was psychology. Who we were learning about? Among others, it was Sigmund Freud (1856-1939). Freud of Vienna believed human behavior was motivated by unconscious drives, primarily by the libido or "Sexual Energy." Freud proposed to study how these unconscious drives were repressed and found expression through other cultural outlets. He called this therapy "psychoanalysis."

"The psychological theories about human nature and the counseling based on these theories have vastly contributed to the ever-expanding fulfillment of 2 Timothy 3:1-5. These psychological theories and therapies have fueled inordinate self-love and thereby served as the seedbed of the twentieth-

century sexual revolution, which has ripped apart families, abolished sexual morality, and led to a redefinition of marriage."[7]

Thought Bombs

America continues to reap the results of the "seeds" of lawlessness which were sown years before the 1960s. The now almost 50-year-old best-seller written by Hal Lindsey, *Satan is Alive and Well on Planet Earth,* contains a profound and almost prophetic chapter entitled, *"Thought Bombs."* Lindsay stated that in the eighteenth and nineteenth centuries a handful of men set off some major "thought bombs" that shape the way people are now thinking. Lindsay said, "The contamination of these explosive ideas has been so devastating that it has completely permeated twentieth century thinking." The men Lindsey listed are still widely known and studied today.

- German philosopher Immanuel Kant (1724-1804)
- German philosopher Georg Wilhelm Friedrick Hegel (1770-1831)
- Denmark's Soren Kierkegaard (1813-1855)
- Germany's Karl Marx (1818-1883)
- England's Charles Darwin (1809-1882)
- Austria's Sigmund Freud (1856-1939)[8]

What has been the results of these "thought bombs"? We have been re-conditioned to think in ways that are

---

[7] Martin and Deidre Bobgan, *Psychology's Influence in the Sexual Revolution,* midnightcall.com

[8] Hal Lindsey, *Satan is Alive and Well on Planet Earth,* pp. 84-97.

contrary to biblical truth and with every step we have taken away from God and the Bible we have created "new norms" for every generation that has followed.

Ruling from the Grave

Eighteen years later in 1990 Dave Breese would write his book, *"Seven Men Who Rule the World from the Grave."* Breese believed, "Though their bodies lie cold and dormant, the grave cannot contain the influence these seven men have had on today's world. They continue to rule because they have altered the thinking of society. They generated philosophies that have been ardently grasped by masses of people but are erroneous and anti-scriptural. Today these ideas pervade our schools, businesses, homes, even churches. As we continue to unknowingly subscribe to their philosophies, we keep the grave open for:

- Charles Darwin (1809-1882), who systematized and advanced the principle that evolution was behind of origin of species.
- Karl Marx (1818-1883), who developed and advocated the notion of modern Communism.
- Julius Wellhausen (1844-1918), who initiated 'higher criticism' and 'modernism.'
- John Dewey (1859-1952), who argued for the educational system focused on problem solving and the growth of the child in all aspects of his being.
- Sigmund Freud (1856-1939), who promoted the view that the sexual instinct is the driving force behind all human action.
- John Maynard Keynes ((1883-1946), who advocated the policies for reducing un-

employment and expanding the economy that today find their expression in deficit spending and governmental activism.

- Soren Kierkegaard (1813-1855), who stressed the obligation each person has to make conscious, responsible choices among alternatives, a major tenet of existentialism."[9]

One Crazy Dude

Let's not overlook a man who wrote directly to the mentality of the 1960s. Wilhelm Reich (1897-1957), an atheist and a second-generation psychoanalyst who had been trained by Sigmund Freud (1856-1939), was the man credited with the concept of "free love." Reich could be said to have invented what was thought to be the second "sexual revolution." It was a phrase he coined in the 1930s in order to illustrate his belief that a true political revolution would be possible only when sexual repression was overthrown.

Reich lived his ideas. He had countless sexual partners, three marriages, and reared his children in absolute sexual freedom. Reich believed that contraceptives should be available to everyone, that childhood sexuality should be affirmed, that sexual relationships between unmarried young adults were healthy, that young people were entitled to have a safe place for the purpose of engaging in sex, that abortion should be legalized, and that having children to bind a marriage harmed them. He said that traditional marriage could

---

[9] Dave Breese, *"Seven Men who Rule the World from the Grave,"* Back cover.

not endure because "sexual dulling" was "the inevitable result of close physical proximity to one partner, and the simultaneous exposure to new sexual stimuli emanating from others." He predicted that the institution of marriage would be replaced by "serial monogamy."[10]

Time magazine called this new "sex-affirming culture" the "second sexual revolution" – the first having occurred in the 1920s, "when flaming youth buried the Victorian era and anointed itself as the Jazz Age." In contrast, the children of the 1960s had little to rebel against and found themselves, the article went on to comment, "adrift in a sea of permissiveness", which it attributed to Reich's philosophy. "Gradually, the belief spread that repression, not license, was the great evil, and that sexual matters belonged in the realm of science, not morals."

Wilhelm Reich's 1945 book, *The Sexual Revolution,* widely regarded as the clarion call for what was eventually manifested as the swinging sixties sought to resurrect the body—including, but not limited to, the full potency of sexuality in both men and women—as a means of healing our "patriarchal culture's dysfunctions." Reich believed the "authoritarian personality" along with many ills of modern society, such as violence, sexism, social injustice, and economic inequities, could be traced to "sexual

[10]https://www.washingtonpost.com/archive/entertainment/books/1983/02/06/wilhelm-reich-a-prisoner-of-sex/10e319e7-fab3-4e69-9ce4-5b93b1e91f8c/

repression."[11] If this sounds familiar, remember he was a student of Sigmund Freud.

One final thing about the weirdness of Reich's belief: he invented and was marketing in the United States a machine that supposedly collected "orgone" from the atmosphere which would help people attain "orgastic potency." The crime for which Wilhelm Reich was convicted was of violation of an injunction obtained by the Food and Drug Administration against interstate transportation of his "orgone accumulator," a metal-and-wood cabinet that Reich said restored human physical powers. The FDA declared it a medical consumer fraud.

Reich died of a heart attack in the federal penitentiary at Lewisburg, Pennsylvania, in 1957. He was 60 years old and had served nine months of a two-year sentence.

One Possessed Woman

Margaret Higgins Sanger (1879-1966) was an American birth control activist, sex educator, writer, and non-licensed nurse. Sanger popularized the term "birth control," opened the first birth control clinic in the United States, and established organizations that evolved into the Planned Parenthood Federation of America.

From Planned Parenthood's website, "Our founder, Margaret Sanger, was a woman of heroic accomplishments, and like all heroes, she was also

---

[11] Deborah Anapol, Ph,D, Whatever Happened to the *Sexual Revolution*, www.psychologytoday.com August 15, 2012.

complex and imperfect. It is undeniable that Margaret Sanger's lifelong struggle helped 20th century women gain the right to decide when and whether to have a child — a right that had been suppressed worldwide for at least 5,000 years (Boulding, 1992). Anticipating the most recent turn of the millennium, *LIFE* magazine declared that Margaret Sanger was one of the 100 most important Americans of the 20th century (LIFE, 1990)."

In a 1966 feature on the birth control pill and morality, the magazine *U.S. News and World Report* asked, "Is the Pill regarded as a license for promiscuity? Can its availability to all women of childbearing age lead to sexual anarchy?" The author Pearl Buck took an even more dire doomsday approach to the Pill when she warned in a 1968 *Reader's Digest* article: "Everyone knows what The Pill is. It is a small object — yet its potential effect upon our society may be even more devastating than the nuclear bomb."[12]

The Real Purveyor of Lies and Deception

In fact, the true father of this revolution is Satan - the liar of all liars, the deceiver of all deceivers. What we have going on around us is more than a cultural war; it is in fact a cosmic war. "Satan continues his efforts to make sin less offensive, heaven less appealing, hell less horrific, and the gospel less urgent."[13]

---

[12] PBS, *The Pill and the Sexual Revolution*, https://www.pbs.org/wgbh/americanexperience/features/pill-and-sexual-revolution/

[13] John MacArthur, https://www.gty.org/library/blog/B110430/the-truth-about-hell

To say that Satan was the one behind these philosophies is usually hard for some to accept, but if we look close enough and long enough, we should come to that conclusion. It has been, indeed, a battle for the mind. A follow-up sequel by Mr. Lindsey would be fitting that could be titled, *Satan is Alive and Well in America.* Satan, the one who came to "kill, steal and destroy," (John 10:10), the murderer and liar of which Jesus warned (John 8:44), the deceiver of the whole world (Revelation 12:9), the one who is roaming about seeking whom he may devour (1 Peter 5:8), is behind *all* of the world's confusion. Is it not amazing that in the enlightened twenty-first century people are confused about something as simple as who are males and who are females?

The Facilitators of the Sexual Revolution

What has facilitated the change of morality in America?

Television

No one can doubt the influence of television, especially the mother who asked her six-year-old son what time he would like his afternoon snack. He replied, "Four o'clock eastern, three o'clock central!"

While television struggled to become a national mass media in the 1950s, it became a cultural force in the 60s. Ninety percent of American households had a television in the 1960s – 52 million TV sets. The present generation cannot image how it was back then. There was no DVR or VCR or TiVo. There was only one set and it was black and white and there was no remote control. There were only three channels – ABC, CBS, NBC – and you watched what they aired live. The programs seemed innocent enough, but they were capturing the minds and time of Americans.

While early television was not telling us what to think, they controlled what we thought about. Television became over time philosophical, political and global. The television in the 1960s brought us Martin Luther King's civil rights movement, the assassination of President John F. Kennedy, the Vietnam war, the moon landing, student protests; and don't forget the Beatles and Tiny Tim.

The goals of the original networks were simple: entertain, escape, educate and make money.

No one can dispute that public opinion was shaped and reset in the 60s. No one can deny that the "prince of the power of the air" (Ephesians 2:2) has been at work.

Anne Marie Sweeney, formerly the co-chair of Disney Media, President of the Disney–ABC Television Group, and the President of Disney Channel from 1996 to 2014, said of the television, it is "the most powerful medium in the world."[14]

Modern Media

Americans are now using internet media more than 7 hours and 50 minutes per household per day; phones,

---

[14] Tim Adler, MISCOM: Disney-ABC, *Deadline*, October 5, 2011.

pads, Facebook, YouTube, Netflix add to that. Six hours a day are spent watching videos.

During the first quarter of 2018 a sizable chunk of the 11 hours per day Americans spent was listening to, watching, reading or otherwise interacting with media. Nielsen's report also examined social media adoption. It found adults are spending an average of 45 minutes per day on social media, with most of that time on smartphones.[15] Considering all the people you see with their heads down that amount of time has grown exponentially.

Added to the access to cable television and internet media there is the multi-billion-dollar influence of Hollywood. Studies have shown that over 90 percent of all sexual encounters on television and in the movies are between unmarried people. Before the average American turns eighteen, he or she has witnessed more than seventy thousand images of sex or suggested sexual intercourse between people who are not wed to each other.[16]

Now, fast forward five decades. There is an "air attack" working together with a "ground war."

The Followers of Sexual Revolution

These "thought bombs" were old school, anti-Christian philosophies from mostly non-American men, which eventually made their way into the American mind,

---

15 2018 Nielsen Total Audience Report.

16 Lee Strobel, *God's Outrageous Claims*, p. 164.

American homes and American schools. Pastor James Love, says, "They were introduced into American thought in the 20th century, were nourished and watered all throughout the 100 years, and have come to fruition in the later part, or we could say we will reap a full harvest in the 21st Century.

- John Dewey's (1859-1952) influence reshaped education.
- Alfred Kinsey's (1894-1956) observations on sexuality redefined who we are and why we are here.
- Benjamin Spock (1903-1998) reshaped family life with his philosophy of permissiveness.
- In a time of depression and war, President Franklin D. Roosevelt (1882-1945) brought socialized government to America called 'the New Deal.'
- Margaret Sanger (1878-1966) brought women into a new role."[17]

How are we to measure the influence of the 1960s?

The first version is the one most often told in the media, and it goes like this: "The sexual revolution was a good thing. It has allowed people to remove the shackles of repression, puritanical morality and experience freedom. People are sexual beings, and they need to explore their sexuality when they feel ready, without fear of guilt or shame."

---

[17] Pastor James Love, personal correspondence.

The second version is different. "The sexual revolution has brought about untold harm. The idea of sexual freedom outside of marriage may appear to be attractive, but the reality is darker. When we live outside the boundaries that God set up for our benefit and protection, we move into a world of risk and danger that is much more profound than many of us realize."[18]

So, which is it?

Judge for yourself.

As to the question in this book's title, *Who Didn't See This Coming?*, many now seem to be surprised by what America has become over the last fifty-plus years.

George Barna (1955-), head of the Barna Research team, saw it coming. His book, *The Frog in the Kettle,* which came out thirty years ago (1990), is revealing when we look back at Barna's prognostications. The subtitle to the book was, *What Christians Need to Know About Life in the Year 2000.* Remember, George Barna is no prophet, but an expert in trends. The book's title is based on the premise that if you place a frog in a kettle of boiling water, it will jump out immediately, aware that the environment is dangerous. But if you place a frog in a kettle full of room temperature water and slowly increase the temperature of the water until it is boiling, the frog will stay in the water until it boils to death. It is the concept of incrementalism.

---

[18] Casualties of the Sexual Revolution, www.familylife.com

Barna believed, "Much of the change that will affect our lives in the new century will be the result of fundamental transformations in what we expect from life, and what we consider to be important and valuable. While the 60s broke through the barriers to change in these areas, the 90s will bring renewed energy to the process of redefining our basic values and assumptions about life."[19] Now, thirty years of changes have taken us further down the road of no return.

---

[19] George Barna, *The Frog in the Kettle*, p. 32

Part II: Looking Around

- 2 -

The Hippies of the 1960s are Today's Grandparents and They and Their Children are the Politicians Now Shaping America

Seminary president Albert Mohler believes *"we are living in an era of moral revolution and seismic cultural change."*[1] Who can deny that?

Yet, somehow, many people did not see this coming.

In 2011 David Jeremiah (1941-) wrote a book entitled, *I Never Thought I'd See the Day.* I agree with the sentiment of the shocking things we have seen come to pass in our lifetime, but we should have known this day was coming if we were reading and believing our Bibles!

Steve Farrar (1949-) recounts two prominent preachers in London in the 1660s: Richard Baxter (1615-1691) and John Owen (1616-1683). Without each other's knowledge, they both began to preach that the judgment of God was about to come down on London. This was completely out of character for these men. They were both Bible scholars and pastors.

---

[1] Albert Mohler, *Answers in Genesis* Magazine, April 1, 2013.

Baxter's book, *Saints Everlasting Rest,* is a classic that is still studied today. John Owen's works on theology are deeply profound. Their common conclusion was if God judged Israel, then He would certainly judge London. For their concern both were ridiculed and scorned. These men could somehow see disease, economic chaos and destruction coming to their city. And it did.

- In 1665, without warning, a smallpox epidemic suddenly swept through London. Within a matter of weeks, thousands were dead. Graves could not be dug fast enough to bury the dead. Bodies were piled high on carts throughout the city. "The Great Plague," as it was called, killed an estimated 100,000 people—almost a quarter of London's population—in 18 months. Proud London was brought to its knees, but they would not repent.

Plague in 1665

- In the middle of the night on September 2, 1666, a crazed man set fire to a row house. Within hours, London was on fire. The city had been without rain for months and the houses and neighborhoods went up like dry tinder. The fire burned uncontrollably for four days. The great city had been reduced to smoldering embers.

What Baxter and Owen saw coming to London they did not see in a spiritual vision or in a mystical dream or from the visit of an angel. They believed what they believed because they saw it in the Bible, the Word of God. *They could see the future by looking to the past.*[2]

If we had been reading our Bibles, we should have seen the coming of present-day America by looking back at those who were raised up in that time of moral permissiveness.

"In contrast to those who see the 1950s as essentially a conservative period, and who view the 1960s as a time of rapid moral change, (there was an) emergence of a liberalizing impulse during the Truman and Eisenhower years. During the 1950s, a traditionalist moral framework was beginning to give way to a less authoritarian approach to moral issues as demonstrated by a more relaxed style of child-rearing, the rising status of women both inside and outside the home, the increasing reluctance of Americans to regard alcoholism as a sin, loosening sexual attitudes, the increasing influence of modern psychology, and, correspondingly, the declining influence of religion in the personal lives of most Americans."[3]

Secularism

The secularization of American society is not just one moral problem we face—it is *the* moral problem we face. Every other moral issue of our day is a manifestation of this one. Secularism is the push for the removal of all religious influences from our country. Another term for secularism is "humanism." Secularism in its milder form in days past just meant the separation of faith and

---

[2] Steve Farrar, *Get in the Ark*, p. 11-13.

[3] Alan Petigny, *The Permissive Society – America, 1941-1965.*

politics. In the 21st century secularism is nothing less than raw atheism. One-fourth of the Millennial generation, those born between 1981 and 2000, identify themselves as religiously unaffiliated, atheist, or agnostic in a 2010 Pew Research Center survey. That works out to about 15 million Americans who describe themselves as "convinced atheists," more than many mainline Protestant denominations, Jews, or Muslims.[4] This new group has a name; they are tagged the "nones." While saying they are "spiritual," they do not call themselves "religious." Assisted by the American Civil Liberty Union (ACLU) we have lived to see the purging of America of religious influence it once had in its past. Now there is no prayer in school, no Ten Commandments in many public places, and no religious symbols even in private colleges that were formerly "Christian." America has become not simply non-Christian, but in many ways anti-Christian.

Who are these secularists?

They are the hippy generation of the 1960s, their children and their grandchildren. Remember, the generation of the 1960s was from Post-WWII parents who promised a better, easier life for their children.

If our current politicians seem like they are from another planet, well, that's close. They are in fact from Woodstock – that's about as far-out as you can get. We have failed to connect the generational dots – present

---

[4] Karen E. Klein, *"Can the Godless Market Evolve Beyond Bumper Stickers?"* Bloomberg Businessweek, Sept. 7, 2012.

day great-grandparents were pre and post WWII, grandparents were the teens and young adults in the 1960s, current parents are grandchildren of the permissive morals which invaded the 1960s and the current teens and young adults are great-grandchildren who are presently living in a culture with few limits. It is a "trickle down" that has turned into a "tsunami."

The movers and shakers of 2020 are the not so distant hippies of the 1960s and their offspring. Predominately, our American government is being led by Baby Boomers (1946-1964), who are between the ages of 74 and 56 and Generation Xers (1965-1981) who are between 55 and 39.

Professor Peter R. Jones (1940-) concluded, "The most radical American Revolution took place not in 1776 but in the last generation of the twentieth century. In those last thirty or so years we witness the First Great Awakening – of Paganism. It deconstructed western Christendom and produced a radical transformation of once-'Christian' America. At the street level, the marginal student revolutionaries of the sixties, who rejected the American political system, took political power in the nineties, and their extreme ideas are now mainstream 'moderate.' They defined sin as social oppression and sought redemption in social structures. This search liberated the individual from personal guilt. For many, redemption became synonymous with sexual liberation. Radical feminists demanded that their sisters be 'sin-articulate,' have the 'courage to sin,' and 'liberate the inner slut.'"[5]

Robert H. Bork makes this same connection in his book, *Sloughing Toward Gomorrah*. "The temporary abeyance of the Sixties temper was due to the radicals graduating from the universities (the ones they had attempted to burn down...jdl) and become invisible until they reached positions of power of influence, as they now have, across the breadth of the culture....The Sixties radicals are still with us, but now they do not paralyze the universities; they run the universities."[6]

Think about the people who are leading our government. The average age of those serving in our federal government at the beginning of the 116th Congress (January 3, 2019) in the House of Representatives was 57.8 years old and in the Senate was 61.8 years old. In the year 2020 the Speaker of the House Nancy Pelosi (D-CA) was 80, Senate Majority leader Mitch McConnell (R-KY) was 78, Senator Dianne Feinstein (D-CA) was 86, and Senate President pro tempore Chuck Grassley (R– IA). These are all hippy holdovers.

During the 2020 Covid-19 pandemic in the United States one of the principle doctors on the President's medical team was Dr. Anthony Facui (1940-). Dr. Facui was chosen because he is the director of the

---

[5] Peter R. Jones, *Sexual Perversion: The Necessary Fruit of Neo-Pagan Spirituality in the Culture at Large*, in *Biblical Foundations for Manhood and Womanhood*, Editor Wayne Grudem, p. 257.

[6] Robert Bork, *Slouching Toward Gomorrah*, p.34, 53.

National Institute of Allergy and Infectious Diseases (NIAID). During the pandemic he gave his strong medical opinion about social distancing. "I don't think we should ever shake hands ever again."[7] Five days later he was interviewed by *Snapchat* on "Good Luck America," and was asked, "If you're swiping on a dating app like Tinder, or Bumble or Grindr, and you match with someone that you think is hot, and you're just kind of like... 'Maybe it's fine if this one [asymptomatic] stranger comes over! What do you say to that person?" Dr. Fauci replied, "You know, that's tough, because that's what's called relative risk. If you're willing to take a risk – and you know, everybody has their own tolerance for risks – you could figure out if you want to meet somebody... If you want to go a little bit more intimate, well, then that's your choice regarding a risk."[8] Did you understand what the doctor said? Shaking hands with friends must not be allowed ever but having casual sex with strangers you meet online is quote, "your choice." That is the advice of a trusted modern scientist/doctor who is conflicted by his lack of basic morals. On the one hand he says he wants to save Americans from Covid-19, yet on the other hand, sees no need to advise people to stay clear of having sex with strangers. Tinder is a dating/hookup app with a reported 57 million users worldwide in 190 countries. According to the Pew Research Center, an estimated 30% of U.S. adults have used Tinder. Grindr is a dating/hookup app primarily for homosexuals. It reportedly has 27 million members and 3.6 million men who use the site daily. According to the CDC, 66% of

---

[7] Amy Gunia, *Time* magazine, April 9, 2020.
[8] Snapchat, April 14, 2020.

new HIV diagnoses are the result of male-to-male sexual contact -- 24,909 new diagnoses in 2018.[9] Dr. Fauci is another hippy holdover.

I am certainly not saying the previously mentioned people were all among the long-haired, dope-smoking, free-loving hippies, but, like myself, they grew up in the decades of moral revision.

Bill Clinton, the first Baby Boomer president, did not know what "is" is. Here's what Clinton told the grand jury.

> "It depends on what the meaning of the word 'is' is. If the—if he—if 'is' means is and never has been, that is not—that is one thing. If it means there is none, that was a completely true statement. ... Now, if someone had asked me on that day, are you having any kind of sexual relations with Ms. Lewinsky, that is, asked me a question in the present tense, I would have said no. And it would have been completely true."[10]

While the modern Millennials catch all the grief for the troubles of present-day America, the real problem was in what the previous generations allowed that preceded them.

Andy Andrews reminds us in his little book, *How Do You Kill 11 Million People?*, that for the 331 million people in America it is only 545 men and women who

---

[9] Michael W. Chapman, *Dr. Fauci on Tinder Hookups During COVID-19: 'If You Want to Go More Intimate ... That's Your Choice'* CNS News.com April 17, 2020.

[10] 1,128 in Ken Starr's report.

enact every law, propose every budget, and set every policy enforced on the citizens of the United States of America: one president, nine Supreme Court justices, one hundred senators, and 435 members of the House of Representatives.[11]

We need to add to those 545 people. James A. Thurber estimates that the actual number of working lobbyists was close to 100,000 and that the industry brings in 9 billion dollars annually.[12] The "influence peddling" by lobbyists is a legal form of bribery or extortion by contributing to the campaigns of current or potential office holders. These political action groups include Planned Parenthood, the National Rifle Association (NRA), AARP, plus countless energy, medical, and environmental groups.

And don't fail to include with the lobbyists the ever-present social activists. They are also affecting change – for good or for bad. Activism consists of efforts to promote, impede, direct, or intervene in social, political, economic, or environmental reform with the desire to make changes in society. Following the surge of so-called "new social movements" in the United States in the 1960s, a new understanding of activism emerged as a rational and acceptable democratic option of protest or appeal.

Before moving on, the answer to Andy Andrew's question is, "You lie to them, over and over again."

---

[11] Andy Andrews, *How Do You Kill 11 Million People?* p. 43.
[12] Lee Fang, *The Nation*, March 10, 2014.

Socialism

It should not surprise us that America is moving beyond secularism to becoming more and more socialistic. By definition "socialism" in theory and practice is the producing and providing of goods owned collectively or by a centralized government that often plans and controls the economy. The final stage is a totalitarian dictatorship. Socialism is all about "big government." Government promises to make things better but ends up making things much worse. Socialism, leading to communism has followed two methods. First, we have seen *socialism by revolution*. Men like Marx, Hitler, and Mao forced socialistic change on people. Those who resisted were murdered by the millions. Second, in America we are seeing *socialism by evolution*. There has been a silent takeover of institutions—the home, education, government, and the church. Socialistic philosophy fosters a "cradle to the grave" society. By the way, they determine the "cradle" [abortion] and they will eventually determine the "grave" [euthanasia] through health care. They create or seize upon chaos then step in to solve the chaos. Their "crisis strategy" is to develop problems that are so large that government is the only perceived solution. Socialism isn't merely an alternative philosophy; it is an aggressive enemy of freedom.

> "The American people will never knowingly adopt socialism. But under the name of Liberalism, they will adopt every fragment of the socialist progress until one day America will be a socialist nation without knowing how it happened."

Norman Mattoon Thomas (1884-1968)
Leader of the Socialist Party USA
Six-Time Presidential Candidate
Founder of the American Civil Leaders Union[13]

Americans have what more than half the world only dreams about—freedom—freedom of speech, freedom of [not from] religion. No one can challenge the fact that our freedoms are being stripped from us, sometimes by our governmental representatives, sometimes by our courts, and, yes, sometimes by our own presidents. We have a choice: dependence on God or government? What current socialists fail to consider is that when communism takes over it does not promote socialists—it eliminates them. The communist reasoning is, "If these socialists betrayed their own country they are not to be trusted. They will betray us too, so let's get rid of them right now before they turn on us." That is the history of communism. What current Americans need to see is that people committed to socialism are not just people with different ideas— they are America's enemies! Strangely, in some ways, socialism is destined to both fail and succeed. It is destined to fail because by nature we are sinners and we are not going to work hard to keep less. Richard Land states, "The reality is that unless people get to keep a

---

13 Quoted by President Ronald Reagan in a speech on Socialized Medicine in 1961. https://www.youtube.com/watch?time_continue=82&v=AYrlDlrLDSQ&feature=emb_title

significant portion of their labor, they're not going to work as hard as they would otherwise."[14]

Does the Bible have anything to say about the far-reaching influence of previous generations? In fact, it does, both in precept and by examples.

"Thou shalt not make unto thee any graven image, or any likeness *of any thing* that *is* in heaven above, or that *is* in the earth beneath, or that *is* in the water under the earth: Thou shalt not bow down thyself to them, nor serve them: for I the LORD thy God *am* a jealous God, visiting the iniquity of the fathers upon the children unto the third and fourth *generation* of them that hate me; And shewing mercy unto thousands of them that love me, and keep my commandments." (Exodus 20:4-6)

This statement has been misunderstood to mean God will punish the children, grandchildren, and great-grandchildren of those who "hate" Him. Some have gone so far as to teach a "generational curse" exists on some people because of what their parents did or believed.

This is obviously *not* what this passage means.

- **"The fathers shall not be put to death for the children, neither shall the children be put to death for the fathers: every man shall be put to death for his own sin."** (Deuteronomy 24:16)

---

[14] Richard Land, *Southern Baptist Texan,* October 1, 2012.

- **"The soul that sinneth, it shall die. The son shall not bear the iniquity of the father, neither shall the father bear the iniquity of the son: the righteousness of the righteous shall be upon him, and the wickedness of the wicked shall be upon him."** (Ezekiel 18:20)
- **"Amaziah *was* twenty and five years old *when* he began to reign, and he reigned twenty and nine years in Jerusalem. And his mother's name *was* Jehoaddan of Jerusalem. And he did *that which was* right in the sight of the LORD, but not with a perfect heart. Now it came to pass, when the kingdom was established to him, that he slew his servants that had killed** (assassinated...jdl) **the king his father. But he slew not their children, but *did* as *it is* written in the law in the book of Moses, where the LORD commanded, saying, The fathers shall not die for the children, neither shall the children die for the fathers, but every man shall die for his own sin."** (2 Chronicles 25:1-4)

In the 1960s, someone came up with the sociological theory of a "generation gap." The reality is there is a "generational connection" between parents and children in every age. What the Exodus 20 passage underscores is the far-reaching influence of all people, especially parents. What each person believes and how they live has a profound influence on their family for generations to come. If a generation chooses to attack ("hate") God and His standards of morality (the context is the moral law contained in the Ten

Commandments), there is the real certainty of direct harm brought upon families, for generations to come. One generation turns its back on God; the next generations grow up without God. All sin has its predictable "domino" effect.

"Examples are legion. To cite one example of each consequence, a son of Bernie Madoff, one of the greatest crooks in American history, committed suicide owing to the shame he felt over his father's crimes. And the worst mass shooting in American history as of this writing – leaving fifty-eight people at an outdoor concert in Las Vegas dead and over five hundred injured – was committed by a man whose father was a lifelong criminal and on the FBI's 'Ten Most Wanted Fugitives List.'"[15]

God does not punish the innocent for another's offense, but those who are innocent often suffer because of what others do or don't do. "Crack babies" are born with an addiction because their mothers smoked freebase cocaine when they were carried in their mothers' wombs. Doctors are able to discover our ailments by asking about our "family history." Drunk drivers kill innocent people by the thousands in America.

There are examples in the Bible about generational degeneration.

Three Generations of Promise Land Possessors

"And if it seem evil unto you to serve the LORD, choose you this day whom ye will serve; whether the

---

15 Dennis Prager, *Exodus – God, Slavery and Freedom*, p. 243.

gods which your fathers served that *were* on the other side of the flood, or the gods of the Amorites, in whose land ye dwell: but as for me and my house, we will serve the LORD." (Joshua 24:15). **"And the people served the LORD all the days of Joshua, and all the days of the elders that outlived Joshua, who had seen all the great works of the LORD, that he did for Israel...And also all that generation were gathered unto their fathers: and there arose another generation after them, which knew not the LORD, nor yet the works which he had done for Israel.** (Judges 2:7, 10)

There are three generations in view in Judges 2:6-15. Generation 1 was Joshua. Generation 2 was the elders that outlived Joshua. Generation 3 was a generation that did not know the Lord.

- The first generation declared, "As for me and my house we will serve the Lord." Joshua and his family were *committed.* The second generation might have said, "As for me without my house, I will serve the Lord." The elders must have been at least somewhat *casual.* The third generation arrogantly responded, "Neither me nor my house will serve the Lord." The third generation was thoroughly *carnal.*
- The *inconsistencies* of the second generation became the *indifference* and *iniquities* of the third generation. How did that third generation turn out? "They did evil in the sight of the Lord and served Baal." (Judges 2:11) "They forsook the Lord God of their fathers...and followed other gods." (Judges 2:12) "They served Baal

and Ashtaroth." (Judges 2:13) "The hand of the Lord was against them... and they were greatly distressed." (Judges 2:15)

- Joshua had experienced the miracle of deliverance from Egypt, the parting of the Red Sea, the daily supply of the manna and more, yet by the third generation "they knew not the Lord" nor had their parents passed on to them the history of God's great works.

Three Generations of Patriarchs

This "generational degeneration" can be seen in lives of the patriarchs.

- The first generation of the patriarchs was Abraham. He obeyed God, left his homeland, and walked by faith. Wherever he ended up he usually did two things: He built an altar and he dug a well. The first act was spiritual, the second physical. It seems wherever Abraham went and whatever Abraham did He put God first. He put spiritual matters ahead of physical matters. Now, Abraham did lie on an occasion to keep a king from killing him and getting his wife. He said Sarah was "his sister," technically a true statement, but she was also his wife.
- The second generation patriarch was Isaac. He, too, dug several wells and sometimes built an altar. He seemed to put the physical ahead of the spiritual most of the time. He had the same God as his father, but not the same convictions. Remember Abraham lied once. Do you know how many times Isaac lied? Twice. He lied two times to protect his life. When God restated His

covenant with Isaac that his seed would bless all nations that it was "because that Abraham obeyed" God's voice (Genesis 26:4-50). We are all affected by the previous generation, for good or for evil.

- The third generation of the patriarchs was Jacob. He was the king of liars. His name meant "supplanter, cheater." The only time be built an altar was when he was in trouble. This is degeneration in three generations.

Three Generations of Priests

This "generational degeneration" was displayed in a family of priests in the first several chapters of 1 Samuel.

- The first generation priest was Eli. He was God's high priest but was far too permissive with his boys. "...He restrained them not" (1 Samuel 3:13)
- The second generation priests were Hophni and Phinehas. 1 Samuel 2:12 says they were "sons of Belial (worthless, corrupt)" and "they knew not the Lord." Their behavior was reprehensible. "Wherefore the sin of the young men was very great before the Lord: for men abhorred the offering of the Lord." (1 Samuel 2:17). Hophni and Phinehas were killed under God's judgment by the Philistines (1 Samuel 4:11).
- The third generation was Ichabod, Phinehas' child, whose name means, "The glory is departed from Israel." (1 Samuel 4:21-22) This was degeneration in three generations.

Three Generations of Kings

This "generational degeneration" was demonstrated in the lives of three kings in 2 *Chronicles 26-28.*

- The first generation King was Uzzah who tried to take over the office and work of a priest and was "cut off from the house of God." (2 Chronicles 26:21). This was *foolish* worship. This man had been *active* in the things of God, but he crossed the line and God kicked Uzzah out of the place of worship. He tried to take over the priest's office. He got out of line. And God judged him, giving him leprosy, but he never repented. So, what happened to his son who would be his successor?
- The second generation King was Jothan. After what Uzzah had his experience in the temple, his son, Jothan, "entered not into the temple of God." (2 Chronicles 27:2) This was *forsaken* worship. Here was a man who was *apathetic* about the things of God. Although Jothan did some good things, he was a "no show" week after week at the house of God. And God wrote it in bold letters and underlined it for us to see. He was a church drop out.
- The third generation King was Ahaz. "**And Ahaz gathered together the vessels of the house of God, and cut in pieces the vessels of the house of God, and shut up the doors of the house of the LORD, and he made him altars in every corner of Jerusalem. And in every several city of Judah he made high places to burn incense unto other gods, and provoked to anger the LORD God of his fathers.**" (2

Chronicles 28:24-25) This was *false* worship. His grandfather was active, his father was apathetic, but he was *antagonistic* toward the things of God. This was degeneration in three generations. It all happened within the space of 84 years.

This decline can also be seen in kings David, Solomon, and Rehoboam.

There is a pattern here that we dare not try to ignore.

"Give ear, O my people, *to* my law: incline your ears to the words of my mouth. I will open my mouth in a parable: I will utter dark sayings of old: Which we have heard and known, and our fathers have told us. We will not hide *them* from their children, shewing to the generation to come the praises of the LORD, and his strength, and his wonderful works that he hath done. For he established a testimony in Jacob, and appointed a law in Israel, which he commanded our fathers, that they should make them known to their children: That the generation to come might know *them, even* the children *which* should be born; *who* should arise and declare *them* to their children: That they might set their hope in God, and not forget the works of God, but keep his commandments: And might not be as their fathers, a stubborn and rebellious generation; a generation *that* set not their heart aright, and whose spirit was not stedfast with God." (Psalm 78:1-8)

While the effects of evil may reach three or four generations, God's mercy can be to thousands. God promises to show **"... mercy unto thousands of them that love me, and keep my commandments."** (Exodus 20:6) "Thousands" of what? From the context it implies thousands of "generations."

God shows His mercy in so many ways to those who love Him and obey His commandments.

- By saving us.
- By preventing many evils from overtaking us.
- By restraining us from sin.
- By directing and protecting our daily decisions.
- By correcting us when we go astray.
- By forgiving us when we confess our sins to Him.
- By cleansing us from the guilt of sins He has forgiven.
- By hearing and answering our prayers.

God desires to show us His mercy in the middle of our mess!

Young people are leaving churches in unprecedented numbers. Many of them are doing so because they want no part of the dispassionate and empty faith of their parents. In fact, they may have never seen authentic Christianity. They reject God because they don't know Him.

Some ask, "Why are churches losing young people?" In fact, churches do not have young people! Parents have children.

People are in crisis. Marriages are in crisis. Families are in crisis. Churches are in crisis. Nations are in crisis.

It is time to break this generational cycle of degeneration and begin a new cycle of regeneration. The Apostle Paul tells us about one family's success story in his final epistle.

"Paul, an apostle of Jesus Christ by the will of God, according to the promise of life which is in Christ Jesus, To Timothy, *my* dearly beloved son: Grace, mercy, *and* peace, from God the Father and Christ Jesus our Lord. I thank God, whom I serve from *my* forefathers with pure conscience, that without ceasing I have remembrance of thee in my prayers night and day; Greatly desiring to see thee, being mindful of thy tears, that I may be filled with joy; When I call to remembrance the unfeigned faith that is in thee, which dwelt first in thy grandmother Lois, and thy mother Eunice; and I am persuaded that in thee also." (2 Timothy 1:1-5)

In these verses we are introduced to three generations. Generation one was Lois, the grandmother. Generation two was Eunice, the mother. Generation three was Timothy, the son and grandson.

Here is what we know about these three generations. They were not suffering from degeneration but were enjoying regeneration. This wasn't a family going down—they were a family going up...I mean all the way up to heaven together.

Do you see what it says in verse 5? It says the grandmother had faith and passed it on to the mother and the mother passed on her faith to her son and her son was passing on his faith to others. That is the way life is supposed to work.

My own faith legacy first dwelt in my great, great grandmother, Tabitha Jowell (1815-1896), a mother of 11 who was a devoted Christian and a Baptist. Her daughter, Mary Carolyn met and married my great, grandfather, Matthew Beal Locke, in 1855 in East Texas. Almost immediately, the young Locke couple made their way 220 miles west in their wagon to the Brazos River in Palo Pinto County, Texas, and built a log cabin. They got busy having 11 children, 7 girls and 4 boys, in the next 21 years. When the tally was finished, they would have 64 grandchildren.

Upon her death at the early age of 63, Mary Carolyn's obituary in the local paper read, "At her death she was a member of the Missionary Baptist church at Mineral Wells. She was a conscientious and willing worker in the church, though for the last eighteen or nineteen years of her life she was an invalid. Through all her afflictions she remained the same kind, patient, and noble woman, affectionate wife and gentle, loving mother." One of my most highly prized possessions is her 1882 King James Bible.

Mary Carolyn's youngest child was my grandfather, Jesse Quinton Locke. He was saved in 1892 at the age of 15 at a Baptist brush arbor meeting under the preaching of G. W. Slaughter (1811-1895). His grandmother, Tabitha Jowell, had taken him there in her buggy. The following was in the back of a 1952 record book written by J. Q. Locke.

> (This May 22, 1952)
> *"I was converted on the night of September 11, 1892 at about 9 O'clock pm under a brush arbor near the Indian Creek School house. Preachers Rev. G. W. Slaughter and Rev. J. D. Clough. I was baptized in Walter Whatley's tank by Rev. J. D. Clough. My Grandmother, J. T. Jowell was present, also Mrs. Laura Russell. I well remember the joy that came into my heart when Jesus came and forgave me my sins. I remember how brightly the moon shone that night when Grandma Jowell, Ms. Laura Russell and I drove slowly in a one-horse buggy to Bro. George Whatley's to spend the night (Grandma drove). I remember very distinctly lying awake till late in the night, praising God and rejoicing. Oh, that everybody could be a Christian."*

J. Q. became a Christian a month before he turned 15. What is remarkable is what you just read was his testimony written 60 years later!

My grandfather was a teacher in 1901 in a one-room school. He took a liking to one of his students who was six years younger, Alice Blocker, so he resigned his teaching position and two years later married his sweetheart when he was 26 and she was 20. They had 8 children in the next 15 years. My dad, Alfred Conner Locke, was J.Q and Alice's last child. My dad's written testimony was, "Clint and Delia Herring asked us to come to church at Salesville (Baptist Church) the next Sunday night. Papa and Mama, Quinton and I went and I was saved that night, May 16, 1937. Quinton was saved also that night and my Mother and Dad joined by statement. My mother shouted when she saw our decision." That is something to shout about! My dad and his brother became Baptists a month later when they were baptized at the Walker stock tank outside of Salesville, Texas, June 20, 1937.

My dad met my mom the next summer and 77 days later they were married. They had 3 boys; I am the last. My brother, David, says I am the reason he didn't have a sister. I remind him he is the reason they had me!

I was saved when I was 10 and surrendered my life for ministry at 18. My wife, Susan and I married when I was 21 and she was 18. Both of us worked to get me through Bible college. After graduation I was called to my first full-time church—Bible Baptist church, Electra, TX. Susan was six and one-half months pregnant with our first child when we moved. She suffered through 16 long hours of labor and would finally require a C-section. I knelt alone in the waiting room at Bethesda Hospital in Wichita Falls, prayed for protection for my young wife and baby (the days before sonograms) and vowed to raise that child to know and serve God.

That baby is my 51-year-old son, Craig, who was saved as a child and surrendered his life to God for ministry at age 19. For the last 21 years he has been the pastor at Willow Springs Missionary Baptist Church in Edgewood, TX. His son, Quinton, our oldest grandson, age 22, has surrendered his life to God for ministry. And our daughter Michelle married James Johnson, whom she first met at church camp. They are parents of our granddaughter Gracie (20) and Gatlin (18) - all are saved and serving God.

Here is a family secret—there are no perfect families. Now, I'll bet that surprised you. Even the families of the Bible were not perfect—Adam, Noah, Abraham, Jacob, Moses...on and on the list goes. Even though they were not perfect, God used them for His glory.

Howard Hendricks stated our challenge so clearly when he said, "We are surrounded by foreign, hostile, home-shattering influences in our world today. The supportive elements of society no longer feed and shade us. The Christian home must blossom in a field of weeds."[16] He wrote that in 1973 and the weeds are worse than they have ever been!

You may be thinking, "That's great for you, but that's not my story. My parents were not Christians. We never went to church. They are divorced."

That is precisely the point. Here you are - it's on you! A generational legacy begins somewhere with somebody. Will you be him or her? Every born-again person can go to the place where their generational testimony began.

---

[16] Howard G. Hendricks, *Heaven Help the Home*, p. 12.

- Zacchaeus had his sycamore tree. He must have been saved somewhere between the limb and the ground.
- The Samaritan woman had her well where she started her generational transformation.
- The maniac of the Gadarenes—the nude dude in a rude mood—had his graveyard.
- The thief had his cross. Though he died the day he was saved, his testimony lives on.
- For Saul, who became the Apostle Paul, it was on the road to Damascus. His spiritual offspring are countless.

Someone has said, "The only thing parents can take to heaven is their children." Think about that; but it is not the parent's choice. Every child has a choice. What parents are involved in is a "give and take" situation. We need to *give* our children every opportunity to know God personally and *take away* any excuse they might pick up from an inconsistent life.

Trust Christ as your Savior today. Turn your life over to the control of the Holy Spirit. Get in a solid, Bible-believing, Bible-preaching Baptist church. Begin living a life of obedience to God's Word.

For some, the story of your generational influence can begin today.

- 3 -

Satan is Alive and Well in America

As I was writing this chapter, I recalled an uncomfortable event that occurred in a church service twenty years ago. I had my share of those being a Baptist pastor for five months short of 50 years. This one may be in the top ten of my most "awkward" moments.

It was the Sunday before our national Presidential election in the year 2000. I was feeling a great spiritual burden about the course our nation was taking morally at the time. The message I delivered that morning was entitled, *The History of Nations – Will America Be Next?* During the message I asked, "Is God blind to the sins of our nation?" I then mentioned the following.

- Homosexuals proudly parading their alternative lifestyle in the streets of America.
- Legalized abortions where millions of unborn babies are killed.
- Sex scandals in the White House that shamed our nation.
- And among other things, the general dishonesty of Americans.

After making those remarks in the introduction, a man with whom I had been slowly building a friendship stood up and walked out of the service, well before the end of the message. I wasn't sure what was going on but presumed he may have gotten ill or had some kind of emergency.

A few weeks later I made a visit at his home to check on him and his family. He was visibly distant at the door and was very quick to say that I had offended him. Even I could see those signs. He invited me in, and I then listened to his personal story.

- On the homosexual matter, he had a son that was gay.
- Regarding abortion, his mother had died because of what he called "a coat-hanger abortion" and he was glad that our nation now offered legal abortions that would have saved the life of his mother.
- Regarding the sex scandal of President Bill Clinton in the White House, he was a yellow dog Democrat. He was sure I wasn't supposed to mix religion and politics in my sermons.
- About general dishonesty in America he offered no opinion, but I knew the business he owned had filed personal bankruptcy leaving a lot of people holding an empty bag.

It seemed to me that *God* gave that man a very personal message that morning, but he took it as *my* message and did not stay around to hear whatever else God had to say. He said he would no longer be attending the church.

I have not written this book with the intention of offending those who may disagree with my conclusions, but neither do I intend to compromise a single word of the clear teachings of the Holy Bible.

One man commented about the changes he had seen in American life, saying, *"Half a century after the sexual revolution, we're still trying to figure out what hit us..."* [1]

It could be said, "Americans know the price of everything, but the cost of nothing," to update a statement Oscar Wilde made more than 125 years ago. We all look closely to the price tag of a house or car or widescreen TV, but seldom think about the cost our beliefs and behaviors will painfully extract from us later.

Some of the metaphors used in the Bible as illustrations no longer relate to our technological culture, but with a little reflection we can clearly make the connection to their spiritual application. Slow down and think about the following Scriptures.

"He that soweth iniquity shall reap vanity:..." (Proverbs 22:8)

"Be not deceived; God is not mocked: for whatsoever a man soweth, that shall he also reap. For he that soweth to his flesh shall of the flesh reap corruption; but he that soweth to the Spirit shall of the Spirit reap life everlasting. And let us not be weary in well doing: for in due season we shall reap, if we faint not." (Galatians 6:7-9)

"But this *I say,* He which soweth sparingly shall reap

---

[1] Robert VerBruggen, *How the Sexual Revolution Unfolded,* The National Review, December 3, 2017.

also sparingly; and he which soweth bountifully shall reap also bountifully." (2 Corinthians 9:6) While this scripture is directly about financial giving, the principle is the same for all areas of life.

These biblical passages inform us of the unchanging laws of sowing and reaping – the laws of harvest.

- The Law of Investment: We will reap because we are *always* sowing.
- The Law of Identity: We will reap *what* we sow.
- The Law of Increase: We will reap *more* than we sow.
- The Law of Immensity: We will reap *in proportion* to what we sow.
- The Law of Interval: We will reap *later* than we sow.
- The Law of Integration: We reap what *others* have sown.
- The Law of Inevitability: We *will* reap in due season.
- The Law of Intervention: We reap because *God* is ultimately overseeing our sowing and reaping.

God created the universe to operate with order and balance – natural laws that have positive or negative results. God doesn't have to intervene directly. We are allowed to consider our options and make decisions, with each decision resulting in positive or negative consequences. A person doesn't have to believe in the law of gravity, however if he jumps off a tall building his mind will be changed, but it will be too late. The Creator imposed order in His creation so that life can flourish when we observe His laws. Francis Collins

(1950-), Director of the National Institutes of Health in Bethesda, Maryland, concluded, "When you look from the perspective of a scientist at the universe, it looks as if it knew we were coming."[2]

God's laws of order are valid for everyone– male or female, young or old, rich or poor, straight or any other distinction we might make, whether we know about the laws or not. These laws operate everywhere – in Africa, Asia and America. These laws exist at all times – first century biblical times and twenty-first century modern times. They operate whether we like them or not. When we sow the wind, we reap the whirlwind (Hosea 8:7). Too many Americans are sowing their wild oats through the week and then show up at church on Sunday and pray a quick prayer for crop failure. That kind of thinking is like trying to stop a forest fire with a toy water pistol or a plague of locusts with a single can of bug spray. **"He made a pit, and digged it, and is fallen into the ditch *which* he made. His mischief shall return upon his own head, and his violent dealing shall come down upon his own pate."** (Psalm 7:15-16)

Over the past sixty years the American mind has been dramatically transformed, but not improved. The way we know this is because of modern behavior in all areas, not just sexuality.

"We continually hear that changes in sexual attitudes

---

[2] Francis Collins, Director of the National Institute of Health, quoted by Adam Mabry, *Life and Doctrine*, p. 70.

are evidence of the march of progress, liberation, and freedom. Opposing the next phase of the glorious revolution, no matter what the next phase may be, is tantamount to opposing civil rights, history, and progress. The proponents of progress never even suggest that we stop, look over our shoulders, and take stock of what the previous steps of the Sexual Revolution have done."[3]

The shock waves from the "thought bombs" mentioned in chapter 1 are beginning to rip our society apart.[4]

Without a doubt, the culture is confused. Nowhere is the confusion more evident than in the area of sexuality, the most basic component of our humanity, and this confusion didn't appear out of nowhere.[5]

"There are always events to which we can point that evidence a merging of ideology into mainstream lifestyle. Those key events are pivotal because we never see them reversed. Teach a little, change a little, move a little, give a little, invent a little, redefine a little, wait a little, and we wake up and it has happened."[6]

There have been intended and unintended consequences of the Sexual Revolution of the 1960s. While some deviance had occurred in decades and centuries before that time, deviance seems to have been turned

---

[3] Jennifer R. Morse, *The Sexual State*, p. 56.

[4] Adapted from Hal Lindsey, *Satan is Alive and Well on Planet Earth*, p. 94.

[5] Travis Gilbert, sermon *Christian Clarity in the Midst of Culture Shift*, October 8, 2019.

[6] James Love, personal correspondence.

into a science in the last fifty plus years. The Bible sums up the perilous times of the last days of our age in 2 Timothy 3:13. **"But evil men and seducers shall wax worse and worse, deceiving, and being deceived."**

In the pages that follow I have put together ideas and concepts that were not generally known before the 1960s, at least regarding their commonality or acceptance.

While you go through the following list do more than process the information. Slow down and take time to put down people's names - family members, friends, work associates, neighbors - whose lives have been forever changed because of the sexual revolution that began in the 1960s. The author gave a considerable amount of time attempting to arrange these blights of the sexual revolution in sequential order but found the task impossible. The reason is simple: there cannot be a logical order for illogical behavior. Jesus prayed, "Father, forgive them, for they know not what they do" (Luke 23:34). Jesus believed there is something inherently stupid about sin. At least on some levels, sinful attitudes and actions are a form of insanity - they make no sense.

Victim Mentality

John MacArthur says in his book, *The Vanishing Conscience,* that "victimism has so infected our culture that one might even say the victim has become the very symbol - the mascot - of modern society... Anyone can escape responsibility for his or her wrongdoing simply by claiming the status of a victim."[7]

"I went to my psychiatrist to be psychoanalyzed,
To find out why I killed the cat and blackened my husband's eye.
He laid me on a downy couch to see what he could find
And this is what he dredged up from my subconscious mind:
When I was one, my mommy hid my dolly in a trunk,
And so it follows naturally that I am always drunk.
When I was two, I saw my father kiss the maid one day
And that is why I suffer from kleptomania.
At three, I had the feeling of ambivalence toward by brothers,
And so it follows naturally I poisoned all my lovers.
But I am happy, now I've learned the lesson this has taught;
That everything I do that's wrong is someone else's fault"

Anna Russell

In order to possess the modern concept of self-esteem many people default to self-exoneration and self-glorification.

Public Immodesty

Immodesty, either intentionally or ignorantly, is about provoking improper sexual thoughts or feelings caused by how one dresses. In some ways, the *intent* is part of what makes something wrong. For example, when I have travelled in Brazil or Africa there was nothing immodest about a woman exposing her breast to feed a baby in public, even while on a crowded airplane. If a woman did that on a bus in the United States it would be terribly out of place. When modern American women flaunts such actions, we perceive she is intending to be immodest and making some statement

[7] John E. MacArthur, Jr., *The Vanishing Conscience*, pp. 28, 21.

about her personal rights. Many of us have donned a hospital gown with the backside of our underwear exposed and it was not presumed to be improper since you are a patient in a hospital. But wearing the same thing to church or school or to Walmart would be terribly immodest. Immodesty is indecently exposing something that is meant to remain private. In the setting of Old Testament worship, God ordered the priests to wear garments under their robes "to cover their nakedness." (Exodus 28:42). The Bible speaks of the "attire of an harlot" (Proverbs 7:10) and the attire of "a bride" (Ezekiel 23:15); two different things altogether. "When it comes to sexual immodesty, the message sent with exposure is far more important than exactly what is seen. So pulling up a robe around the waist in order to run or work is not immodest (1 Kings 18:46; 2 Kings 4:29; 9:1; Jer. 1:17), but seeing the same bit of leg or thigh under a priest's robe is considered immodest (Ex. 20:26)."[8] It should not surprise us to see the rise in horrific sexual crimes in response to such an "undressed society." For the Christian, 1 Corinthians 6:19-20 is what makes modesty important. **"What? know ye not that your body is the temple of the Holy Ghost *which is* in you, which ye have of God, and ye are not your own? For ye are bought with a price: therefore glorify God in your body, and in your spirit, which are God's."**

Sexual Lust

Lust is desiring what God has forbidden for our good. Lust is big business in America and around the world. The majority of advertisement is sexualized.

---

[8] Daniel R. Heimbach, *True Sexual Morality*, p. 214.

Restaurants, such as Twin Peaks and Hooters, are offering more to their customers than good food. Super Bowl halftime entertainment has not been "G" rated in years. You have surely noticed, don't say you haven't, that the current television news and current interest shows that the men are generally shot from the neck up, but the entire bodies of women are often shown. Have you ever wondered why you have never seen the calves or cleavage of Walter Cronkite or Dan Rather? It is the sexual images of women that sells. On my way to the DFW airport recently a giant billboard for MINT Dentistry read, "I make Sexy Teeth." Is that a conversation you have had with your dentist recently? The worst thing? We are so accustomed to sexualized advertisement we hardly ever give it a second thought, but the first thought was enough. Women are being publicly objectified. Where is the outrage by the modern women's movements? Promoting a standard of the 'ideal' or 'perfect' body puts pressure on women to conform, whatever the cost. "Ultimately, sex is everywhere. On advertisements, billboards, magazines and social media galore. It definitely shows no signs of going away even though it usually is unnecessary and inappropriate. After all, if your product is really as good as you claim, you won't need a semi-naked woman plastered all over your ad to make it sell. That's just the easy way out."[9] One old country preacher lamented, "You can't sell hog feed without them putting a picture of a naked woman on the bag!"

---

[9] Alexandra Jones, *Sex Sells: It's Everywhere, but Does it Make it Right?* Medium.com. May 4, 2018.

Radical Feminism

A new role and attitude that was initiated and expressed in the 1960s grew as many agitated women got what they wanted, but now many are not that "happy" with what they got. Going to the grave lonely and childless wasn't worth "burning their bras" after all. Traditional women who were faithful wives and loving mothers had it right all along. True feminism holds and extends dignity and rights for women, but modern feminism is about the right of women to be free to control sexual reproduction, which is code for contraception and abortion. The first step of feminism was only to gain legal equality with men. It is now the full-fledged "liberation from heterosexual tyranny" with special privileges expected because they are women.[10] Chapter nine will have more you will want to read on this topic.

Promiscuity

Casual sex has become the recreation of too many teens and adults. Although between 1991-2015, the proportion of students who ever had sexual intercourse decreased from 54% to 41%, who can be happy knowing 4 of 10 teens have prematurely engaged in sex? "Until the mid-1960s, college dormitories were all single-sex and parietal rules were enforced with suspensions and expulsions."[11] As early as 1969, 150 colleges including Brown University, Stanford University, The University of Pennsylvania, Oberlin College, Clark University, and the California Institute of Technology, are providing

---

[10] Rene Denfeld, *The New Victorians*, p. 45, quoting Chery Clarke, *This Bridge Called My Back.*

[11] Christopher Caldwell, *The Age of Entitlement*, p. 46.

co-ed dorms – now called gender-neutral housing.[12] "There's now 'sex week' on a large smattering of college campuses, and condoms, while occasionally controversial, are not hard to find at the vast majority of university health centers. In other words, we have more or less embraced the reality that young people have sex before they get married, so they might as well be doing it safely."[13] C. S. Lewis believed that "if a healthy young man indulged his sexual appetite whenever he felt inclined, and if each act produced a baby, then in ten years he might easily populate a small village."[14] Is it any wonder that dating is out and hooking up is in?

Teen Pregnancy and Parenting

There has been a recent decline in teenage pregnancies in America, but still, the numbers are staggering and life changing. Some of that lower number is because of abortion. Help should be given to the young women who wants to carry their unborn baby and care for it after birth. Many school districts offer alternative classes, but the push now is to mainstream them into regular classes and activities the same as their non-pregnant peers. There is a real balance that needs to happen. The pregnancy of students should not be celebrated nor shamed – not celebrated by other students who see them as an acceptable model, nor shamed as though not having value, potential or a future. The balance is seldom reached.

---

[12] https://www.collegexpress.com/articles-and-advice/student-life/articles/living-campus/co-ed-dorms-sleeping-together/

[13] Hannah Seligson, *"The Case for Cohabitation,"* www.TheDailyBeast.com, April 18, 2012.

[14] C. S. Lewis, *Mere Christianity*, p. 49.

Unwed Childbearing

Women who are bearing children outside of marriage have expanded the welfare systems of American government beyond reasonable limits. "In 1960, roughly 5 percent of all births were to unmarried women, by 1970, the year President Richard Nixon introduced family planning into U.S. federal policy, roughly 10 percent of all births were non-marital. Since 2011, over 40 percent of all births are to unmarried women."[15] As of 2018, half of all children born to women under the age of 30 in America now are illegitimate. Three in 10 white children are born out of wedlock, as are 53 percent of Hispanic babies and 73 percent of black babies.[16]

Dead-Beat Dads

This is a pejorative term referring to parents of any gender who do not fulfill their parental responsibilities, especially when they evade court-ordered child support obligations or custody arrangements. According to CNN Business, deadbeat dads owed $100 billion in 2009 in unpaid child support - nearly half of that to taxpayer supporting children on public assistance costing taxpayers 53 billion dollars in back payments owed to deserving spouses.[17]

Home Alone

A recent U.S. Census report shows that 7 million of the nation's 38 million children ages 5 to 14 are left home

[15] Jennifer R. Morse, *The Sexual State*, p. 235.

[16] There are no illegitimate children; it was the man and woman who were illegitimate.

[17] https://money.cnn.com/2012/11/05/news/economy/unpaid-child-support/

alone regularly. For many parents, this is not a happy or freely chosen decision. The increase in single-parent households, the need for both parents to work in two-parent families, the lack of availability of affordable and constructive childcare, the fact that older relatives are working themselves, are too far away, or are unwilling to help, and the fact that school days are out of sync with workdays all create an untenable situation. For many families, there are gaps in child supervision that seem impossible to fill.[18]

Trial Relationships

This is the "drive before you buy" mentality, which has further compromised the institution of marriage. Many times, this is initiated only for shared financial reasons. The idea is that two can live more cheaply than one. Trial relationships are more "trial" than "relationship," they are bad, not good for couples. What does beginning a relationship with the expectation that it might not last say? Such relationships are "sexually-based," "emotion-based," "needs based," but not "commitment-based."

Cohabitation

Those choosing to live together without a legal marriage do so because marriage is no longer seen as obligatory, necessary or beneficial. Men and women have "live-in" partners which compromise any sense of morality. There is an interesting statement Jesus made in his conversation with the Samaritan woman in John 4. In response to the woman saying she had no husband,

---

[18] Marie Hartwell-Walker, Ed.D., *Children Who are Home Alone*, pyschcenteral.com, October 8, 2018.

Jesus said. **"Thou hast well said, I have no husband: For thou hast had five husbands; and he whom thou now hast is not thy husband: in that saidst thou truly."** (John 4:17-18) Jesus recognized the woman's five failed marriages but did not recognize her "live in" relationship as a legitimate marriage. Financial institutions have eased any marriage requirement for couples to purchase a house together, so they do many of the same things married people do without a commitment to permanent and pure marriage. Couples have come to the self-serving conclusion that "marriage is unimportant."

Single Parents

The stand-up singles who conceived a child outside of marriage and are now taking the responsibility of caring for the child or the "reluctantly divorced" singles whose marriages blew up against their intentions are some of the real heroes of our broken world in my estimation. What kind of adults have we become where we do not believe we owe our biological offspring a caring relationship with both parents (if possible and reasonable)? Single parents before the 1960s were for the majority men or women who became widowed because of an unexpected death. In the "old days" there was nothing intentional on the part of a woman or a man to take on parenting alone.

Blended Marriages

Many families in America are now made up of children who are "his, hers and ours." They are making the best out of bad situations, but no one should assume it is easy. While "the Brady Bunch" had their tensions and troubles, do not expect yours to be corrected in thirty minutes. There will always be a next episode.

Multi-Generational Families

Five percent of children and young people have grandparents who have assumed the job of parenting by default. The "golden years" of many grandparents have lost some luster because they have been forced back into a role they did not choose. They should be the ones being cared for in their advanced years, not the other way around.

Contraception and Condoms

These products are often distributed to teens by "thoughtful" adults, many of them parents. They are sold as "protection" from pregnancy and sexual diseases for those who want to have the freedom and fun involved with sex without the consequences. Their failure rates tell a different story.

Abstinence Mocked

Not having sex is no longer considered practical, yet it is the only reliable way to avoid pregnancy and sexually transmitted diseases. The benefits of entering a monogamous marriage as virgins are far-reaching. A girl who was being shamed for being a virgin said to her sexually active mockers, "I can be like you in fifteen minutes, but you can never be like me for the rest of your life." I would presume that movies like *Forty-Year-Old Virgin* that highlight the most "uncool" things for anyone, especially a male, is sexual restraint and sexual abstinence.

Fornication

God's "F" word for all pre-marital sex is "fornication" (Romans 1:29; 1 Corinthians 6:18). God has commanded sexual abstinence until a person is married (1 Thessalonians 4:2-6). "Every negative limitation on sexual behavior guards something tremendously positive and good. So, even though sexual temptation is deceptive and always whispers the opposite, sexual prohibitions in the Bible do not actually prevent anyone from truly enjoying God's gift of sex. Rather, they ensure that we will never lose the best by corrupting something God made to bless us."[19]

Adultery

Number seven in God's 10 Commandments is, "Thou shalt not commit adultery," the sexual unfaithfulness of those who are married. Adultery is viewed in the Bible as a serious moral violation. In the current culture adultery is viewed as a couple of consenting strangers who got carried away with their "passion" that results in few, if any, prolonged consequences. Adultery needs to be seen for what it can be – a person-killing, marriage-killing, child-killing, nation-killing act of divine defiance. Adultery was once considered a capital offense, but because it required two witnesses, the law served only as a deterrent.

Internet "Hookup Sites"

People of any sexual orientation can "cruise" the internet for a one night or casual encounter. It should not be called a "relationship"- that would cheapen the

---

[19] Daniel R. Heimbach, *True Sexual Morality,* p. 177.

term. It is about as debased as pets copulating in a dog park.

"Open Relationships"

The concept of an open relationship, inside or outside of marriage, involves casual sexual involvement without any of the responsibilities required in a genuine relationship. Females want "love with benefits" of a relationship. Men want "the benefits" without a relationship. Even if a couple agree on an *open* relationship it is the Creator's plan for married couples to have an *only* relationship.

Abortion

Abortion was the leading cause of death worldwide in 2019 with 42 million killed.[20] This is more than twice the number of all worldwide deaths caused by cancer, smoking, alcohol, traffic accidents, malaria and HIV-AIDs combined. 60 million babies have been murdered in America since *Roe vs. Wade* made abortion legal in 1973 by the Supreme Court of the United States. Writing for *The Cut,* Sarah Miller describes her fourth abortion, calling her latest "the best abortion ever." She wrote graphically and in profane terms about the ending of human life as if it were simply a somewhat distressful medical procedure.[21] The modern sonogram tells a story the abortionists have denied for decades – what is in the womb of the mother is not a fetus, but a baby with

[20] Adam Ford, DISRN.com. These numbers are accord to *Worldometers,* an organization that keeps a running tally on major world statistics. They calculate abortion numbers based on the latest statistics published in the World Health Organization (WHO).

[21] *The Cut,* June 19, 2019.

a heartbeat. Now, the issue of the sanctity of human life has been redirected as "a war for women's health." However, God recognizes life before birth (Psalm 139:13-16; Jeremiah 1: 4-5; Psalm 51:5).

"No Fault" Divorce

On September 4, 1969, California governor Ronald Reagan signed the "Family Law Act of 1969" into law, abolishing the fault grounds for divorce, replacing it only with "no-fault." "Virtually no one, even the most conservative traditionalist, realized just how radical this legal innovation really was. No one foresaw the many new threads of laws and social practices that would come into being as the new non-permanent, no-sexually exclusive version of marriage worked its way through the culture."[22]

The divorce rate in America has decreased over the last decade for this simple reason - many people are choosing not to get married at all. As one person profoundly observed, "Before you can get divorced, you have to get married first." It has never been as easy to sever a marriage as it is today with "no-fault divorce." There are so many false and destructive beliefs that attempt to justify divorce. (1) "If we are not happy, it is better for everyone if we go ahead and divorce." (2) "The kids will be alright." Try this. Ask them. Hands down, the children will beg their parents not to divorce. And in order to take up the slack created by a selfish divorce, parents and grandparents, teachers and coaches have to work double duty because of the inevitable neglect. (3) "We will work this out

---

[22] Jennifer R. Morse, *The Sexual State*, p. 226.

respectfully." Judges and courts are the ones who work it out. How about a quick math equation for those considering divorce? When 1 man and 1 woman marry, the 2 become 1. When they divorce, the 1 becomes 2 halves, not 2 whole people again.

Domestic Violence

"Intimate partner violence," as we are now encouraged to call it, is higher among cohabiting, divorced or casual partners, than among those who are in a faithful marriage. Conduct your own survey from the regular news stories on the evening local TV news. I do not think you will find this wrong. When men and women have not been taught to respect others you can expect domestic disturbances. Domestic violence is usually symptomatic of the wrong kind of relationship.

Binary Gender

Binary means something that can be divided into two categories. Sexually, that means there are only males and females. However, the new idea is that a person's biological sex is not an objective reality but something "assigned at birth." But wait. Could there be more? Some suggest, "After being taught in school that there are only two genders, it can be challenging to hear how broad the gender spectrum really is. As you focus on building a more inclusive culture at your company, don't worry if you occasionally get terms mixed up or forget what a word means. Recognizing that you've still got more to learn is part of the process. Acknowledge your slip-ups, extend the same level of respect to everyone, and be open to hearing more about the lived experiences of others whose genders vary from your own."[23] Facebook allows for 71 gender options. *National Geographic* surveyed 1,000 Millennials (ages 18-34) about gender. 50 percent believed gender to be a spectrum and not biologically determined at birth.[24]

PGP

PGP Stands for "Preferred Gender Pronoun." In 2020 my granddaughter served on the orientation staff for the University of Oklahoma during her sophomore and junior years. On her official name tag, under her name, Gracie Johnson, were her preferred pronouns "she, her, hers." This is an accommodation for transgender and gender nonconforming people. This is the way the LGBTQ propagandists want people to separate sexual deviance from gender.

Homosexuality

Homosexuals are males who are attracted sexually only to other males. "Our word homosexuality is not a Bible term. It is man's term intended to remove the moral and spiritual connotations of sin. The act is unconditionally condemned... The Bible uses fifteen different terms to refer to such an act: sodomy (1 Kings 14:24); abomination (Lev. 18:22; 20:13); vile affections (Romans 1:26, 27); burning with lust, (Romans 1:27); dishonoring the body (Romans 1:24); violating nature (Romans 1:26); shameful lusts (Romans 1:27); wickedness (Judges 19:23); lusting for strange flesh (Jude 7); filthy dreamers (Jude 8); abusers of

---

[23] Samantha McLaren, *15 Gender Identity Terms You Need to Know to Build an Inclusive Workplace*, May 20, 2019, LinkedIn Talent Blog.

[24] Robin Martinez Henig, *Rethinking Gender*, National Geographic, January 2017.

themselves (1 Corinthians 6:9); effeminate (1 Corinthians 6:9); defilers of themselves (1 Timothy 1:9-10); inordinate (Colossians 3:56); reprobate (Romans 1:28)."[25]

> "Even in purely nonreligious terms, homosexuality represents a misuse of the sexual faculty and, in the words of one... educator, of 'human construction.' It is a pathetic little second-rate substitute for reality, a pitiable flight from life. As such it deserves fairness, compassion, understanding and, when possible, treatment. But it deserves no encouragement, no glamorization, no rationalization, no fake status as minority martyrdom."
>
> This appraisal comes from *Time* Magazine, January 21, 1966.

As recently as 1972 the American Psychiatric Association (APA) treated homosexuality as a disorder deserving of psychiatric treatment. Now those who oppose homosexuality are sent off for therapy.

Lesbianism

Lesbianism refers to females who are attracted sexually only to other females. It has been typically said that women are the most virtuous of the genders. The last stages of a culture that is disintegrating is when females become profane in their language, dishonest in their affairs, and deviant in their sexuality. A survey conducted by Whitman Insights Strategies and BuzzFeed News, in 2018, found of the LGBTQ community only 16 percent claimed they were

---

[25] Nelson L. Price, *The Emmanuel Factor*, pp. 58-59.

lesbians.[26] What remains strange to me is that lesbians say they are attracted only to other women, but usually one of them in the relationship dresses, looks and acts like a male.

Bisexual

Bisexuals are people who are attracted sexually to both males and females. They represented 46 percent of the LGBTQ who were polled in the previously quoted Whitman-BuzzFeed survey.[27] The governor of Oregon since 2015 is Kate Brown (1960-) who is openly bisexual and lives with her husband, Dan Little and two stepchildren.

Transgender

This is a gender identity or gender expression that differs from their sex assigned at birth, previously called "sexual diaspora." Dr. Paul McHugh, former head of psychiatry at Johns Hopkins, surveyed people who had undergone "transgendering" and found they're typically no happier than they were before. Dr. McHugh said, "At the heart of the problem is confusion over the nature of the transgendered. 'Sex change' is biologically impossible."[28] Male-to-female transsexualism, especially as it related to sexuality and fetishes, was initially

---

[26] Shannon Keaton, *Polls Find Lesbians Are only 16 Percent of the LGBTQ Population in America*, BuzzFeed, June 15, 2018.

[75] Dominic Holden, *Most LGBTQ Americans Actually Love Having Cops and Corporations In Pride Parades,* Buzzfeed, June 24, 2019. https://www.buzzfeednews.com/article/dominicholden/lgbtq-poll-pride-month-cops-coprorations

[28] Robert Royal, *Transgenderism and Perfect Freedom,* www.thecatholicthing,org, June 17, 2019.

seen as a perversion, then a disorder. Now it's an identity, covered under a much larger umbrella term, "transgenderism." More information on transgenders is in Chapter Seven.

Questioning

The sexual confusion has reached new lows. Now the long-held understanding that is being challenged is there are more than males and females – gender binary. Facebook allows users to describe themselves as any one of seventy-one genders. People can also select their preferred pronoun. The idea is that a person's biological sex is *not* an objective reality but something "assigned at birth." Description now allow for 122 gender options.

Intersexual

Intersex is a group of conditions where there is a discrepancy between the external genitals and the internal genitals (the testes and ovaries). Sometimes, a baby can have genitalia with some male characteristics and some female characteristics. And even deeper than external appearance, some people are born with a mix of male and female biological features (such as a uterus and testicles) that can't be seen on the outside. When a person doesn't fall exactly into the "male" or "female" sex designation, the term "intersex" may be used.[29]

Pansexual

People who are attracted to or can be attracted to people of all genders, presuming there are more than

---

[29] Healthline.com, *Here's What to Know About Having a Baby Who Is Intersex.* https://www.healthline.com/health/baby/what-does-intersex-look-like#considerations

two. Miley Cryus (1992-) American child star Hannah Montana, singer, songwriter, and actress, identifies as a pansexual. "My whole life, I didn't understand my own gender and my own sexuality. I always hated the word 'bisexual,' because that's even putting me in a box. I went to the LGBTQ center here in L.A., and I started hearing these stories. I saw one human in particular who didn't identify as male or female. Looking at them, they were both: beautiful and sexy and tough but vulnerable and feminine but masculine. And I related to that person more than I related to anyone in my life."[30] It is somewhat interesting that when she wanted to get married in 2018, she did so to the male Australian actor Liam Hemsworth (1990-).

Deadnaming

Deadnaming is referring to a person by their birth name or the name they went by before transitioning or changing their name for their new identity. It is considered to be extremely disrespectful and harmful, as one trans said, "the ultimate insult." Huffpost headlined an article, *Deadnaming a Trans Person is Violence – So Why does the Media Do it Anyway?* The article believed deadnaming "denies trans not just from their identity, but their humanity."[31]

Churches Ordaining Homosexuals/Lesbians as Pastors/Priests

Many denominations that are dying, like the

---

[30] Francesca Bacardi, *Miley Cyrus Talks Coming Out as Pansexual*, ENews, October 11, 2016.

[31] Huffpost, *Deadnaming a Trans Person is Violence*, March 17, 2017.

Episcopalians, United Church of Christ, Presbyterians, Methodists, and some so-called Baptists, are caving to cultural pressure and are ordaining homosexuals and lesbians as ministers.

Same-Sex Marriage

The same-sex marriage push was not going well until it was rebranded to "marriage equality." Who could be against marriage equality? Same-sex marriage was made legal on June 26, 2015, by a United States Supreme Court ruling.

Degenderizing Babies

It is now being advocated that instead of celebrating the addition of a "boy" or "girl" baby, parents should hold the baby's gender open until they or their children affirm their sexual identity.

Same-Sex Couples Adopting Children

Obviously, the LGBTQ crowd do not produce children themselves. So, they take babies from men or women who were previously in heterosexual relationships where children were born. The United States courts are now sympathetic toward these kinds of adoptions to modern same-sex couples.

Gay Pride Parades

Many of the behind the scenes antics at "Gay Pride" parades are not covered by the news because they are so openly vile. They are publicly X-rated and proud of it. It started 50 years ago, June 28, 1970, and where else but in New York City.

Suicide Among the LGBTQ

Suicide is significantly higher in the LGBTQ community than among the general population. This is often attributed to bullying or isolation. In many cases, it is because of a confused and compromised mentality about their sexual identity. Suicide rates are even higher among transgenders.

HIV and STDs

In 2018, Sexually Transmitted Diseases (STDs) surged for the fifth straight year, reaching an all-time high.

At present approximately 1.1 million people in the U.S. are living with Human Immunodeficiency Virus (HIV) today. About 14 percent of them (1 in 7) do not know it and need testing.[32] HIV continues to have a disproportionate impact on certain populations, particularly racial and ethnic minorities and gay and bisexual men.

Poz-Friendly

This is a person who does not have HIV and is willing to have sex with someone who is HIV positive.

Reproductive Technology

In vitro fertilization (IVF) at first offered hope to married couples when the males were sterile with the wife using donor sperm. For the sterile wife, it turned to egg-harvesting and a rent-a-womb surrogate. Now, high wage-earning homosexuals and lesbians can outsource the baby-making business to the professionals and a low

---

[32] https://www.hiv.gov/hiv-basics/overview/data-and-trends/statistics

wage-earning surrogate. Afterwards, they can also hire a nanny and not miss a day of work if they don't wish to.[33]

The Heritage Society reported on July 3, 2018, "Political and social support for the sale of infants by women who need money is increasing in the United States, despite human rights campaigns to ban surrogacy and the parallel practices of organ sales and prostitution. Women who need money rent out their wombs to people who can pay as much as $200,000. This practice is promoted by a burgeoning fertility industry and uncritically cheered on by an expanding cadre of neoliberal LGBT activists. The public, our lawmakers, and even some health professionals are relatively fact-free regarding the adverse consequences of surrogacy for everyone except the purchasing parents and the businessmen who control fertility clinics."[34]

Sexual Assault Scandals

The "Me-Too" movement exposed predatory males like Bill Cosby, Harvey Weinstein, Al Franken, Matt Lauer, Charlie Rose, Jeffery Epstein, and other men who all professed to be "pro-woman."

The numbers of sexual assault – date rape, gang/group rape, child abuse cases– are numerically off the chart. The Federal Bureau of Investigation has put out an alert about the increase of in-flight sexual assaults. Typically, men are the perpetrators, and women and

---

[33] Rod Dreher, The American Conservative, *Victims Of The Sexual Revolution,* July 3, 2018.

[34] *Causalities of Surrogacy,* The Heritage Society, Video, May 16, 2019.

unaccompanied minors are the victims. The report said, "It's safe to say that many incidents occur that are not reported."[35]

Prostitution

Should prostitution be considered a job like any other, whose practitioners could be empowered by workplace protections if it were made legal? Or is it inherently harmful — a form of violence predicated on racial, gender, and income inequality from which women should be set free? Female empowerment through sex work has become a surprising liberal rallying cry amplified worldwide by billionaire George Soros, whose Open Society Foundations funds organizations that promote it. Groups from Amnesty International, the Human Rights Watch, the ACLU, and even the Women's March have embraced it, and measures that would decriminalize all aspects of prostitution are being pushed in Washington, D.C., and New York state. "Decriminalizing sex work would improve the health and safety of sex workers and put them on the path to greater stability," US Representative from the 7th District of Massachusetts, Ayanna Pressley said in an interview. She has embraced the argument that sex work is the only work available to some marginalized people — particularly transgender women of color — and that they would be less vulnerable if they could better advocate for themselves and report crimes committed against them.[36] It is well

[35] https://www.fbi.gov/news/stories/raising-awareness-about-sexual-assault-aboard-aircraft-042618

[36] Stephanie Ebbert, *Sex Work or Sexual Abuse?* Boston Globe, Dec. 16, 2019.

documented that prostitution is what finances much of organized crime. Prostitution is one of the most dangerous professions in the country, worse than Alaskan fishermen, or loggers, or oil rig workers. In fact, in the U.S., prostitutes get busted more often than Johns or pimps by a huge margin. Every year in the U.S., between 70,000 and 80,000 people are arrested for prostitution, costing taxpayers approximately $200 million.[37]

Human Trafficking and Sports

At all the annual major sporting events like the NFL's annual Super Bowl, the NBA's Finals, and the Soccer World Cup, there is an increase is sex-trafficking. Prostitutes are brought in to meet the demand for this perversion.

Child Sex Trafficking

Geoff Rogers, co-founder of the *U.S. Institute Against Human Trafficking,* on how sex-trafficking across the U.S., while primarily targeting girls, also targets boys as young as 10-years-old and dresses them as girls. San Diego, known as one of America's most beautiful cities, is also making news because of a Department of Justice study estimating that its underground sex trafficking economy exceeds $800 million a year.[38]

Planned Parenthood Selling "Baby Organs"

In a strange twist of responsibility, Liberty Counsel is having to defend Sandra Merritt, the lady who exposed PP's purchasing baby parts to sell to researchers. She is

---

[37] HG.org/prostitution.

[38] https://usiaht.org/about-us/

being sued in nine felony charges by California Attorney General Xavier Becerra for their undercover journalism work which exposed Planned Parenthood's trade in baby body parts. The suit is for $58 million dollars for invasion of their privacy.[39]

Pornography

For many people, any attempt to define the word *pornography* calls to mind the oft-quoted line from Supreme Court Justice Potter Stewart in 1964: "...I know it when I see it." While compilers of dictionaries might wish to be granted such latitude in explaining the meaning of certain words, they are held to a higher standard. *Pornography,* which has been used in English since the middle of the 19th century, comes from the Greek *pornographos* ("writing about prostitutes"), and initially referred to visual or written matter designed to cause sexual arousal, a meaning that is still the most common one employed today. *Pornography* has taken on an additional, non-sexualized sense: one that refers to a depiction of sensational material (such as violence) in order to elicit a reaction. The phrase "pornography of violence," for example, began to be used in the early 1950s.[40]

There was a *New York Times Magazine* cover story on May 18, 2001 called "Naked Capitalists: There's No Business Like Porn Business." Pornography is big business--with $10 billion to $14 billion in annual sales.

---

[39] https://lc.org/sandra2

[40] https://www.merriam-webster.com/dictionary/pornography

The author, Frank Rich, says pornography is "no longer a sideshow to the mainstream...it is the mainstream."[41]

By 2017, the porn industry's net worth was about $97 billion. That is enough money to feed at least 4.8 billion people a day. Every year Hollywood releases roughly 600 movies and makes $10 billion in profit. And how much does the porn industry make? Porn turns out 13,000 films and has revenue of close to $15 billion in profit. The porn industry makes more money than Major League Baseball, the NFL and the NBA combined.[42]

According to recent numbers, the leading porn website made the top 10 list of the most popular websites in the United States and gets more traffic than eBay, Wikipedia, Instagram, Reddit, Craigslist, Pinterest, New York Times, and Netflix.[43]

A veritable sewer pipe has broken throughout the nation and the world.

Here is a curious side note. Don't expect to get any help from the world's health experts. While the American Psychiatric Association (APA) recognizes all kinds of marginal addictions for treatment, "porn addiction" isn't an official diagnosis recognized by the APA, so no definitive diagnostic criteria guide mental health professionals in a diagnosis. Here is their conclusion:

---

41 Forbes, *How Big is Porn?* May 25, 2001.

42 Medium.com *How Big is the Porn Industry,* February 10, 2017.

43 SimilarWeb, March 1, 2020.

"Some people aren't interested in it, and some are deeply offended by it. Others partake of it occasionally, and others on a regular basis. It all boils down to personal preference and personal choice."[44]

Pedophilia

Pedophilia is sex with children. Child molesters are excused as having a different "sexual orientation," and a preference for "intergenerational sex." Michael Peterson, who treats pedophile Catholic priests at the St. Luke Institutes, says, "We don't see heterosexual pedophiles at all."[45] Pedophiles are all homosexuals. There is an alarming number of both molesters and victims.

NAMBLA

NAMBLA is an acronym for National Association Man Boy Love Association whose agenda is to repeal laws prohibiting adult men from having sex with boys under the age of consent, and to repeal laws regarding age of consent in general.

Bestiality

Bestiality, also called zoophilia, is a human having sex with an animal. One man argued that his having sex with his dog should be accepted because, when a person forms a deep emotional bond with an animal, it can sometimes "develop to be a sexual one."[46]

---

[44] https://www.healthline.com/health/pornography-addiction

[45] Mary Eberstadt, *The Elephant in the Sacristy*, Weekly Standard, June 17, 2002, p. 22.

[46] Daniel R. Heimbach, *True Sexual Morality*, p. 172.

Language Modification/Accommodation

Language has been changed to protect the guilty. "Sexual preference" is now "sexual orientation." "Same-sex marriage" is now "marriage equality." "Cohabitation" is now "Co-residing." "Promiscuous" is now "sexually active." "Surrogates" are "sex care providers." "Prostitutes" are "sex workers." "Perverts" are "sexually dysfunctional." "Unborn "babies" are now "fetuses." "Abortion" is now a matter of "women's health" and "Reproductive Freedom." "Pro-abortion" is now "Pro-Choice." "Sex Education" is now "Reproductive Health Education." The redefinition of these terms is an attempt to direct people away from the truth and the self-condemning human conscience.

Sensitivity/Diversity Training

Every business of any size will have their Human Resource department require their employees to be regularly trained (brain washed) about the treatment of fellow employees with a significant list of "dos" and "don'ts" regarding people of diversity.

Lawsuit Conformity

The LGBTQ mob have intimidated non-conformists by suing those who would not provide services based on their religious convictions. This includes bakers, florists, photographers, event venues...the list is endless.

Colleges and Universities Offer Degrees in Queer Studies

Colleges and universities that are heavily funded by the United States federal government are offering LGBTQ courses and degrees in "Queer Studies" (their terminology).

Inappropriate Sex Education

Federally funded programs in public schools demand students of all ages be required to attend sex education classes. "Sex education in the schools appears to operate more as an incitement to sexual activities than as a heeded caution."[47] Check out Chapter Six, the Shameless Super-Sexualization of Children."

Birth Rate Decline in America

The nation's population grew by less than 0.5 percent in 2019 - part of a steady decline since 2015. This decline is because parents are having fewer and fewer children - the average family consisted of 3.14 persons in 2019. Only four million babies were born in America in 2019 (total population 328 million), compared to 4,257,850 in 1960 when the American population was much smaller (total population 180 million). Part of the diminishing population is due to more and more abortions. 18 percent of pregnancies (excluding miscarriages) in 2017 ended in abortion. Approximately 862,320 abortions were reported in 2017. This is a decline in the years preceding but the numbers are still heart-breaking.

Abortion clinics, liquor stores, and marijuana shops were considered essential during the 2020 Covid-19 pandemic in America, while churches and mom and pop stores were classified non-essential.

---

[47] Robert Bork, *Slouching Toward Gomorrah*, p.159.

Radical Ecologists

The idea is that too many people living on planet earth are creating an ecological disaster and a future economic breakdown. On the www.youmatter.world it asks, *Should we Stop Having Children in Order to be Truly Sustainable and Save the Planet?* The site says, "In order to meet our demand, human activities are changing and destroying ecosystems at an incredible speed that is actually 100 to 1000 times faster than natural selection would be. Deforestation, biodiversity loss, the immeasurable usage of disposables, greenhouse gases and climate change are, to name a few, some of the reasons why planet Earth could say we're not really making a brilliant job down here."[48]

Just the opposite can be argued. Without an increase in births, in combination with the increasing aging of the elderly, and the horrific loss of millions of unborn babies who are aborted, a real economic crisis does loom.

Conclusion

Raquel Welch (1940-), a Golden Globe-winning film, TV and stage actress who starred in 45 films, at the age of 70 wrote an opinion article on May 8, 2010 for CNN.

> "Margaret Sanger opened the first American family-planning clinic in 1916, and nothing would be the same again. Since then the growing proliferation of birth control methods has had an awesome effect on both sexes and led to a sea change in moral values.

[48] Andre Goncalves, *Should we stop having children in order to be truly sustainable and save the planet?* September 19, 2018. www.youmatter.world.

And as I've grown older over the past five decades -- from 1960 to 2010 -- and lived through this revolutionary period in female sexuality, I've seen how it has altered American society -- for better or worse.

One significant, and enduring, effect of The Pill on female sexual attitudes during the 60's, was: 'Now we can have sex anytime we want, without the consequences. Hallelujah, let's party!'

It remains this way. These days, nobody seems able to 'keep it in their pants' or honor a commitment! Raising the question: Is marriage still a viable option? I'm ashamed to admit that I myself have been married four times, and yet I still feel that it is the cornerstone of civilization, an essential institution that stabilizes society, provides a sanctuary for children and saves us from anarchy.

In stark contrast, a lack of sexual inhibitions, or as some call it, 'sexual freedom,' has taken the caution and discernment out of choosing a sexual partner, which used to be the equivalent of choosing a life partner. Without a commitment, the trust and loyalty between couples of childbearing age is missing, and obviously leads to incidents of infidelity. No one seems immune. As a result of the example set by their elders, by the 1990s teenage sexual promiscuity -- or hooking up -- with multiple partners had become a common occurrence.

Seriously, folks, if an aging sex symbol like me starts waving the red flag of caution over how low moral standards have plummeted, you know it's gotta be pretty bad. In fact, it's precisely because of the sexy image I've had that it's important for me to speak up and say: Come on girls! Time to pull up our socks! We're capable of so much better."[49]

[49] Raquel Welch, CNN opinion article, *It's Sex O'clock in America*, May 8, 2010. https://www.cnn.com/2010/OPINION/05/07/welch.sex.pill/index.html

- 4 -

The Insanity of the Modern Non-Thinking "Reprobate Mind"

You have probably heard the statement, "The mind is a terrible thing to waste." It is even sadder to see someone lose their mind – that, too, is a terrible thing. This happens to people we know, and many are not able to do anything about it.

Some mind issues are just a part of old age. As you age there are physical things that you no longer can do, and if you try to do them, you regret it for days. Old people who are confined to living alone or in a nursing facility often repeat themselves three or four times in a thirty-minute visit. They see so few people and never engage the world outside, so their world becomes very small.

My mom had a stroke late in her life that rewired her memory. She still had a great mind but could not remember the thirty years she had previously lived. She could be so funny at times. She was always wondering why God wasn't taking her to heaven. In trying to console her I said, "Mom, you're just going to have to be patient." In a flash she said, "What has this family ever known about patience!" This was the lady who knew who I was but could not remember my name.

Some who I have known had a severe head injuries and their brains shut down. After the swelling on their brain came down, in different cases, all, some or none of their brain function was restored.

Who of us do not have a first-hand experience with the devastating, life-changing disease called Alzheimer's? I have personally seen most of the stages: mild confusion, progressive memory loss, anger, finally being completely unaware of their surroundings. The disease disconnects the nerves from the brain but does not kill the person – it is other complications that lead to death. Five million people currently have the disease, with the numbers expected to triple to 16 million by 2050.

Others we know have damaged their brains through illegal drug use. Drug overdose is now the leading cause of death for Americans under the age of 50 and has lowered the average life expectancy in the United States.[1] Over the next decade as many as half-a-million people in the United States will die from opioid substances that include heroin, painkillers such as morphine and oxycodone, and synthetic agents such as fentanyl.[2]

In this chapter we will discover a mind malfunction that is far more serious.

---

[1] Shelia Kaplan. *C.D.C. Reports a Record Jump in Drug Overdose Deaths Last Year, New York Times,* Nov. 3. 2017.

[2] Max Blau, *STAT forecast:* Opioids could kill nearly 500,000 Americans in the next decade," June 27, 2017. https://bit.ly/2OQVCAY.

Have you ever overheard what someone said, or observed what someone was doing and asked yourself, "What were they thinking?" We unsuccessfully try to find some hidden rhyme or reason for it, but it just doesn't calculate. In fact, what many people are doing makes no sense at all. Here is the answer. You can't figure it out because it is beyond figuring out. We presume they have a mind, but it seems to not be functioning at present.

Why do homeless people live on the street, defecate and urinate on public sidewalks, dig around in dirty trash cans to find something to eat, scrounge enough money by begging to do drugs...yet they refuse to go to a free night shelter to eat a hot meal and sleep in a clean and safe environment? They do it because they want their "freedom." Where is the logic in that? It is illogical for us to propose a logical solution for those who choose to be illogical.

Where is the slightest bit of logic for 20-year-old Adam Lanza killing 20 children between the ages of six and seven, plus six adult staff members at Sandy Hooks Elementary School on Dec. 14, 2012, in Newtown, Connecticut? If you need your logic to be further confused, add to this dozens of other senseless mass murders. It defies logic or reason. Something more is at play.

Why did Kenneth Lay (1942-2006) the founder, CEO and Chairman of Enron, make the choice to bankrupt a multi-billion-dollar company and causing 20,000 employees to lose their jobs and in most cases their life savings, not counting the billions of dollars lost by investors. And then comes along Bernie Madoff (1938-) who is presently serving a 150-year prison sentence for his 65-billion-dollar investment fraud. What were they thinking?

How does one get to these places in life?

Find a Bible and follow the trail that is laid out in Romans chapter one. Speaking of America, John MacArthur wondered, "Who can read the verses of Romans 1 and deny that they describe our own society right now with an uncanny precision."[3] And how much more so since that statement was made twenty-five years ago.

The Conflict

God Openly Stands Against All Sin

"The good news" of the gospel in Romans 1:16, which is "the power of God unto salvation to every one that believeth," is offered only against the dark backdrop of Romans 1:18. **"For the wrath of God is revealed from heaven against all ungodliness and unrighteousness of men, who hold the truth in unrighteousness; ..."**

- Sin ignores God's honor; it embarrasses us.
- Sin disobeys God's commandments; it condemns us.
- Sin violates God's law; it makes criminals of us.
- Sin corrupts God's health; it sickens us.
- Sin steals God's blessings: it robs us.

---

[3] John MacArthur, *The Vanishing Conscience*, p. 73.

- Sin disrupts God's peace; it makes us guilty.[4]

Leon Morris defines "wrath" as "a strong and settled opposition to all that is evil arising out of God's own nature. It is the holy revulsion of God – being against that which is the contradiction of His holiness."[5]

The word "ungodliness" points to our condition, while "unrighteousness" points to our conduct.

The idea of the word "hold," as it regards the truth, means people "suppress," they "resist" the truth that sin is serious and is offensive to God. "The Scriptures teach that the problem of human unbelief is not the absence of evidence; rather, it is the suppression of it."[6]

God's wrath that has always been revealed against sin is seen in His response to Adam and Eve in the Garden of Eden, to Cain after he murdered his brother, to Noah's day and the universal flood, toward the Tower of Babel project where language was multiplied and the people scattered, and the utter destruction of Sodom and Gomorrah because of their wickedness.

We should not wonder if America is waiting for the wrath of God to come. Ungodliness and unrighteousness are signs that God has already brought a degree of His wrath on us.

---

[4] Elmer Towns, *Praying the Lord's Prayer,* p. 150.
[5] Leon Morris, *The Apostolic Preaching of the Cross,* p. 35.
[6] Ravi Zacharias, *Can Man Live Without God?* p. 183.

People Openly Stand Against God

There are increasingly large segments of 21st century American society where God is not welcome in their personal lives or in the public square. The more often a person says "no" to God, the more easily he says "yes" to sin.

The "God" references in Romans 1:16-32 clarify for us that God is at the center of this conflict, and mankind does not like it.[7]

- God is ignored and denied as Creator (Romans 1:20). People do not see what they refuse to see. A believer in the Almighty sees a sunrise and says, "What a God!" An unbeliever sees the same sunrise and says, "Let's go fishing."
- God is not recognized as Most Glorious (Romans 1:21). While segments of mankind are deified, God is defamed.
- God is not thanked for His goodness and gracious gifts (Romans 1:21).
- God is marginalized and made more manageable by being recreated as an idol (Romans 1:23-25). Idolatry is not just oversight of the true God; it is full-blown rejection and rebellion against the True and Living God.
- God eventually "gives up" the rejectors to their own desires (Romans 1:14, 26, 28).
- God is "hated" (Romans 1:30).
- God will judge (Romans 1:32).

---

[7] "God" 16, 17, 18, 19 (2), 21(2), 23, 24, 25, 18 (2), 30, 32; "God head" 20; "Creator" 25; Him 20; "His" 20.

While a general belief in God as our Creator is not enough to save a person, it is enough, if rejected, to condemn a person. All of mankind is "without excuse." God will accept your confession, but He will not tolerate your rejection.

The Culprit

Throughout Romans 1 the "thinking" part of man - the mind and heart – is exposed as the problem. The heart of the human problem is the human heart. **"The heart *is* deceitful above all *things,* and desperately wicked: who can know it?"** (Jeremiah 17:9) There has always been a battle for the mind.

With your Bible open, scan through Romans 1 and underline the words and concepts relating to the "mind."

- "Know" (Romans 1:19). This is a reference to human cognition. Divine disclosure is made by God which allows mankind to make human discoveries.
- "Understood" (Romans 1:20). God has given every person an internal witness – a conscience. Notice, this knowledge is "in" us. This is innately known truth about God – His reality, His character, His standards of right and wrong, and good and evil.
- "Knew" (Romans 1:21) God has also given every person an external witness – creation. This revelation "around us" is "clearly seen." When it comes to empirical evidence, that which is around us, the world in which we live, it should

be obvious. The universe and those who live in it should cause us to see its magnificence, beauty, and order and conclude there is a God and He is powerful.

- "Vain imaginations" (Romans 1:21). The speculations and opinions of mankind are empty.
- "Foolish heart was darkened" (Romans 1:21). When a person walks away from the divine light of truth he is walking into the darkness of error.
- "Professing themselves to be wise, they became fools." (Romans 1:22). People who reject or ignore God's truth are mental idiots to be pitied regardless of how many letters follow their name. "Sin is the biggest confidence game in town. No one is so thoroughly fooled as the so-called liberated (thinking) person."[8] It is possible to be educated beyond our intelligence.
- "Hearts" (Romans 1:24).
- "Did not like to retain God in their knowledge" (Romans 1:28). There is no place for God in the modern, non-thinking mind.
- "Mind... reprobate" (Romans 1:28).
- "Without understanding" (Romans 1:31).
- "Knowing" (Romans 1:32). They see where things are heading but will not turn back.

Bible commentator John Phillips says mankind was "consciously irreligious and consequently irrational."[9]

---

[8] J.W. MacGorman, *Romans: Everyman's Gospel*, p. 25.

[9] John Phillips, *Exploring Romans*, p. 28.

The Consequences

Three times in Romans 1 the writer declares, "God also gave them up... God gave them up... God gave them over to a reprobate mind." (Romans 1:24, 26, 28).

> "A country that has been now since 1963 relentlessly in the courts driving God out of public life shouldn't be surprised at all of the problems we have.
> Because we've in fact attempted to create a secular country, which I think is frankly a nightmare."
>
> Newt Gingrich, November 21, 2011
> Former Speaker of the U.S. House of Representatives

God Removes Divine Restraints

People often get what they want but end up not wanting what they get. In the summer before I became a senior in high school, prayer in public school was deemed unconstitutional on June 25, 1962 in the Engel v. Vitale decision of the United States Supreme Court. During the summer after I graduated from high school, Bible reading in public school was no longer allowed by a ruling of the United States Supreme Courts on June 17, 1963, in the Abington School District v. Schempp. In Stone v. Graham, November 17, 1980, the United States Supreme Court ruled a Kentucky law that required the posting of the Ten Commandments on the wall of every public school classroom in the state violated the establishment clause of the First Amendment because the purpose of the display was essentially religious. Now in the place of the Ten Commandments public schools have metal detectors, alternative classes for pregnant students and homosexual and lesbian clubs.

Will America join the graveyard of nations who have destroyed themselves?

Edward Gibbon, the famed author of *The Rise and Fall of the Roman Empire* cited the leading causes of the fall of Rome.

- Sexual immorality was at the top of the list.
- The mad craze for more brutal forms of entertainment.
- Public overspending.
- The decline of religion.

Someone else put it this way, "Rome dug her grave with her teeth, killed herself with illicit sex, and embalmed herself with alcohol." Historian Titus Livius (59 BC-17AD), known as Livy in English, wrote in *Ab Urbe Condita,* "Rome could neither bear its ills nor the remedies that might have cured them." This sounds disturbingly too familiar.

GOD GAVE THEM UP TO SENSUALISM AND SUPERSTITION

"Wherefore God also gave them up to uncleanness through the lusts of their own hearts, to dishonour their own bodies between themselves: Who changed the truth of God into a lie, and worshipped and served the creature more than the Creator, who is blessed for ever. Amen." (Romans 1:24-25) Religion in all of its forms are man-made, a matter of human invention. The idea of some is that religions have evolved. They started by worshipping idols (animism). Then, people saw others believed in different expressions of deities, so they moved to polytheism (the worship of multiple gods). Finally, polytheism gave way to monotheism, which led them to worship only one God.

In fact, it is just the opposite. Idolatry is not the first step toward God; it is the first step away from God! Idolaters have a form of godliness but deny the real power behind it - Satan. Idolatry is a matter of demonic deception. Idolatry is an assault on God who has already revealed Himself. In Psalm 106:36-37 the psalmist informs us that those who offer sacrifice to idols are in fact making sacrifices to devils (demons).

When people exclude the true and living God, they become "gods" unto themselves where any decision or action is justified. The new religion they established was unrestrained and deviant "s-e-x."

If that seems like a stretch, consider GLADD (Gay & Lesbian Alliance Against Defamation) and their guidance on how to participate in their annual "Spirit Day" and compare it to Christianity.

GLADD	CHRISTIANITY
1. Take the Pledge.	1. Confess your faith in Christ.
2. Learn the Facts.	2. Study the Bible.
3. Spread the Word.	3. Tell others about Jesus.
4. Go Purple in October.	4. Openly live for Jesus.
5. Donate.[10]	5. Give to spread the Gospel.

[10] gladd.org/spiritday#how

GOD GAVE THEM UP TO SEXUAL PERVERSION

"For this cause God gave them up unto vile affections: for even their women did change the natural use into that which is against nature: And likewise also the men, leaving the natural use of the woman, burned in their lust one toward another; men with men working that which is unseemly, and receiving in themselves that recompence of their error which was meet." (Romans 1:26-27) Without moral and mental control, sex breaks out in wild and wicked perversions. Sex is God's gift to heterosexual, monogamous couples in marriage. Homosexuality is a sorry perversion of God's sacred gift (Hebrews 13:4; 1 Corinthians 6:19-20). Sexual attraction for those of the same gender are "vile affections" and "against nature" (Romans 1:26). When this passage refers to homosexuality as being "against nature" it means deviant sexuality is against the intention of the Creator whom they have disavowed. "Unique to humans is we have the freedom to choose courses of action that do violence to what it means to be humans."[11]

GOD GAVE THEM OVER TO ANTI-SOCIAL BEHAVIOR

"And even as they did not like to retain God in *their* knowledge, God gave them over to a reprobate mind, to do those things which are not convenient; Being filled with all unrighteousness, fornication, wickedness, covetousness, maliciousness; full of envy, murder, debate, deceit, malignity; whisperers, Backbiters, haters of God, despiteful,

---

[11] Richard H. Howe, Southern Evangelical Seminar Video Series.

proud, boasters, inventors of evil things, disobedient to parents, Without understanding, covenantbreakers, without natural affection, implacable, unmerciful:..." (Romans 1:28-31) Similar behaviors are listed in Galatians 5:19-21 as "the works of the flesh" and in 2 Timothy 3:1-5 as what will occur in "the last days" which will be "perilous times."

God Reprobates Human Reason

When sinful people dismiss God from their thinking, their minds become functionally defective.

"And even as they did not like to retain God in *their* knowledge, God gave them over to a reprobate mind, to do those things which are not convenient;..." (Romans 1:29)

WHAT IS A REPROBATE MIND?

The word "reprobate" (adokimos) means "rejected." There seems to be a play on words in Romans 1:29. God was rejected from their knowledge, so God rejected them. They believed it was "worthless" to maintain a God-consciousness, so God gave them a morally "worthless" mind, a mind that was both unwilling and unable to think right. Confirmed sinners cannot think logically or biblically about moral issues. They victimize themselves by their own behavior. People with a reprobate mind manage to not notice the obvious.

When human minds are cesspools of immorality, they cannot be sanctuaries for God.

"Having the understanding darkened, being alienated from the life of God through the ignorance that is in them, because of the blindness of their

heart: Who being past feeling have given themselves over unto lasciviousness, to work all uncleanness with greediness." (Ephesians 4:18-19)

What would be some evidences of a modern non-thinking reprobate mind?

If you believe...

...the wild fantasy that there are more than two genders

...all consensual sexual behavior is never inappropriate and is generally enjoyable

...a 14-year-old who has had sex with a man ten years her senior, becomes pregnant, and confides in a school nurse, but the nurse cannot report to the authorities (check this out) or the parents of their daughter's pregnancy and/or her potential abortion which she can get without parental consent

...a 10-year-old should be compelled to go through public school sex education

...a 3-year-old is mature enough to decide an alternate gender

...college co-ed dorms are reasonable and appropriate for young adults

...self-identified transgenders should compete in athletic events of their new group and have access to the bathrooms/lockers/showers of their new sexual identity

...injecting cattle with hormones would be evil but injecting kids with hormones to alter their gender identity is just fine

...Bruce Jenner, the 1976 male Olympic decathlon

winner, is now a woman, Caitlyn Jenner

...the current state of dress (or undress) of Americans has little or nothing to do with the sexualization of children

...60 million abortions are just "women's health" issues and have no negative physical, psychological or social consequences

...the saving of a "whale" is more important as saving the life of the "unborn" human baby

...the previous banning of women from military combat was gross stereotyping

...since the Supreme Court of the United States has ruled in matters of life, marriage, and faith, all discussion and debate should cease, and we should just learn to get along

...women who do not follow the modern feminist script aren't true to their womanhood

...government cannot and does not legislate morality.

If you believe any of the above, you have a non-functioning mind. Look over the list again. This list consists of non-thinking ideologies from those who are set on aggressively tearing down long-standing realities in their overt rebellion against God. For a person or two to hold these ideas is one thing, but America, as a nation, is bordering on collective insanity as they affirm these ideologies.

DOES A PERSON WITH A REPROBATE MIND REACH A PLACE OF NO RETURN?

No one can deny the damage the Sexual Revolution has done to the moral standards of the American home, the American education system, and to American churches.

I think all of us wonder if an individual or our nation can reach the point of no return.

There is a natural and biblical tension in my answers: "Yes," there is a point of no return. "No," there is always hope for those who will repent of their sins and trust Christ.

Don't play games with God or your eternity. Is God willing to extend more time for people who have heard the truth to be saved? In studying the following list of scriptures be sure to ask yourself, why did God refuse to be held hostage to a person's stubbornness and unbelief. Draw your own conclusion from these scriptures.

- God made this warning in Genesis 6:9. **"My spirit shall not always strive with man…"** And what followed that warning? The judgment of the flood in Noah's day when only eight people were delivered.
- God warned the people in the days of the Judges, **"I will deliver you no more."** (Judges 10:13)
- Samson had compromised his life repeatedly and then he **"wist** (knew) **not that the LORD was departed from him."** (Judges 16:16-18).
- Read closely the warnings in Proverbs 1:20-33. **"Wisdom crieth without; she uttereth her voice in the streets: She crieth in the chief place of concourse, in the openings of the gates: in the city she uttereth her words, *saying,* How long, ye simple ones, will ye love simplicity? and the scorners delight in their scorning, and fools hate knowledge? Turn**

you at my reproof: behold, I will pour out my spirit unto you, I will make known my words unto you. Because I have called, and ye refused; I have stretched out my hand, and no man regarded; But ye have set at nought all my counsel, and would none of my reproof: I also will laugh at your calamity; I will mock when your fear cometh; When your fear cometh as desolation, and your destruction cometh as a whirlwind; when distress and anguish cometh upon you. Then shall they call upon me, but I will not answer; they shall seek me early, but they shall not find me: For that they hated knowledge, and did not choose the fear of the LORD: They would none of my counsel: they despised all my reproof. Therefore shall they eat of the fruit of their own way, and be filled with their own devices. For the turning away of the simple shall slay them, and the prosperity of fools shall destroy them. But whoso hearkeneth unto me shall dwell safely, and shall be quiet from fear of evil."

- **"He, that being often reproved hardeneth *his* neck, shall suddenly be destroyed, and that without remedy."** (Proverbs 29:1)
- **"Ephraim is joined to idols; let him alone."** (Hosea 4:17)
- As Judea drew near when they would be taken captive by the Babylonians look closely at their casualness and their eventual irreversible condition. **"Moreover all the chief of the priests, and the people, transgressed very**

much after all the abominations of the heathen; and polluted the house of the LORD which he had hallowed in Jerusalem. And the LORD God of their fathers sent to them by his messengers, rising up betimes, and sending; because he had compassion on his people, and on his dwelling place: But they mocked the messengers of God, and despised his words, and misused his prophets, until the wrath of the LORD arose against his people, till *there was* no remedy." (2 Chronicles 36:14-16)

- Just before the seventy disciples were sent out in Matthew 10:12-15, Jesus instructed them regarding those who would and would not receive them. The ones who were "worthy" were those who were open to the truth and welcomed it. This is where the focus of Christian ministry should start. It is not to be the *only* people we reach out to, but fruit comes from those who want the truth. Those in the audience of the apostles (family, friends, co-workers, community) who stubbornly refused the truth, when given repeated opportunities yet continued to refuse. What do you do? You withdraw after a time and move on. Jesus wasn't saying we should forsake people who do not immediately come to saving faith. There is a place for prayer (Romans 10:1-4), patience (2 Peter 3:9), and persistence (2 Corinthians 5:20). But, when people adamantly persist in opposing, corrupting, and refusing the truth, we are called to turn our efforts to others. While the gospel is "the power of God unto salvation" it is only so to "every one that believeth" (Romans 1:16).

- The rich young ruler showed interest in "eternal life," but when told of the cost "went away sorrowful." (Matthew 19:16-26). While Jesus "loved" this young man (Mark 10:21), He did not chase after him.
- King Herod showed interest in seeing a miracle to satisfy his curiosity, but Jesus **"answered him nothing."** (Luke 23:7-9) Jesus refused to be a side-show to entertain people.
- Concerning the religious leaders of His day Jesus said, **"Let them alone: they be blind leaders of the blind. And if the blind lead the blind, both shall fall into the ditch."** (Matthew 15:14)
- Of the people of the city of Jerusalem, it is said they had missed the **"time of thy visitation."** (Luke 19:39-40, 42-44)
- While it wasn't too late for one of the thieves who was crucified with Jesus, it was too late for the other thief – the one who did not repent. (Luke 23:39-42)
- Acts 14:16 records the story of human history. God **"...who in times past suffered** (allowed) **all nations to walk in their own ways."** God moves in... God moves out... God moves on.
- 2 Thessalonians 2:10-12 makes a sobering warning to people living during the time of the introduction of the anti-Christ. **"And with all deceivableness of unrighteousness in them that perish; because they received not the**

love of the truth, that they might be saved. And for this cause God shall send them strong delusion, that they should believe a lie: That they all might be damned who believed not the truth, but had pleasure in unrighteousness." When a person is presented the truth, it is not a choice between truth and error, but truth and sin. When the decision is made to refuse the Savior and hold on to sin, God steps in and becomes involved in preventing that person from ever coming to salvation.

There is a time we know not when,
A point we know not where,
That marks the destiny of men to glory or despair
There is a line by us unseen
That crosses every path,
The hidden boundary between God's mercy
and God's wrath.
Oh, come today, do not delay, too late it soon will be.
To Jesus fly, for mercy cry, He waits to welcome thee.

"The lost enjoy forever the horrible freedom they
have demanded and are therefore self-enslaved."[12]
C.S. Lewis, *Joyful Christian*

One of Aesop's famous fables concerns an old lion and a fox. The lion was getting too old to hunt. He said to himself, "I've got to eat, but I'm too old to hunt. So, I will spread the word that I'm sick and my friends will

[12] C.S. Lewis, *Joyful Christian*, p. 226.

come to see me." The kingly lion put the word out and all the animals came and, of course, he would grab them and devour them. An easy way to hunt and to live. The fox came over to see the lion one day saying, "Yoo Hoo, Mr. Lion." And the lion answered, "Yoo Hoo, Mr. Fox. Come in and see me. I'm sick and tired." Mr. Fox said, "I believe I'll just visit you through the window." "Oh, do come in," said Mr. Lion. Mr. Fox said, "No, I'll just visit from the outside." The lion asked, "Mr. Fox, why won't you come it?" The fox answered (this is the punch line for those who have become distracted), "Mr. Lion, I have been noticing the tracks. They all lead in and none lead out."

THERE DOESN'T NEED TO BE A POINT OF NO RETURN

"...where sin abounded, grace did much more abound." (Romans 5:20) No one should doubt that God's grace is always greater than man's sin. Someone said, "Jesus delights not only to forgive the messer, but to unmess the mess." That's sounds right, but with this amendment. While God removes the *condemnation* of our sins, He doesn't always eliminate the *consequences* of our sins when moving us away from the *contamination* of sin. Jesus said to the paralytic at the pool of Bethesda, **"Wilt thou be made whole?"** (John 5:6). After the man was healed Jesus warned, **"Behold, thou art made whole: sin no more, lest a worse thing come unto thee."** (John 5:14). To the adulterous woman Jesus said, **"Where are those thine accusers? Hath no man condemned thee?" She said, No man, Lord. And Jesus said unto her, "Neither do I condemn thee, go and sin no more."** (John 8:10-11) Paul made a long list of those who would not inherit the kingdom of God, then he reminded them, "such were some of you..." (1 Corinthians 6:9-11) The full answer of God's grace is not experienced apart from repentance of the sins that have separated us from Him.

The Condemnation

"Who knowing the judgment of God..." Many people know more than they often let on. Most people have some sense of justice. Every heyday has a payday.

God's judgment is sovereign, and He often gives no accounting of His intentions. **"The LORD hath prepared his throne in the heavens; and his kingdom ruleth over all."** (Psalm 103:19) God rules over all – all people, all circumstances, all beings, all nations, all the time. **"But our God is in the heavens: he hath done whatsoever he hath pleased."** (Psalm 115:3) **"For the kingdom is the LORD'S: and he is the governor among the nations."** (Psalm 22:28)

God told Jeremiah that even if Moses and Samuel interceded in their behalf it would not change what He was going to do (Jeremiah 15:1).

God told Ezekiel that if Noah, Daniel and Job lived in that time, they would only deliver their own souls from the judgment that was coming (Ezekiel 14:14, 20).

God's judgment sometimes centers not on individuals, but on a nation as a whole. In the case of national judgment, both the righteous and the unrighteous are touched. George Mason, the Father of the Bill of Rights, believed, "As nations cannot be rewarded or punished in the next world, they must be in this [one]. By an inevitable chain of causes and effects, Providence punishes national sins by national calamities."[13]

The Celebration

"...not only do the same, but have pleasure in them that do them." (Romans 1:32)

What was scandalous, shameful, and secret in past generations is now approved, accepted, and applauded.

"The shame of the situation ought to be overwhelming. A sense of repentance and grief ought to permeate the human scene. A great reaching out for righteousness, restoration, and renewal ought to be the greatest human longing, but such is not the case. The appalling truth is that those who could reasonably be expected to react towards God in such a way do exactly the opposite."[14]

Not only does the absence of repentance expose a problem, but the presence of celebration exposes an even greater problem!

- Annual Gay Pride parades, which began in New York in 1970, are now nation-wide events numbering into the hundreds, participated in by thousands.
- June 25, 2015, the then 65-year-old Bruce Jenner, Olympic gold medalist, was celebrated on the

---

[13] Jonathan Elliot, *Debates of the Adoption of the Federal Constitution* – Vol. 5, 1787.

[14] D. Stuart Briscoe, *The Communicator's Commentary*, pp. 51-52.

cover of Vanity Fair as transgender Caitlyn Jenner.[15]

- Shortly after the June 26, 2015 announcement of a U.S. Supreme Court decision affirming same-sex marriage as a constitutional right, the White House was bathed in Gay Pride rainbow-colored lighting as a national celebration. This was done with National Park Service and U.S. Secret Service permission.
- For decades educators have celebrated atheists and evolutionists as profound thinkers, yet a child who reads a Gideon Bible knows more about life's origin than most intellectual elites.
- Now federally funded universities offer degree programs on "Queer Studies" to encourage and celebrate deviant sexuality.
- GLAAD (formerly the *Gay & Lesbian Alliance Against Defamation*) published its annual *Where We Are on TV* report on November, 2019, which examines the number of LGBTQ characters on television. They demanded that of the regular characters of television series 20 percent be LGBTQ by 2025, with half of them being people of color by 2022. "These two steps are key moves toward ensuring that entertainment reflects the world in which it is created and the audience who consumes it."[16]
- During the 2020 Covid-19 pandemic, Planned Parenthood shut down most of the women's

---

[15] https://www.vanityfair.com/hollywood/2015/06/caitlyn-jenner-bruce-cover-annie-leibovitz

[16] https://www.dailywire.com/news/glaad-we-want-20-of-series-regular-characters-to-be-lgbtq-by-2025

> health clinics but kept open their abortion mills which were considered "essential" by the government.[17]

Deviant sexual behaviors are not new. They have been a part of human history for millennia. What is new is that beyond being normalized, it is now institutionalized and openly celebrated.

May God have mercy on America!

---

[17] Washington Examiner, *Coronavirus Exposes Planned Parenthood's Biggest Lie*, April 2, 2020.

- 5 -

The Mystery of Morality

Since this is a book about the continuing consequences of the Sexual Revolution of the 1960s, it is only natural that we should investigate morality – morality in general and morality relating to sexuality.

"Every society must regulate sex. It is not healthy for any society to be so saturated with sex that it dominates the political system. When sex becomes a society's political currency, then public life comes to be dominated by those willing to use sexuality as a weapon to acquire power. In retrospect, the notion that a society could simply dispense with the mores and restrictions that have kept sex under control in this and every civilization for millennia, and instead adopt the sexual morality of Woodstock hippies, and that this could be done with no adverse social or political consequences, seems breathtakingly naïve. It is not possible to rearrange matters as fundamental as the relationships between men and women, sexuality, and family structure without far-reaching consequences that cannot possibly be foreseen. In the decades since we began this experiment, little effort has been made to step back and assess the wisdom of what we are doing. Rather than heed the warning signs, we seem determined to plough on regardless, willfully oblivious to the consequences."[1]

What exactly is morality?

Morality speaks of a system of behavior that sets standards of right or wrong. The word carries the concepts of:

- Standards that govern our individual and collective behaviors.
- Responsibility regulated by our conscience.
- Identifying those who are doing good from those who are doing evil.

The "NO" Standard of Morality

The notion that "one-morality-fits-all" is rejected by many people in our current culture. The whole idea of a universal morality is debunked based on the size of the world's population and the countless cultures that exits within it. No two people are alike, and no two societies are alike, so it is absurd that there is only one moral standard for all. That's the tune some sing.

Many people will say there is no standard morality until... a moral code violation is made against them.

- If Ken Lay was your former boss at Enron, you would not invite him over for Christmas (you would have to dig him up because he is deceased, but you get my point).

---

[1] Stephen Baskerville, *The New Politics of Sex*, p. 337.

- If Bernie Madoff trashed your retirement future, you would not want to give him a minute of your time, unless it was an unsupervised moment in his jail cell.
- If Matt Lauer violated your granddaughter, you would not think of it lightly and deem it only as a moment of slight "indiscretion."

Somehow, we suddenly become real moral when we are the victim.

But wait a moment. If there is no standard of morality, who can say what Ken or Bernie or Matt did was wrong?

To declare there is "no" absolute moral truth is in itself a statement of absolute truth. Such a statement is self-refuting.

This proposition has been made: if you were stranded in a crime-ridden part of town at midnight and as you stepped out of your car you saw a half dozen big young men walking in your direction, would it make any difference to you to know whether they were coming from a bar or a Bible study?

When given the choice, most people want others to have some kind of standard of morality. But which standard?

The "ME" Standard of Morality

For many people morality is based on each person's view and with each situation. Morality is merely an opinion or a preference. Very often we declare ourselves the arbitrator of what is right and what is wrong. We reason, "Why should another person's personal view of morality be preferred over my view? You can have your truth and I will have mine."

We are very much living in an ego-centric time when it comes to many things. Individuals prefer certain models of automobiles, in a certain color, with certain options. Other makes of cars will provide our basic transportation, but we have our preferences, if it fits our budget. You have heard of the guy who loved new Cadillacs but only had a used car budget. One car is no better or worse when it comes to getting us from point A to point B, but we have our preferences.

Many times, morality is no more than what we prefer as judged by our own standard of decency. Decency cannot be judged by what we see people wear to Walmart, but I digress. When having to make decisions it's often not about what's right, but what's right for *me* in this moment.

If a person suggests there is a standard beyond one's own opinion the response will likely be, "I'm glad that works for you, but I'm searching for my own truth."

Of a generation of people in the Bible it is said, "Every man did that which was right in his own eyes," (Judges 17:6; 21:25), yet they were in fact doing "evil in the sight of the Lord" (Judges 2:11).

When the concept of "situational ethics" was introduced in the mid-nineteen-sixties, *Time* magazine ran an article, "Between Law and Love." "To the modern-day existentialist, all guidelines are irrelevant; he argues that any authentic decision must arise spontaneously from man's inner sense of what the moment demands. Today, several Christian theologians expound a third way—halfway between the two previous paths—which they call 'situation' or 'contextual' ethics."[2]

When morality is based on a person's intellect and experience, it is deeply flawed.

Here are some of the problems with the "Me" standard of morality. We are all capable of being victims of our own delusion.

- Instead of thinking that desires for sex should never be trusted, you can begin to think your sexual desires should never be questioned.
- Instead of thinking of sex in terms of relationships, you think of sex in terms of recreation.
- Instead of feeling guilt about aberrant sex, you celebrate it as acceptable.
- Instead of measuring sex by God, you measure God by sex.
- Instead of salvation being freedom *from* sexual sin, you abuse grace to indulge *in* sexual sin.
- Instead of your sex-life being ruled by God, your sex-life overrules God.

---

[2] *Time* magazine Vol. 87, No. 3, *"Between Law and Love,"* January 21,1966.

> *If morality can mean anything for anyone,*
> *then it means nothing to everyone.*

It is difficult for most of us to comprehend how a man like Adolf Hitler could have a girlfriend. Well, he did. Her name was Eva Anna Paula Braun (1912-1945). She was Hitler's longtime companion and, for less than 40 hours, was Hitler's wife. She died at age 33, alongside Hitler who shot himself, when she bit down on a cyanide capsule. How could anyone live intimately and faithfully for a decade with a man who was one of the world's worst human beings of all time? The answer? She had a "me" standard of morality.

That's the problem with the "me" standard of morality – everything is up to you. You have noticed, haven't you? We are always hard on others, but easy on ourselves. We want an "anything-goes" morality if it goes our way. And when it doesn't go our way, we protest that our rights have been violated. We become victims. Life is not like a huge buffet where you can make up your own personal rules for living. Try that at the restaurant and walk out without paying because you don't believe in the morals of honesty. Try that the next time you are stopped by a police officers for speeding and declare you operate with different driving laws. After the officer stops laughing, you may find yourself on your way to jail.

"The moral relativists say that all's fair when it comes to morals. There is no absolute standard of morality. They say that having total freedom from moral restraint is the surest way to happiness. Parties, sex, booze, drugs, whatever else – go for it, dad! Eat, drink, and be merry, for tomorrow we die. The sad thing is that people who live like this are miserable."[3]

The "US" Standard of Morality

On what can we collectively agree? Usually, not much. The collective opinions of people are all over the place. One week it is one way, the next week it is something else.

Morals by Polls

In modern America, morality is largely determined by majority consensus. The majority removes things that were once on the immoral list because they seem out-of-date and add them to the moral list because the majority says its okay now. This is all done by "the survey of the day." It is morals by opinion. The problem with morals by the majority is they are always changing – and usually not for the better.

Morals by Peers

In the days of the holocaust which led to the mass murders of millions with peer approval in Germany, theologian Dietrich Bonhoeffer (1906-1945) stood up against Hitler and spoke out against what was accepted by others. Bonhoeffer was executed by hanging for his moral convictions. Corrie ten Boom (1892-1983) was a Dutch watchmaker and later a writer who worked with her father, Casper ten Boom. Their family helped many

---

[3] Ryan Dobson, *Be Intolerant*, p. 44.

Jews escape the Nazi Holocaust during World War II by hiding them in their home. She was among the Dutch resistance and her defiance led to imprisonment, loss of family members, who died from maltreatment while in German custody. She and her sister Betsie were held at three different prisons during the following ten months, until they were finally sent to the Ravensbrück concentration camp, near Berlin, in Germany. Before Betsie died, she told Corrie, "There is no pit so deep that He [God] is not deeper still." Fifteen days later, Corrie was released. Afterwards, she learned that her release was because of a clerical error and that a week later, all the women in her age group were sent to the gas chambers.

Morals by Business

I serve as a volunteer chaplain at a local hospital and on one occasion I served on an ethics advisory board. It was during the debate over universal health care in America. The question debated was – is universal health care a right or a privilege?

- As a right, everyone is entitled to it regardless of their ability to pay.
- As a privilege, everyone takes the responsibility to live in such an economic way to buy health care on their own.
- Is health care a *product* offered by hospitals that exist in order to make a profit?
- Is health care a *provider* that hands out free stuff regardless of the cost?

Herein lies the dilemma: those who don't purchase health insurance on their own, are covered by people who pay for their health care.

There is a moral issue inside that debate that is still not settled.

Morals by the Government

Government is established for the protection of its citizens and to provide for their good. Therefore, representatives, lobbyists and lawyers influence what is deemed bad, government protects us from those things, and determines what is good, so government provides for those things. In so doing, some people are deprived of their rights. Equal protection is not always easy to achieve. Who gives the government the authority to make things legal or illegal? The authority comes from the citizens who vote for people to represent them. It is government by the consent of the people.

"Give all power to the many, they will oppress the few. Give all power to the few, they will oppress the many."
Alexander Hamilton, 1787

> "From the nature of man, we may be sure that those who have power in their hands... will always, when they can... increase it."
>
> George Mason, 1787

Attorney General William P. Barr (1950-) frames how the government responds to a lack of national morality. "We call on the State to mitigate the social costs of personal conduct and irresponsibility. So, the reaction to growing illegitimacy is not sexual responsibility, but abortion. The reaction to drug addiction is safe injection sites. The solution to the breakdown of the family is for the State to set itself up as the ersatz husband for single mothers and the ersatz father to their children. The call comes for more and more social programs to deal with the wreckage. While we think we are solving problems, we are underwriting them. We start with an untrammeled freedom and we end up as dependents of a coercive state on which we depend."[4]

Morals by Religion

Some of the most evil people on the earth have been and are religious people. Religion is and can be completely separated from orthodoxy. It is hard for us to process, but Adolf Hitler believed he was following a form of the teachings of Christianity.

Islamic terrorists kill people in the name of their god - Allah. Professed Christians conducted crusades to "convert and kill" people on their way to visit holy sites in the Middle East.

On a couple of my ministry trips to Ghana, West Africa, I visited one of the most famous castles in the city of Cape Coast. At first the structure was a trade lodge constructed by the Portuguese, in 1555, in their pursuit of gold. Years later it was captured by Swedes, Danes, Dutch and finally the British and they began trading in another resource – people. Before slavery was abolished from West Africa it is estimated that six million slaves had been shipped to other countries. About 10-15 percent perished at sea during the so-called Middle Passage, never reaching their final destination.

---

[4] William P Barr, Attorney General, The United States Department of Justice, October 11, 2019.

Up to 1,000 males and 500 female slaves were shackled and crammed in the Cape Coast castle's dank, poorly ventilated dungeons, with no space to lie down and very little light. Without water or sanitation, the floor of the dungeon was littered with human waste and many captives fell seriously ill. The men were separated from the women, and the captors regularly raped the helpless women. The castle also featured confinement cells — small pitch-black spaces for prisoners who revolted or were seen as rebellious. Once the slaves set foot in the castle, they could spend up to three months in captivity under these dreadful conditions before being shipped off to the New World.

In an environment of harsh contrasts, the castle also had some extravagant chambers, devoid of the stench and misery of the dungeons, only a couple of meters below. The British governor and officers' quarters were spacious and airy, with beautiful parquet floors and scenic views of the blue waters of the Atlantic.

Here is the moral irony that I have never forgotten. There was also a chapel in the castle enclosure for the officers, traders and their families as they went about their normal day-to-day life somehow completely detached from the human suffering around them. They "worshipped" in the chapel that was directly above the dungeon where the male slaves were kept.[5]

---

[5] Lilian Diarra, *The Culture Trip*, January 24, 2017, https://theculturetrip.com/africa/ghana/articles/ghana-s-slave-castles-the-shocking-story-of-the-ghanaian-cape-coast/

When there are a lot of "us" involved in deciding what's moral, there will be hundreds of contradictory opinions and preferences.

People believe in standards, but they try not to believe those standards relate to things that are moral and spiritual. Engineers set the standards for highways and bridges. Health departments set the standards for restaurants. Police officers enforce the standards for lawfully driving a motor vehicle.

At least on some level, most people believe you should "help" people when you have opportunity and not "harm" people if you can avoid it.

- But who says we should "help" people?
- And who says we should not "harm" people?
- Are these moral obligations for everyone, or just for some, or is it just an opinion?
- From where does that sense of obligation to help or not harm people come?
- Who cares if we do or don't?
- Who is to say its right to help, but wrong to harm?
- Why should we care at all?

The "US" standard of morality isn't as neutral as it may first sound. If society at large determines what is moral, then anyone who doesn't go along is viewed as immoral. Political columnist Charles Krauthammer (1950-2018) observed, "As a part of the vast social project of moral leveling, it is not enough for the deviant to be normalized. The normal must be found to be deviant."[6]

"Woe unto them that call evil good, and good evil; that put darkness for light, and light for darkness; that put bitter for sweet, and sweet for bitter." (Isaiah 5:20)

"The "GOD" Standard of Morality

Max Hocutt, professor of philosophy emeritus at the University of Alabama, says:

> "The fundamental question of ethics is, who makes the rules? God or men? The theistic answer is that God makes them. The humanistic answer is that men make them. This distinction between theism and humanism is the fundamental division in moral theory."[7]

Have you made the same observation? The further our nation has moved away from a God-consciousness the more immoral we have become.

Take this quick quiz.

- Spiritually, have things gotten *better* or *worse* in America in the last fifty years?
- Emotionally, do you feel *safer* or more *uneasy* in America in your normal day's routine?
- Morally, in which direction is America going, *up* or *down*?

---

[6] Robert H. Bork, *Slouching Toward Gomorrah*, p. 3.

[7] Richard E Simmons III, *Who Decides Morals?* https://thecenterbham.org/2018/10/04/who-decides-what-is-moral/

Morality describes the principles that govern our behavior.

Moral Truth is Exclusive

When Supreme Court nominee Brett Kavanaugh was under consideration for his appointment he was accused of sexual assault by Christine Blasey-Ford. She said he did, he said he didn't. Of this we can be sure, they both could not have been telling the truth. By its very nature, truth is exclusive. Two statements that are contrary cannot be true.

"Surveys by George Barna show that a minority of born-again adults (44 percent) and an even smaller proportion of born-again teenagers (9 percent) are certain of the existence of absolute moral truth. Even more disturbing is the fact that by a three-to-one margin adults say truth is always relative to the person and their situation.

George Barna concludes in his book, *Boiling Point: Monitoring Cultural Shifts in the 21st Century,* that moral anarchy has arrived and dominates our culture today. His argument hinges on a substantial amount of attitudinal and behavioral evidence, such as rapid growth of the pornography industry, highway speeding as the norm, income tax cheating, computer hacking, increasing rates of cohabitation and adultery, and Internet-based plagiarism."[8]

[8] Kerby Anderson, *Point of View Radio Talk Show,* January 22, 2016, https://pointofview.net/viewpoints/absolute-truth/

Moral Truth is Universal

Murder is understood in every culture to be wrong for everyone, everywhere. It is wrong in America and wrong in Africa. It is wrong in India and wrong in Indonesia.

> *"A man does not call a line crooked unless he has some idea of a straight line."*[9]
> C.S. Lewis (1898-1963)

Moral Truth is Timeless

Truth is truth no matter the century or time-zone.

When God established boundaries, they were not just to keep us *from* something prohibited, but to keep us *for* something preferred. Every choice has a consequence.

Visiting a zoo allows you to get up close and personal with lions. The barriers which have been erected between you and the lions are very comforting and allow you to enjoy the experience.

On a Colorado fly-fishing trip, a buddy and I encountered a cow Moose and twin calves in the stream we were fishing. Initially, it was a beautiful thing, a photographic moment. But knowing how territorial the mamma Moose can be, we gave her all the stream she wanted... immediately!

Which of the following describes your view of life?

---

[9] C.S. Lewis, *Mere Christianity,* p. 45.

The "Minus God" Worldview

1. We are random.
2. Truth is relative.
3. People are basically good.
4. You can change your own life.
5. The goal of life is self-satisfaction and self-promotion.

The "Plus God" Worldview

1. God is in control and nothing is random.
2. The Bible is absolute truth.
3. All people are innately sinful.
4. Only Christ can change your life.
5. Selfless submission to Christ and the ultimate glorifying of God are the goals of life.

Without God, morals are meaningless. God exists above the realm of those He created as the source of objective and absolute moral standards.

God's Answer for the Moral Shortcomings of Mankind

Morals? Who Gets to Decide what is Good or Evil?

"Who makes the rules? Who tells other people what is right and what is wrong? It is a good thing to think about. No one enjoys living where there are no laws or rules, and no people to enforce, or make people keep, the rules. If the government tells people what to do, what is there to make the men in the government make the right rules? People who think there is no one in the whole universe watching them, treat other people with cruelty very easily, just as boys and girls often kick each other or knock each other down when they think no teacher or older person is watching.

If there were no Creator God who really made all things and all men, then the religions of men are only made up by men and are of no use whatsoever. The only thing that would be worth anything would be trying to have as good a time as possible for the short time you could live, before someone ruined your good time with their idea of an opposite way of living!...What a mess it would be if all the crying and seeking for help, just ended in an empty echo, like calling into a cave and hearing an echo. Happily, this is not so!... There is God the Father, God the Son, and God the Holy Spirit, and the Bible, God's word, has been given to us to give us explanation as to what the universe, and our lives are all about... What is sin? Is it just something a lot of men have decided is wrong? Is sin just something seventy-five percent of people voted we shouldn't do? No. We have a personal God, who is perfect in holiness, and perfect in his love. He is holy, and he is love. He has made the rules, he has made the laws. Anything we do which is against the *character* of God is sin. It is breaking the laws of God, yes, but in breaking his laws we are doing something against his character.[10]

We tend to divide humanity into two groups: the good and the bad.

---

[10] Francis and Edith Schaeffer, *Everybody Can Know*, pp. 217-218.

Billy Graham
(1918-2018)

VS.

Charles Manson
(1934-2017)

Billy Graham preached to live audiences of 210 million people in more than 185 countries and territories through various meetings during his lifetime. He was a man of such honor and integrity that many pastors and Christian leaders adopted what has been called "the Billy Graham Rule," refusing to spend time alone with women to whom they are not married.

Charles Manson formed what became known as the "*Manson* Family," a quasi-commune based in California, whose followers committed a series of nine murders at four locations in July and August of 1969.

This is usually how we divide the human family. The bad, like Charles Manson, go to hell because of their bad deeds and the good, like Billy Graham, go to heaven because of their good deeds.

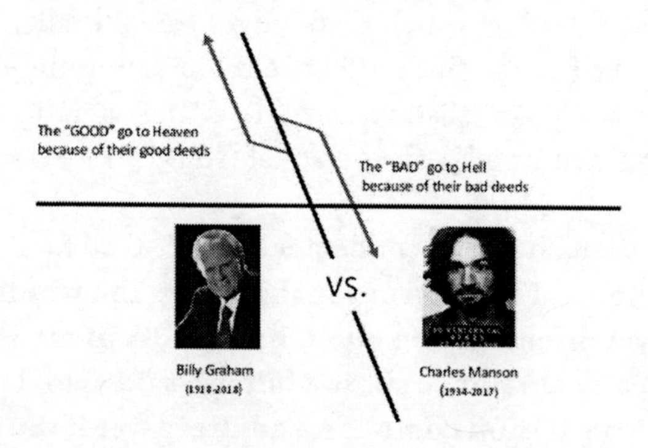

But God's moral law declares **"there are none that doeth good, no not one,"** (Romans 3:12). All people are sinners. **"For all have sinned, and come short of the glory of God."** (Romans 3:23)

Even though we are flawed sinners, all people are impressed with a fundamental sense of right and wrong. While the moral law does not describe how we *actually* live, it does tell us how we *ought* to live.

[11]

---

[11] Illustrations adapted from *I Don't Have Enough Faith to Be an Atheist*, Chapter 7.

The standard by which God judges true morality is not by other people, but by Himself. Sin is not merely the violation of an abstract law; it is the violation of a personal command of a personal God.[12]

Every person stands condemned before God for a single violation. **"For whosoever shall keep the whole law, and yet offend in one *point,* he is guilty of all. For he that said, Do not commit adultery, said also, Do not kill. Now if thou commit no adultery, yet if thou kill, thou art become a transgressor of the law."** (James 2:10-11)

God is the ultimate standard, so God is both our judge and our only hope. The One whom our sins have offended is the One who is the remedy.

The Holy Son of God, Jesus Christ, Was Sent to Earth to Die so our Sins Could be Forgiven

"But now the righteousness of God without the law is manifested, being witnessed by the law and the prophets; Even the righteousness of God *which is* by faith of Jesus Christ unto all and upon all them that believe: for there is no difference:..." (Romans 3:21-22) What we are not able to accomplish, God has accomplished for us in Christ. Jesus was born by a *perfect birth,* lived a *perfect life,* died a *perfect death* and was raised by a *perfect resurrection* so that every believing sinner might have a *perfect salvation* through Him. By simply trusting in Him alone, we become beneficiaries of His gift of eternal salvation.

---

[12] Genesis 39:9; Psalm 51:4; Luke 15:21; 1 Corinthians 6:18.

The Holy Spirit Indwells Believers to Change Them

God's gift at the point of faith is not only eternal life but also His indwelling presence by the Holy Spirit. **"...Now if any man have not the Spirit of Christ, he is none of his. And if Christ *be* in you, the body *is* dead because of sin; but the Spirit *is* life because of righteousness...For as many as are led by the Spirit of God, they are the sons of God....The Spirit itself beareth witness with our spirit, that we are the children of God:..."** (Romans 8:8-9,14,16) Christianity is an inside job – a life of the Spirit in Christ which has a moral implication. **"Flee fornication. Every sin that a man doeth is without the body; but he that committeth fornication sinneth against his own body. What? know ye not that your body is the temple of the Holy Ghost *which is* in you, which ye have of God, and ye are not your own? For ye are bought with a price: therefore glorify God in your body, and in your spirit, which are God's."** (1 Corinthians 6:18-20)

The Holy Bible Remains Our Moral Foundation

Where can we find the standard moral will for all people on planet earth? The answer is, the Bible. The Bible tells us what God wants us to *believe* and how God wants us to *behave.* This aspect of God's will is the same for all. Right is right and wrong is wrong, no matter who is involved.

For two-thousand years Christians have believed, taught and lived according to the teachings of the Bible. Without going into depth regarding the compelling historical, scientific and archaeological evidence for accepting the Bible as divine truth, let's just say millions confess there is something supernatural and divine about the Bible. Mankind's responsibility is not to *develop* moral truth, but only to *discover* it in the Bible and live accordingly.

It is often taught that the source of authority for sexual morality is the Bible. While that is right to a degree, the actual authority is the God of the Bible.

For example, family is not a social experiment. No individual or group advises God on what His standards should or should not be. God is God over all! God is the One whose principles shape us, whose prohibitions guard us and whose promises bless us.

Sometime back the adult daughters of former Vice-President of the United States Dick Cheney were having a spat. One daughter, Liz, was running for political office in Wyoming as a conservative Republican and was for biblical marriage. Her sister, Mary, a lesbian married to her wife, Heather Poe, said to her sister, "Liz - this isn't just an issue on which we disagree, you're just wrong - and on the wrong side of history," alluding to the fact that history has changed on the rights of women to vote, the equal rights of blacks in America, on the legality of abortion, and that the American public will change on the issue of gay-rights as well. Liz Cheney may eventually be on the "wrong side of history" but a matter of greater significance is she is on the "right side of the Bible."

Avowed atheist Richard Dawkins still doesn't believe in God but recently conceded "religion may help people behave morally – and may even help lower crime rate." "Whether irrational or not, it does unfortunately seem plausible that, if somebody sincerely believes God is watching his every move, he might be more likely to be good," Dawkins wrote in his 2019 book, *Outgrowing God*. Dawkins referenced an experiment conducted by Melissa Bateson at the University of Newcastle. She set up an "honesty box" in a school coffee room to pay for drinks and also placed a price list on the wall. She decorated the price list with either pictures of flowers or a depiction of eyes. People paid "nearly three times as much for their drinks when eyes were displayed," she wrote in a paper about the experiment. Dawkins said it would be bad to get rid of religion. "People may feel free to do bad things because they feel God is no longer watching them." Ken Ham, founder and president of *Answers in Genesis*, added, "The only way we can have an ultimate standard for morality is if God exists and the Bible is true. Without it, morality is simply arbitrary."[13]

---

[13] Southern Baptist Texan, December 2019, www.texanonline.net

- 6 -

The Shameless Super-Sexualization of Children

Can someone accurately determine how far a nation has walked away from a God-centered culture? Remember, a nation is the collective consciousness of its individual people.

During the presumed overpopulation of Egypt in the days of the Pharaohs, the government ordered that male babies were to be murdered at the time of their birth (Exodus 1:22).

Some of the apostate kings in Israel sacrificed their children to the "fires" of the pagan god, Molech (2 Kings 16:3; 21:6; Leviticus 18:21; 2 Kings 23:10).

Following the birth of Jesus, King Herod ordered the massacre of all babies in Bethlehem under the age of two (Matthew 2:16-18). The population of Bethlehem at the time of Jesus' birth has been estimated at only about 300 people, so the number of babies might have been

10-20 in Bethlehem and the surrounding area. This low number of deaths is the likely explanation for why there exists no secular historical accounts of the massacre. Simply put, a handful of children killed by a local ruler was not noteworthy enough for human historians. Regardless of how few children were killed, their deaths were a horrible atrocity and God had already taken note of it in a prophecy by Jeremiah 600 years before (Jeremiah 31:15). "Those innocent and precious babies of Bethlehem were the first casualties in the new-intensified warfare between the kingdoms of this world and the kingdom of God's Christ, God's Anointed."[1]

A nation that has removed God from their center is one that no longer values and protects its children.

The poet Ralph Waldo Emerson (1803-1882) believed, "We find delight in the beauty and happiness of children that makes the heart too big for the body."

Children are a priceless treasure and a deep well of joy. They are God's gift to a couple, to a church and to a nation.

There was a time when childhood was presumed to be a time of innocence, with the expectation that adults would protect them from inappropriate exposure to damaging influences.
In the United States minors are not allowed to....

- Drive a car legally before age 16
- Join the military

[1] John MacArthur, *MacArthur New Testament Commentary - Matthew 1-7*, p. 44.

- Purchase tobacco
- Sign contracts
- Vote in local and national elections
- Get tattoos without parental consent
- Purchase or consume alcoholic beverages
- Have sex or for anyone to have sex with a minor
- Carry a single aspirin to school without proper authority
- Marry without parental consent
- Inherit an estate until they are 18

Yet, our twenty-first century American culture is saturated with sexual content that was once considered too risqué for children. Almost everything in America is creating an environment for deviant sexual identity and behavior. Advertisements, social media, television, movies, celebrities, and educators are propagandizing and brainwashing children.

Stephen Baskerville wrote, "It is worth posing the question of whether we are now caught in a vicious cycle, whereby dysfunctional families are the breeding ground and mechanism for recruiting children into radical ideologies... We have certainly reached the point where sexual confusion is codified in law, and citizens now face legal punishment for failure to choose words consistent with the most extreme manifestations of sexual ideology."[2]

---

[2] Stephen Baskerville, *The New Politics of Sex*, p. 89.

At the heart of this vicious cycle is the education and exploitation of children.

When non-Christian psychologist, Fred Kaeser, admits, "We are creating a generation of super-sexualized children,"[3] who could disagree with him?

Is there anything related to sexuality that is inappropriate for a child? Evidently not! And if it is inappropriate today, just wait...it will likely be approved soon.

In the sexualization of children, there is hardly a blurring of boundaries anymore; it is totally blatant and obvious. How can you not notice the latest, most despicable, most devastating LGBTQ trend? This mob is no longer in the shadows but is targeting and openly exploiting the most vulnerable in every society – children.

Youth Organizations

On October 11, 2017, the Boy Scouts announced that girls would be allowed to become Cub Scouts (K-3rd Grade), followed by a name change in February 2019 to Scouts BSA. In the same year, a separate program for older girls was introduced, enabling girls to earn the rank of Eagle Scout. This is more than letting girls and boys hang out and have fun together. It is another not so subtle step in the attempt at de-gendering children and becoming gender neutral.

---

[3] Fred Kaeser Ed.D., *Psychology Today*, September 23, 2011.

Consider LGBTQ's intrusion and capture of the Boy Scouts of America who were founded in 1910.

Look at the following timeline.

- 1980 – Tim Curran was outed because he was gay as an assistant Scoutmaster.
- 1988 – After a 14-year court battle, Catherine N. Pollard won the right to be the first female Scoutmaster.
- 2013 – Ended the ban on gay Scouts.
- 2014 – Transgenders who identified as boys were allowed membership.
- 2015 – The ban on gay scout leaders was lifted.
- 2017 – Girls allowed to join the Boys Scouts.
- 2019 – The Boys Scouts of America officially became the Scouts BSA.
- 2020 – The BSA filed for Chapter 11 Bankruptcy due to the sexual abuse lawsuits against previous scout leaders.

It is not surprising that membership in the Scouts has sharply declined by nearly one-third since the year 2,000 when it boasted of 3.5 members. In 2018 the number was down to 2 million members. It will likely not survive, even after filing bankruptcy.

Don't be shocked, if BSA does survive, the day will soon come when "duty to God" goes and agnostics and atheists are welcomed. It's only a matter of time.

Media

With the advent of social media, there has been an acceleration of the spread of pornography to younger and younger viewers. The American Academy of Pediatrics reports that in the United States, 42 percent of children between 10 and 17 have viewed pornography online.[4]

Amanda McKenna, now "Mike," has one million subscribers on YouTube. Why? McKenna came out as a trans boy, went on testosterone, got a double mastectomy and was transformed into a purportedly "happy, healthy young man." "When you're a closeted transgender teen it's really important to have people to look up to," says Leo, a 16-year-old in the Pacific Northwest. 'Mike' has created this support for people who maybe don't know who they are or aren't totally sure."[5]

Television

In the transgender debate, even Bert and Ernie are puppets for the LGBTQ mob. Incredibly, "Sesame Street," the once-beloved kids' show, is making the best case for defunding PBS yet: inviting drag queen Billy Porter on to teach kids the virtues of gender confusion. Wearing a "tuxedo dress," Porter, the star of "Kinky Boots," tweeted about the appearance. "I was tickled to

---

[4] Rebecca L. Collins, Victor C. Strasburger, Jane D. Brown, Edward Donnerstein, Amanda Lenhart and L. Monique Ward, *Sexual Media and Childhood Well-being and Health,* American Academy of Pediatrics, November 2017.

[5] Taylor Lorenz, *The Atlantic,* June 22, 2018.

meet Elmo and the gang," he posted. Parents, on the other hand, aren't nearly so thrilled.

"Sesame Street has a long commitment to multi-culturalism and diversity," said Sesame Workshop Director of Communications Bethany Mill-bright, reading from a prepared statement. "So as you might imagine, adding a transgender character to our huge cast of diverse Muppets was a no-brainer. We understand that there will be some who don't understand this addition, but Sesame Street has long been a vanguard of children's television, and we believe history is on our side."

When word of the backlash made its way to Porter, he hit back at parents. "Stay out of my bedroom, and you'll be fine. That is none of your business."

It wasn't that long ago that LGBTQ activists were trying to get the government out of their private lives. Now they want to throw their private lives into our faces, our children's faces, and every classroom in between.[6]

"It just defies common sense," said Missouri Republican Vicky Hartzler, who represents the State's 4th District and has proposed several anti-LGBTQ laws. "It's like allowing a 3-year-old to drive a car. If we allow a transgender puppet to be in front of our children every day, they're going to begin to think that's normal. And we all know this is a part of the gay agenda. You know how this falls into place. If you care about somebody and you have a committed relationship, why not allow one man and two women, or three women to

---

[6] Tony Perkins, *The Daily Signal,* February 13, 2020.

marry? Why not allow an uncle to marry his niece? Why not allow a 50-year-old man to marry a 12-year-old girl if they love each other and they're committed? And allowing this thing onto Sesame Street is just a way of creeping this agenda into the commonplace."[7]

On May 3, 2020, the NBC's Sunday night primetime show for children, *Little Big Shots,* featured a girl, Ella Briggs, who had been voted by her student friends to serve as the 2019 Connecticut Kid Governor. This fifth grader now identifies as a boy. Ella had been elected by 6,500 of her student friends on a platform supporting LGBTQ rights. As the Kid Governor she crisscrossed the state meeting dignitaries and giving speeches to crowds ranging from small classrooms of fifth graders to a room full of 2,000 people at the True Colors Conference.[8] Ella started a group she called *Pride-Hope-Love Club* to help students feel pride in who they are. To further her work, NBC made a $10,000 donation to her club.

Common Examples of Sexualizing Behaviors in Children's Media are...

- Wearing clothing that reveals or exposes sexualized body parts
- Animal-type behaviors (e.g., crawling, purring)

---

[7] Roy Riffle, *Sesame Street Announce New Transgender Character.* Gish Gallop. https://www.gishgallop.com/sesame-street-announces-new-transgender-character/

[8] Vin Gallo, *State's Kid Governor is Making Her Mark,* Journal Inquirer, September 12, 2019.

- Performance-related occupation where appearance is emphasized (e.g., background dancer, beauty product salesperson)
- Move, reposition, grab, or otherwise physically treat an individual as an object rather than a person
- Unwanted sexual touching, kissing, hugging, caressing, etc.
- Comments about weight, weight loss, fatness, etc.[9]

Movies

The Disney film *Onward,* which hit theaters in March 2020, features a self-identified lesbian heroine with a girlfriend, the first-ever animated LGBTQ character in the Disney-Pixar universe. The character, named Officer Specter, will be a Cyclops cop, voiced by openly gay screenwriter and actress Lena Waithe, Yahoo Entertainment reported. "It just kind of happened," the film's producer, Kori Rae, was quoted as saying. "The scene, when we wrote it, was kind of fitting and it opens up the world a little bit, and that's what we wanted." Director Dan Scanlon stated, "It's a modern fantasy world and we want to represent the modern world."

Ellen DeGeneres, who voiced the popular character Dory in the 2003 hit animated film *Finding Nemo,* repeated the role in the release of *Finding Dory* which has a trans character — the first one to ever be featured in a Disney film. "There's a stingray that's

---

[9] Elizabeth McDade-Montez, PhD, *New Media, Old Themes: Sexualization in Children's TV Shows,* March 18, 2017.

becoming sting-Rhonda, so there's a trans sting in the movie," DeGeneres told *USA Today*.[10]

In the 2017 live-action remake of *Beauty and the Beast*, LeFou, Gaston's sidekick played by Josh Gad, was presented as gay.

In the 2019 *Toy Story 4*, viewers saw two mothers dropping off and picking up their daughter from a day care center in the background.

Marvel Superhero movies will get a transgender Superhero "very soon," its president Kevin Feige promised. Be looking for a wave of "diversity" in upcoming productions. Feige said that more transgender characters will be featured in the future.

GLAAD, the L.G.B.T. advocacy organization, applauds their narrative. "Over the past few years, L.G.B.T.Q. characters and stories have become common in the kids and family entertainment space with little controversy, but with large celebration from L.G.B.T.Q. families with children who have longed to see themselves represented," said Jeremy Blacklow, director of entertainment media at GLADD.[11]

---

10 Bradford Richardson, *The Washington Times*, June 14, 2016.

11 Johnny Diaz, *Pixar Short Film 'Out' Features Studio's First Gay Main Character*, New York Times, May 24, 2020.

Celebrities

Former Miami Heat basketball player Dwyane Wade said on a February 2020 appearance on *Good Morning America* that his 12-year-old child, a biological male named "Zion," has known he was transgender since the age of three and was now switching genders.

Wade's child, now called, "Zaya," has "known it for nine years, since she was three years old," Wade said.

"Zaya started doing more research. She was the one that sat down with us as a family and said, 'Hey I don't think I'm gay.' And she went down the list and said this is how I identify myself: I identify myself as a young lady. I think I'm a straight trans, because I like boys,'" he continued.

In a separate interview on *The Ellen DeGeneres Show,* who herself is a lesbian, Wade announced that he and his wife were the parents of a child in the LGBTQ community.

"We're just trying to figure out as much information as we can to make sure that we give our child the best opportunity to be, you know, her best self," Wade said.[12] "I am ready to live my truth," the 12-year-old said. "What's the point of being on this earth if you're gonna try to be someone you're not."[13]

---

[12] Zachary Evans, *National Review,* February 19, 2020.
[13] Chuck Schilken, *L.A. Times, Feb. 11, 2020.*

Would it surprise you to discover that Gabrielle, Zion's stepmother, had taken the 12-year-old to participate in a Miami Gay Pride Parade the year before?

Movie Star Natalie Portman has been in the public eye since she became a teenager. The actress, now 37, is speaking out about the inappropriate ways' society treats young celebrities.

"I know I was sexualized in the ways that I was photographed or portrayed, and that was not my doing," she recently told *People* of the early days of her acting career. "That becomes a part of your public identity."

Portman's first acting credit, "Leon," was released in 1994, when Portman was just 13.

The actress, who is currently starring in "Vox Lux," previously opened up about receiving a particularly inappropriate piece of fan mail as a young teenager.

"I understood very quickly, even as a 13-year-old, that if I were to express myself sexually I would feel unsafe and that men would feel entitled to discuss and objectify my body to my great discomfort," she said at the Women's March last January. "I felt the need to cover my body and to inhibit my expression and my work in order to send my own message to the world that I'm someone worthy of safety and respect."

"I remember being a teenager, and there was Jessica Simpson on the cover of a magazine saying 'I'm a virgin' while wearing a bikini, and I was confused. Like, I don't know what this is trying to tell me as a woman, as a girl," she said.[14]

United States Politics

A 9-year-old Colorado boy got kudos from openly gay Democratic presidential hopeful Pete Buttigieg when he asked him during a rally for help telling the world that he's also gay. "Thank you for being so brave," Zachary Ro's question read. "Would you help me tell the world I'm gay too? I want to be brave like you." Zachary's question - which he wrote on a piece of paper as he entered the Aurora, Colorado, rally Saturday night - was met with cheers and chants of "Love means love" from the nearly 4,000 people in attendance. "I don't think you need a lot of advice from me on bravery, you seem pretty strong," Buttigieg said as he began to answer the boy. "It took me a long time to figure out how to tell even my best friend that I was gay, let alone go out there and tell the world. And to see you willing to come to terms with who you are in a room full of thousands of people you never met, that's really something," he added.

The former South Bend mayor went on to warn Zachary that, while "it won't always be easy," what's really important is that "you know who you are," because when you have that, "you have a center of gravity that can hold you together when all kinds of chaos is happening around you."[15]

---

[14] Hannah Yasharoff, *USA Today*, December 27, 2018.
[15] Emily Jacob, *New York Post*, February 24, 2020.

When Pete Buttigieg finally withdrew from his candidacy for president, he acknowledged the historic nature of his campaign as the first openly gay Democrat to run for president. "We sent a message to every kid out there," he said, "wondering if whatever marks them out as different means they are somehow destined to be less than, to see how someone who once thought that very same thing can become a leading presidential candidate with his husband at his side."

Chasten Buttigieg spoke first, growing emotional as he introduced his presumed husband. He recalled being overcome when Pete Buttigieg said he was considering a run for president. "After falling in love with Pete," Chasten said, "Pete got me to believe in myself. I told Pete to run because there were other kids out there who needed to believe in themselves too."

Buttigieg declared, "I hope that everyone who has been a part of this in any way, knows that the campaign you have built and the community you have created is only the beginning of the change that we are going to make together."[16]

2020 Democratic presidential candidate Elizabeth Warren gave a round of applause to a 9-year-old transgender child who was introduced to her at a CNN presidential candidate forum about gay and transgender issues. "My name's Jacob, and I'm a 9-year-old transgender American," the child said.

"All right, Jacob!" Warren said, applauding. Jacob asked what the Massachusetts senator would do in her first

[16] Chris Sikich, *Indianapolis Star*, March 1, 2020.

week as president to ensure transgender children "feel safer in schools," and what she thinks schools should do to make sure that Jacob would not have to "worry about anything but my homework."

"Let me start by saying I want to have a secretary of education that who both believes in public education and believes in the value of every one of our kids and is willing to enforce our civil rights laws," Warren said. "We've had some secretaries of education who've been better, and we've had one that's been a whole lot worse. Her name is Betsy DeVos. So, when I'm president, she'll be gone."

Warren indicated that she wanted Jacob to help her vet her pick for secretary of education. "I want to make sure that the person I think is the right secretary of education meets you and hears your story, and then I want you to tell me if you think that's the right person and then we'll make the deal," Warren said.

Jacob gave a thumbs-up in agreement.[17]

Physicians and Psychologists

The increasing prevalence of transgender ideology in culture and education has narrowed the treatment options for children with gender dysphoria. A study was initiated in the UK as to why referrals for "Gender

---

[17] Emily Larsen, *Elizabeth Warren claps as CNN invites 9-year-old Transgender Boy to ask her a Question,* Washington Examiner, October 10, 2019.

Dysphoria" in children had increased over 4,000 percent in 10 years.[18]

Transgender activists' pressure both doctors and parents to consent to "gender-affirming medical treatment" for children who otherwise likely would grow to accept their bodies. Such treatment typically starts with puberty blockers at age 8, cross-sex hormones at 14, and genital surgery for boys as young as 17. In one case, a 13-year-old girl was given a double mastectomy.

The detrimental side effects of hormones, such as increased depression, loss of bone density, and sterility, are well-known. Yet, 15 states have banned counseling for gender-dysphoric children that would help them become comfortable with their biological sex.[19]

The Tavistock Centre in north London, a clinic that specializes in gender transition, is being sued for "fast-tracking" young people into changing gender. A former patient, who is now 23, says she was severely harmed as part of a gender transition in her teen years.[20] One observer noted, "It is malpractice for psychologists, counselors, surgeons, endocrinologists, and other assisting medical personnel to give minors hormones, sterilizing puberty blockers and Mengele[21] operations."

---

[18] Christian Post, September 18, 2018.

[19] The Heritage Foundation, *We Must Fight the Sexualization of Children by Adults*, Oct 5, 2019.

[20] Brandon Showalters, *The Christian Post*, March 3, 2020.

[21] Dr. Josef Mengele was the infamous Nazi doctor who performed medical experiments at the Auschwitz death camps.

At this facility, Gender Identity Development Service, 2,590 young patients were referred to them in 2019, compared with just 77 patients a decade ago.

One psychologist, who wished to remain anonymous, said: "Our fears are that young people are being over-diagnosed and then over-medicalized." Former staff said they were unable to properly assess patients over fears they would be branded "transphobic."[22]

Marcus Evans, one of the governors of The Tavistock and Portman NHS Foundation Trust has resigned, after accusing its management of having an "overvalued belief in" the expertise of its Gender Identity Development Service (GIDS) "which is used to dismiss challenges and examination." Thirty-five other staffers have resigned in a three-year period.

The trend toward trans has come to America. In 2013 there were only three gender clinics. By 2019 there are 41. These clinics report a 400 percent increase in children and teens identifying as transgender.

In 2018 in Ohio, a judge removed a biological girl from her parents' custody after they declined to help her "transition" to male with testosterone supplements. The Cincinnati Children's gender clinic recommended these treatments for gender dysphoria (the condition of being distressed with one's biological sex).

22

https://www.theguardian.com/society/2019/feb/23/child-transgender-service-governor-quits-chaos; https://www.bbc.com/news/health-51676020;

When her parents wanted to treat her with counseling instead, the county prosecutor charged them with abuse and neglect, while transgender activists and pro-trans doctors compared their decision to denying treatment for asthma or even cancer patients.

That all happened without federal legislation.

One of House Speaker Nancy Pelosi's top legislative priorities in 2020 is the Equality Act which could give the transgender community a vice grip over the medical profession. It could open the floodgates for lawsuits against doctors who don't fall in line with transgender ideology.

Politicizing the medical treatment of gender dysphoria could lead to more prosecutions against parents who refuse to aid in the sterilization of their children. As more doctors recommend that children take puberty blockers at age 11, cross-sex hormones at 16, and undergo "sex-reassignment" surgeries at 18, parents who resist could face charges of child abuse and lose custody of their children.

The tragedy in Ohio could be repeated in families across America.[23]

---

23 Emilie Kao, The Heritage Foundation, January 15, 2019.

Educators

Mansfield, Texas, art teacher Stacy Bailey had been an art teacher at Charlotte Anderson Elementary School for 10 years and was twice named teacher of the year. But in 2017, she was placed on leave after discussing in class about her fiancé who was another woman. She noted that other colleagues had not been disciplined for speaking about their marital status in class. District officials said then it was not discrimination but about whether or not Bailey broke district policy that required controversial subjects be taught in "an impartial and objective manner."

Bailey said she believes there is nothing political about simply speaking about one's family. But she said too many gay teachers end up lying to their students because they're afraid what they say will be taken out of context. "If you're a gay teacher and you decide to live your life out loud, I want you to know that it may not be easy," she said. "You may get pushback. And if what happened to me happens to you, I want you to know that you can survive it." In November, a federal judge ruled in her favor, but the district appealed the case. As part of the settlement, Mansfield ISD will require training for human resource officials and counselors on LGBTQ issues in schools, and trustees will vote on whether to add "sexual orientation" to the district's anti-discrimination policies. Bailey, who was awarded $100,000 in the settlement, resumed teaching duties in 2018. She hopes training and policy changes sparked by the settlement will make things better for students and other teachers.

She plans to continue teaching at a high school in the district for at least a few more years. "I have some sophomores and juniors who would be very upset if I left before they graduated," she said.[24]

Public Schools

"Education apparently exists not to transmit learning and culture from one generation to the next but to inculcate politically approved right thinking in the young."[25]

California mandates gay and lesbian history in its required curriculum and Massachusetts schools teach children as young as five about gay and lesbian relationships.[26]

Sexualizing children is a multi-billion-dollar business for Planned Parenthood and other similar organizations. These organizations get their foot in the door by offering what is in their opinion "age appropriate" sex education. Children are "prospects" once sexualized and become PP "customers" who become dependent on their services.

---

[24] nbcdfw.com, February 25, 2020.

[25] Stephen Baskerville, *The New Politics of Sex,* p. 295.

[26] OHCHR Report on Sexual Orientation and Gender Identity, Family Watch International, 2011.

As *CBN News* reported in April 2019, a participant at a Drag Queen Story Time event in Houston, 32-year-old Albert Garza, was convicted of multiple sexual assaults against four young children (ages 4, 5, 6, and 8) in 2004. He was incarcerated and is listed as a "high-risk sex offender."

That man was part of a local drag queen group called the "Space City Sisters" who were invited by the Houston Public Library to read stories to little children during an event promoted as "Drag Queen Story Hour." The convicted sex offender served as a greeter for the event, according to LifeSite News. Activists later uncovered that the man had worked as a transgender prostitute and a porn actor.

Austin Independent School District's elementary school, Blackshear Fine Arts Academy, hosted at the school's library a drag queen who had previously been convicted of prostitution charges (October 24, 2019). The school had invited Miss Kitty Litter ATX (real name David Robinson) to spend time with the school's children even though he was reportedly charged with breaking the law as a prostitute.

According to the Family Research Council, in texts to Roger Grape, the school librarian, Robinson admitted that he might not pass the school background check.

"The guidelines for submission automatically disqualify me if the deferred adjudication for prostitution is considered a conviction... so I don't know if it's ethical to submit," he wrote.

"So, either the school didn't go through with the background check - or ignored it altogether. Either option is equally distressing," writes the Family Research Council's Tony Perkins.

The drag queen reportedly spent the entire day at the school, walking in dressed head-to-toe as a woman at 7:25 am, even though the book-reading was scheduled for 11:00 am. FRC says he didn't leave until right before the final bell at 2:11 pm.

"Usually, the fact that a district is willing to host one of these drag queen events is sickening enough. Imagine finding out that the person they invited wasn't even vetted - or worse, a confirmed sex trafficker. Schools are supposed to be safe learning spaces, not a catwalk for prostitutes," Perkins noted on the Family Research Center website.

"Their actions would suggest that Austin officials are more interested in the sexual exploitation of kids than their actual wellbeing. In any classroom, including this one, the only thing these drag queens should be reading are the directions to the nearest exit," Perkins continued.

Five days after the drag queen library episode, October 29, 2019, Austin ISD's district's trustees voted to implement a pornographic sex-education policy that includes instruction on homosexual sex and how to place a condom on the male anatomy. The radical sex-education policy will provide graphic instruction on gender identity and mandated support of the LGBTQ movement. Students in grade school and middle school will also be taught how to get an abortion or obtain birth-control pills without parental permission or consent.

"Use gender inclusive language," the district's material mandates. "It is important to avoid terms which refer to only 'male' or 'female' identities when speaking with young children as this can limit their understanding of gender into binaries and can exclude children who may not identify within these identities." The district's curriculum recommends "integrating" words like parents or guardians instead of mom or dad. "To force this kind of pornography on school children is nothing more than government-sanctioned child abuse. The district's policy is all about grooming children for sex."[27]

Inside public schools are clubs to represent and service its students. For the LGBTQ student body there is the Gay Straight Alliance. The GSA is there to encourage student to "come out" as whatever they wish. Since gender is now considered fluid, they may be anything they wish. Bisexuality is cool in many high schools so teens can keep their options open. "Changing the moral sensibilities of the next generation will certainly change history."[28]

---

[27] Todd Starnes, Oct 29, 2019, https://patriotpost.us/opinion/66420-texas-school-district-mandates-teaching-kids-how-to-have-anal-sex-2019-10-29

[28] Wayne Gruden Editor, *Biblical Foundations for Manhood and Womanhood,* p. 270.

LGBTQ Advocates

In order to break down the "binary" boundaries that there are only two sexes – male and female, the LGBTQ propagandists have targeted children with cute, age-attractive figures to make their point. The figures used below are not copyrighted, so it can be used and distributed without charge.

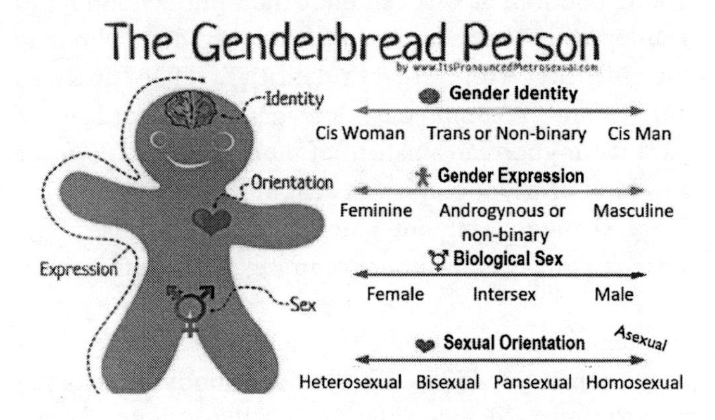

So, isn't it pretty simple? There are males and there are females. Their maleness and femaleness define both their gender and their sexual options. Not according to Trans Student Educational Resources at www.reachout.com. "Gender, sex and sexuality are all pretty complicated ideas – and definitely not as black and white as some people might think. The most important thing to realize is that you're not defined by your sexuality or gender. You're *you*, and that's awesome."

On the same page they have this popup.

Been feeling 😖 or 😟 lately?

What you say in research will help us understand what young people need
to get through tough times. It involves doing quick, online quizzes over
12 weeks and every week you get a chance to score $50 in prizes! Tell me more.

Then they have a cute illustration.

"How much do you feel like a man, a woman, or something else? This is your gender identity. This is a spectrum, because you could feel a little like a man, a lot like a woman, and maybe also a bit like something else. Or you could feel like none of these. That would make you *agender*, meaning that you don't feel any of these gender identities fit you. That's okay, too!"[29]

[29] Trans Student Educational Resources, www.reachout.com

When you think about it, the LGBTQ group must recruit because they have no children of their own.

Online Predators and Child Sexual Abuse

Online predators create and share their illegal material, which is increasingly cloaked by technology. Tech companies, the government and the authorities are no match for them.

An investigation by *The New York Times* reporters Michael H. Keller and Gabriel J.X. Dance, September 29, 2019, found an insatiable criminal underworld that had exploited the flawed and insufficient efforts to contain it. As with hate speech and terrorist propaganda, many tech companies failed to adequately police sexual abuse imagery on their platforms or failed to cooperate sufficiently with the authorities when they found it.

Law enforcement agencies devoted to the problem were left understaffed and underfunded, even as they were asked to handle far larger caseloads.

The Justice Department, given a major role by Congress, neglected even to write mandatory monitoring reports, nor did it appoint a senior executive-level official to lead a crackdown. And the group tasked with serving as a federal clearinghouse for the imagery - the go-between for the tech companies and the authorities - was ill equipped for the expanding demands.

A paper recently published in conjunction with the group, the *National Center for Missing and Exploited Children,* described a system at "a breaking point," with reports of abusive images "exceeding the capabilities of independent clearinghouses and law enforcement to take action." It suggested that future advancements in machine learning might be the only way to catch up with the criminals.[30]

Here are some staggering numbers to process.

- In 1998, there were over 3,000 reports of child sexual abuse imagery.
- Just over a decade later, yearly reports soared past 100,000.
- -In 2014, that number surpassed 1 million for the first time.
- By 2018 there were 18.4 million, more than one-third of the total ever reported which included over 45 million images and videos flagged as child sexual abuse.[31]

Parents Need to Wake Up, Stay Alert, Get Involved

In an attempt to shift responsibility, parents have been asking, "What's wrong with churches? Why are they in decline? Will churches survive?"

Those are the wrong questions.

---

30 Michael H. Keller and Gabriel J.X. Dance*, The New York Times*, September 29, 2019.

31 Rich Harris, *The National Center for Missing and Exploited Children.*

Faith is practiced and learned first and foremost in the home. "Disrupting the classroom of the home amounts to losing the 'language' of faith itself."[32]

Under King Solomon's reign, he commissioned the making of 300 shields of beaten gold (1 Kings 10:17). Under his son King Rehoboam's reign, Shushak, the king of Egypt, came to Jerusalem and stole the "gold shields which Solomon had made" (1 Kings 14:26). Instead of storming the enemy's strongholds and retrieving the priceless golden shields, King Rehoboam chose a safer path. He commissioned 300 brass shields to be made as a replacement for the gold shields of his father, cheap imitations of the real things (1 Kings 14:26-27). "Rehoboam was both unwilling to live for a great cause or die for a great idea. He would not take the risk! He would not buck the crowd. He would not fight for anything. Thus, the last recorded act of Rehoboam was to compromise! He had substituted shields of brass for shields of gold."[33]

Along the way, parents have replaced their "golden shields" with "brass shields." Parents have turned over the responsibility of teaching and training their children to Christian schools, church youth groups, summer camps and Bible clubs at public schools.

It should be obvious to all that it is the biological parents who are to be the principle providers, protectors and teachers of their children.

---

[32] Mary Eberstadt, *How the West Lost God.*
[33] Jack R. Taylor, *After the Spirit Comes*, p. 65.

"Now these *are* the commandments, the statutes, and the judgments, which the LORD your God commanded to teach you, that ye might do *them* in the land whither ye go to possess it: That thou mightest fear the LORD thy God, to keep all his statutes and his commandments, which I command thee, thou, and thy son, and thy son's son, all the days of thy life; and that thy days may be prolonged. Hear therefore, O Israel, and observe to do *it;* that it may be well with thee, and that ye may increase mightily, as the LORD God of thy fathers hath promised thee, in the land that floweth with milk and honey. Hear, O Israel: The LORD our God *is* one LORD: And thou shalt love the LORD thy God with all thine heart, and with all thy soul, and with all thy might. And these words, which I command thee this day, shall be in thine heart: And thou shalt teach them diligently unto thy children, and shalt talk of them when thou sittest in thine house, and when thou walkest by the way, and when thou liest down, and when thou risest up. And thou shalt bind them for a sign upon thine hand, and they shall be as frontlets between thine eyes. And thou shalt write them upon the posts of thy house, and on thy gates." (Deuteronomy 6:1-9)

For days after JonBenet Ramsey was found murdered in 1996, Americans watched in amazement at the images of a 5 year-old girl decked out as a mini-show girl, wearing full make-up and "big hair," as she strutted her stuff, dancing and singing across the stage of a beauty pageant.

A 5-year-old is a child who should be protected by responsible parents who are not afraid to make tough decisions. In this confusing age when children are exposed to overt and ubiquitous sexual messages, parents need to step up and take their parenting role seriously and not cave in when pressured - whether from peers, celebrities or advertising – who are relentlessly attempting to drag our children towards premature adulthood.

Adults Need to Search Their Hearts

On-going surveys of "church-going people who say they are Christians" continue to find there is virtually no difference between them and those outside of churches in areas of basic morality. But many people are missing the real conclusions of those surveys. The real truth of the surveys isn't that Christians aren't living right. What the surveys reveal is that many people who say they are Christians must not in fact be Christians at all! The Christian gospel is being cancelled out by the way professed Christians live! The problem with Christianity in America is not the unbelieving world outside; it is the people on the inside who "...profess that they know God; but in works they deny him, being abominable, and disobedient, and unto every good work reprobate." (Titus 1:16)

It happened before and it is happening again. When the Puritans came to America, they were serious about their faith [they were often very wrong, but not because they were careless]. The second generation of Puritans tended to live off their parents' beliefs. By the time the third generation came around they were only a skeleton without any life. But even the third generation wanted some pretense of Christianity, like having their babies christened.[34]

By that time the Puritans came up with what they called "The Halfway Covenant" which allowed unconverted parents to have their babies baptized, but the parents were not allowed to take Communion. They were "half in and half out." We would call them fence-riders.[35] By that time their religion was a mere sham.[36]

Adults Need to Reach Their Children

Here is the second bone-jarring reality for present-day believers in America: there are children in our lives who will one day enter eternity. It is not just the happiness of children that is at stake – the eternity of our children is in the balance. If it were only stubborn adults who are determined to live and die in defiance to God we could just step out of their way and let them "crash and burn," but there are children on board. The problem is adults create a "new norm" for their children when they live out of the will of God. Their eternal souls are affected by parents' obedience or disobedience.

An Ivy League professor says we need to end homeschooling because parents who homeschool their children are "authoritarian." An article in the April 2020 edition of *Harvard Magazine,* Harvard law professor Elizabeth Bartholet, faculty director of the Law School's

---

34 Puritans practiced infant sprinkling; what old Baptists called merely a "water ceremony."

35 Steve Farrar, *Get in the Ark, pp. 58-59.*

36 Turn back to chapter 2 and look again at the degeneration that occurred in three Generations again and again.

Child Advocacy Program, blasted homeschooling as "dangerous" and appealing to those who seek "authoritarian control over their kids." One solution offered by the conference was to simply ban homeschooling altogether.

Illustration by Robert Neubecker

The magazine cover is my favorite part: The illustration shows a child imprisoned in a "house" made of books as his public and private school friends frolic happily outside. The books are, of course, titled Reading, Writing, Arithmetic, and—my personal favorite—the Bible.

Not only did the fantastic illustrators at Harvard Magazine spell "arithmetic" wrong (as "artithmetic") and later corrected it, but the insinuations are obvious: Homeschooled children are imprisoned by religious zealots who educate their kids at home because they fear the outside world, with all its secularization and happy children.[37]

How bad does it have to get before God's people see how our sins have offended God and what our sin has brought into our lives, our families, and our nation?

There is an undeniable pattern in Scripture: God blessed His people. Those who were blessed got distracted by their blessings - spouses, children, health, property, prosperity, peace- and ended up forgetting the very One who blessed them. They then quickly descended the slippery slope of "no return" and God brought on them His judgment. God is given no other choice. Do we presume God has a different response to sin now than He did before? Steve Farrar reminds us, "Scripture tells us that America is ripe for judgment. In fact, we are more than ripe: We are overdue."[38]

"Remember ye the law of Moses my servant, which I commanded unto him in Horeb for all Israel, *with* the statutes and judgments. Behold, I will send you Elijah the prophet before the coming of the great and dreadful day of the LORD: And he shall turn the heart of the fathers to the children, and the heart of the children to their fathers, lest I come and smite the earth with a curse." (Malachi 4:4-6)

---

[37] Jarrett Stepman, *The Left's Long War on Parents Over Schooling Their Kids*, The Daily Signal, April 23, 2020.
[38] Steve Farrar, *Get in the Ark*, p. 2.

Parents remember, your highest priority is not just to raise children for matury, but for eternity!

- 7 -

The Civil Rights vs. Gay Rights Debate

The now 350-year-old words of John Owen (1616-1683), a Puritan theologian and academic administrator at the University of Oxford, have never seemed more insightful.

> "Sin aims always at the utmost; every time it rises up to tempt or entice, might it have its own course, it would go out to the utmost sin in that kind. Every unclean thought or glance would be adultery if it could; every covetous desire would be oppression, every thought of unbelief would be atheism, might it grow to its head. Men may come to that, that sin may not be heard speaking a scandalous word in their hearts - that is, provoking to any great sin with scandal in its mouth; but yet every rise of lust, might it have its course, would come to the height of villainy: it is like the grave that is never satisfied."[1]

When it comes to sexual sin, we now find ourselves at "the utmost – the height of villainy."

Almost every month there is another letter added to the acronym of the LGBTQCIAA group. Here are the current meanings: Lesbian, Gay, Bisexual, Transgender,

---

[1] John Owen, *Sin and Temptation*, p. 12.

Queer (or Questioning), Curious, Intersexual, Asexual, Androgynous. For the purpose of this book I have chosen to simply go with LGBTQ.

In 2005, James Dobson, then the director of *Focus on the Family,* described the homosexual agenda as follows:

> "Those goals include universal acceptance of the gay lifestyle, discrediting of scriptures that condemn homosexuality, muzzling of the clergy and Christian media, granting of special privileges and rights in the law, overturning laws prohibiting pedophilia, indoctrinating children and future generations through public education, and securing all the legal benefits of marriage for any two or more people who claim to have homosexual tendencies."[2]

Fifteen years later he sounds like a prophet.

The LGBTQ spirit has become so authoritarian that no one can openly question, challenge or disagree, whether you are inside or outside the movement. This class who cried "tolerance" for years shows no tolerance toward those who do not support their beliefs or behaviors. "If you don't believe that Caitlyn Jenner is a woman, you're the worst kind of hateful. If you think a child deserves a mother and a father, you are a bigot. If you think a gender-dysphoric boy should not be treated as a girl, you're evil. If you think a man should use the men's restroom, regardless of what sex he thinks he is, you are discriminatory. If you think parents' desire to get their children counseling help for their same-sex attraction is okay, you're very dangerous. If your church teaches that

---

[2] Dr. James Dobson, *Marriage Under Fire*, Focus on the Family, 2005.

homosexual activity is wrong, your church is bigoted. You must agree with every part of LGBTQ values or be slimed. This dictatorial absolutism is not sitting well with many Americans."[3]

When Adrian Rogers spoke of the sinfulness of our days he said, "It is not a new day; it is the end of an age and the beginning of the judgment of God. A new day has not dawned. Rather, the sun has almost set."[4]

The problem of deviant sexual behavior is one thing, but the affirmation and celebration of it is beyond understanding.

In 1985 the New York City Department of Education opened the Harvey Milk High School in the East Village of New York City. The high school is located on the third floor of a nineteenth-century high-rise at 2 Astor Place, and with its chic multi-million-dollar renovation it could be mistaken for the hip headquarters of a downtown ad agency. Eighteen magnificent glass-walled classrooms, many outfitted with state-of-the-art computers, are arrayed along a curving hallway lined with candy-colored orange lockers. In the year 2020 the school had only 62 students and 10 teachers. So, what's up with this small 35-year-old school in the NYC Department of Education that serves more than 1.1 million high school students who are taught in more than 1,700 public schools with a budget of nearly $25

---

[3] Glen Stanton, *Is America Running Out of Patience with LGBT Activism?* February 13, 2018. https://www.thepublicdiscourse.com/2018/02/21030/

[4] Adrian Rogers, *God's Way to Health, Wealth and Wisdom*, p. 71.

billion? This school is designed for, though not limited to, gay, lesbian, bisexual, and transgender young people, as well as those questioning their sexuality. Harvey Bernard Milk (1930-1978) was the first openly gay elected official in the history of California who would later move to New York City amid a migration of gay and bisexual men. In 1977, he won a seat as a city supervisor during which he sponsored a bill banning discrimination in public accommodations, housing, and employment based on sexual orientation. On November 27, 1978, Milk and New York City Mayor George Moscone were assassinated by Dan White, another city supervisor, so Milk has become a martyr for the LGBTQ movement.

The building of a new monument in New York City was announced in 2019 that will commemorate Marsha P. Johnson (1945-1992) and Sylvia Rivera (1952-2002), transgender activists, drag performers and close friends who played central roles in the 1969 Stonewall Uprising. The statue - one of six commissioned by public arts campaign *She Built NYC* for its first wave of women-centric installations - will be the "first permanent, public artwork recognizing transgender women in the world," according to the City of New York."[5] The Associated Press reported that $750,000 would be allocated to the project as part of "an initiative to increase the diversity of the statues and monuments in public places around New York City." New York City

[5] Melian Sally, Smithsonian Magazine, June 3, 2019. https://www.smithsonianmag.com/smart-news/new-york-city-monument-will-honor-transgender-activists-marsha-p-johnson-and-sylvia-rivera-180972326/

Mayor Bill de Blasio said in a statement, "Transgender and non-binary communities are reeling from violent and discriminatory attacks across the country. Here in New York City, we are sending a clear message: we see you for who you are, we celebrate you, and we will protect you."[6]

Maybe the monument will be built near the Museum of Sex (MOsex) which opened on New York City's Fifth Avenue in 2002. The museum's building is appropriately in the area of New York City formerly known as the "Tenderloin," a district of NYC made notorious in the 19th century for its bordellos, dance halls, theaters and saloons, and now serves as a New York City landmarked site. The one-of-a-kind (thank God) museum celebrates prostitution, strips shows, pornography and homosexual behavior. They proudly advertise featured videos entitled, *The Illicit Origin of Pornography, Superfunland: Journey into the Erotic Carnival,* and the *On Abortion: And the Repercussions of Lack of Access.*

Homosexual activist Fred Kamney (1925-2011) looked back on the LGBTQ movement and said, "We started with nothing and look what we have wrought!" To celebrate Kamney the Smithsonian's National Museum of American History, which is funded with government money, American tax-payer money, has artifacts from his early days in the gay rights movement in its

[6] Zachary Smith, Hyperallergic.com, May 30, 2019. https://hyperallergic.com/502763/marsha-p-johnson-and-sylvia-rivera-are-getting-a-permanent-monument-in-new-york-city/

collection. It was through Kamney's efforts in 1973 that the American Psychiatric Association removed homosexuality from its list of mental illnesses. In 2011, his former house in Washington D.C. was listed by the National Park Services as a National Register of Historic Places.

How did sexual choice and behavior become a civil right?

The History of those who Codified the Civil Rights Acts of 1964

On February 8, 1964, as the House of Representatives debated passage of the bill, Howard Smith, an ardent segregationist from Virginia, rose to propose changes to four pages of Title VII, the section of the bill barring hiring and firing "because of race, creed, religion, or color (national origin)." After the word *religion,* they inserted the word *sex.* Smith drawled, urging his colleagues to rectify "this grave injustice... particularly in an election year."

The bill passed in the US House of Representatives 289-126 and in the Senate 73-27 and was signed into law by President Lyndon B. Johnson. This bill was seen as a memorial to the recently assassinated President John F. Kennedy who had originally led the effort to ban discrimination.

The word "sex" in 1964 would only mean people who were either biologically "male" or "female." It was not addressing "sexuality." It referenced biology, not behavior.

"Would Hubert Humphrey, Everett Dirksen, Mike Mansfield, and the other legislative lions who shepherded the 1964 Civil Rights Act ever have imagined that the law might one day be invoked to safeguard the rights of LGBTQ people, a then-unheard-of abbreviation that they might have taken for a mashed-up mix of New York subway lines?"[7]

The Hijacking of the Original Intent of the Civil Rights Acts of 1964

Because of the inclusion of the word "sex," the Civil Rights Act would later be hijacked by the LGBTQ advocates to demand the approval of their deviate sexual behavior. Again, the word "sex" in 1964 was a reference to sexual "gender," male or female, and did not have in view sexual "behavior" nor any modern view of "gender identity."

> Equal protection of the law is guaranteed by the Fifth and Fourteenth Amendments and reinforced by hundreds of local, state and federal civil rights laws. Although the Fourteenth Amendment, ratified at the end of the Civil War, was designed to ensure legal equality for African Americans, Congress wrote it as a general guarantee of equality, and the courts have interpreted the Equal Protection Clause to prohibit discrimination on the basis of gender, religion and disability. The ACLU believes the Equal Protection

---

[7] Todd S. Purdum (1959 -), Staff writer, *The Atlantic, April 26, 2019.*

> Clause prohibits discrimination based on sexual orientation as well.[8]

In August 2019, the Trump administration sent a brief to the Supreme Court. The brief, from Solicitor General Noel Francisco, argues federal prohibitions on employer discrimination do not extend to protect individuals from being fired or otherwise disenfranchised in the workplace because of their sexual orientation.

The Supreme Court of the United States decided differently on June 15, 2020. In a 6-3 majority decision they disallowed any employer the right to discrimination on the basis of a person's sexual preference and identity.

Justice Department spokesperson Kelly Laco had previously told *TIME* magazine that, "the government argues that the law can only be enforced as it is currently written. Since Title VII's original enactment 55 years ago, Congress has repeatedly declined every year to pass bills to expand the scope of the statute to add sexual orientation. Any change to protections under Title VII must go through Congress, which remains free to legislate in this area, not the courts. The proper role of the judiciary, which the rule of law requires, is to fairly enforce the laws as written, not re-interpret or re-write them."[9]

---

[8] https://www.aclu.org/other/rights-lesbian-gay-bisexual-and-transgender-people

[9] https://time.com/5660956/trump-administration-anti-gay-brief-title-vii/

"If the justices open up the arsenal of our civil rights law for the gay rights establishment to plunder, we will see a degree of legal intimidation and social control unparalleled in our history."[10] This is exactly what is happening.

The Civil Rights Act of 1964 had not enhanced the Constitution as it had once been understood but had in its own way replaced it. The civil rights law has become a de facto constitution. Civil rights meant affirmative action and court-ordered approval of whatever judges deemed legal. "Civil rights gradually turned into a license for government to do what the Constitution would not previously have permitted....The new system for overthrowing the traditions that hindered black people became the model for overthrowing every tradition in American life, starting with the roles of men and women."[11]

On the official ACLU (American Civil Liberties Union) website it says they are "taking on the fight for transgender equality as part and parcel of our lesbian and gay rights work, the ACLU Lesbian & Gay Rights Project will further equality for everyone who experiences discrimination and fear of violence for not fitting tidily into the uncomfortably narrow definitions of 'man' and 'woman.'"

Before moving on, take a couple of quick tests.

---

[10] R.R. Reno, First Things, October 9, 2019.

[11] Christopher Caldwell, *The Age of Entitlement*, pp. 34, 35.

What is the percentage of blacks who make up America's population? In a 2001 Gallup poll people believed it was 33 percent. A sixth of Americans believed America was a majority black country. The U.S. Census found blacks made up only 14 percent of the country's population – only one-seventh.

What is the percentage of homosexuals in America? In the second decade of the century, Americans on average, came to believe that the country was between 23 and 25 percent gay, bisexual or transgender – about 1 in 4. In fact, gays, bisexuals, and transgender people make up 3.8 percent of the population, closer to 1 in 25.[12]

How could so many be so wrong in their perspective? Where did this distorted view originate? The answer is, it came from the media, the government, the universities, special interest lobbyists and activists, and the ever-present political correctness police. Without necessarily attempting to conspire, together they have created a false reality.

The Path of LGBTQ

1. They were living quietly in the "shadows."
2. Gay activists came out of the "closet," while others did not want the notoriety.
3. They refused to practice sexual "restraint" of their same-sex attraction.
4. They demanded their "rights."

---

[12] Ibid, p. 250.

5. They took the position of "victims" of other people's prejudices.
6. They demanded that everyone "recognized" and "celebrate" them.
7. They do not allow discussion, debate or disagreement with their sexual choices.
8. They strip away the rights of those who opposed them.
9. If possible, they would put those who oppose them into the "shadows."

The Havoc Caused by the Misapplication of the Civil Rights Act of 1964

The LGBTQ group *saturate* and *educate* people to their new agenda and thus have created a new normal. This group who at first just wanted to be left alone behind the closed doors of their bedrooms to exercise their right to privacy now intends for no one else to be left alone.

The colleges and universities now influence, educate and radicalize the troops that followed the Sexual Revolution of the 1960s. The first ethnic studies departments in the United States was established at San Francisco State University in 1968. Now, state universities, like Yale, Oregon State, Oklahoma University, Brown University, operating out the departments for Women's and Gender Studies, offer minors, majors, and doctoral programs on "Queer Studies." These degree programs advertise that they touch on LGBTQ history, queer theory, and experiences of LGBTQ individuals. Universities also have ally groups who are not LGBTQ but are positive about those who aim at "changing the culture on campus, one person at a time." Who can't see this is all about recruitment?

"A radical understanding of race and gender arrived on campus at the same time as Baby Boomer professors. It has been tempting to trace P.C. (political correctness) to a 'takeover' of the universities by 1960s radicals. That is not exactly how it worked. In 1990, Baby Boomer professors were between their late twenties and their mid-forties. They were not...the maker of the 1960s revolution. They were what the sociologist Max Weber called 'successors' – a generation that undertakes the routinization, the bureaucratization, of the charismatic movement that preceded it."[13]

There is now a saturation of our national culture surrounding racial and gender politics – at every level you can imagine. School curriculum, Pre-K to Ph.D., include sexual identity material. The goal is to propagate their conclusion that all kinds of 'families" are loving and caring households (except those that follow the biblical model). Local, state and federal governments do their business primarily through lawyers and lobbyists, many of whom favor no sexual restraints. Businesses now conduct regular Human Resource training on how to treat favorably the LGBTQ group and keep everyone else in tow.

The LGBTQ group have created for themselves a new religion. The www.itgetsbetter.org, LGBTQ website

[13] Ibid, p. 164.

reads like a religion. They post testimonials, sell products, challenge people for financial support and even have a pledge to stand up and speak out against hate and intolerance and to be steadfast. If you are not a devout LGBTQ follower, you must celebrate their agenda, or pay a price. When you think about it, they are on a mission. They must convert people to their way of life because they do not biologically reproduce people on their own.

The LGBTQ group now *dominates* major aspects of our world. GLAAD (Gay and Lesbian Alliance Against Defamation) set a goal that demanded 10 percent of primetime TV characters be LGBTQ. The organization recently reported that this goal was achieved. The new goal is now 20 percent. According to GLAAD CEO Sarah Kate Ellis, this is to ensure that "entertainment reflects the world in which it is created and the audience who consume it."[14] Four percent of the population identifies as gay. In what universe does a group capable of compelling fivefold overrepresentation in the media require anti-discrimination protection?

The LGBTQ group *intimidates* all nonconformists. Any subversive opinions to the contrary have special protection and punishment by civil rights laws. Previously, universities were places where people were challenged with new ideas, but now any ideas that do not fit the modern narrative are not allowed. No one can deny it, the policy is clearly to "purge and punish" nonconformists.

---

[14] Martin Mawyer, Christian Action Network, Nov. 20, 2019.

How are dissenters or nonconformists punished? The government usually doesn't need to get involved. Companies who exist off of their bottom line, fearing bad press or lawsuits, self-enforce. Then the lawyers get involved. People's lives are destroyed for being on the wrong side of the new civil rights issue. Bakers, photographers, florists – you got it - are sued, usually out of existence.

- Barronelle Stutzman, the owner of Arlene's Flowers, in Richland, Washington, was sued for refusing to provide flowers for a gay wedding because of her Christian convictions.[15]
- Nationally, several municipalities and states have barred foster and adoption agencies from refusing to place children with same-sex couples. In 2019, Michigan banned organizations that contract with the state from refusing same-sex couples. Faith-based adoption and foster care agencies in states like Massachusetts, California, Illinois and the District of Columbia have halted their adoption services because of such rules.
- Fines are now being imposed on individuals who refuse to use the preferred pronouns when addressing those who are sexually fluid.
- An LGBTQ group sued YouTube for discrimination against their sexually oriented videos.[16]

---

[15] USA Today, October 8, 2019.
[16] Washington Post, August 14, 2019.

- Goldman Sachs was sued by a former gay executive who alleged sexual orientation discrimination.[17]
- A Fuller Theological Seminary student was expelled because of his same-sex marriage, joining another 1-million-dollar suit for violating anti-discrimination laws.[18]
- In 2020 evangelist Franklin Graham was dis-invited from speaking appearances in the United Kingdom and Scotland because he takes a position on the sin of homosexuality.

The Hard Questions Regarding the Gender Identity Philosophy of LGBTQ

No one is naive enough to believe a page or two of questions and answers about the LGBTQ issues will settle it for all people forever. It is my hope that we can keep the discussion open and moving in an appropriate direction.

Are Homosexuals "Born" Gay?

In one sense, all people are "born" the way they are - sinners. **"Behold, I was shapen in iniquity; and in sin did my mother conceive me."** (Psalm 51:5) All people have a sin nature. Some are drawn by their sin nature toward dishonesty, drunkenness, violence, adultery, stealing, pride, self-righteousness – and, yes, homosexuality. All tendencies toward sin are inherited.

---

17 CNBC, June 5, 2019.
18 Christian Today, January 7, 2020.

There is no empirical evidence that a person is born homosexual in a genetic sense. Doctors and scientists have looked long and hard and have discovered no "gay gene."

Even if a person was genetically wired to certain identities or behaviors it would not make their immoral acts moral.

If homosexuality is a fixed orientation, what do you do with the pedophile? If the pedophile says it is his sexual orientation to have sex with a child, who is to say it is not? If that is so, then the promiscuous are free to have sex with all kinds of women or men – it's their orientation. And the women or men who are married to them just have to get over it.

If sexual orientation is inborn, it seems homosexuals should be enraged that potentially millions of homosexual babies are being aborted with their permission. At least they should be consistent and become anti-abortion.

Is Sexual Orientation a "Choice"?

For discussion purposes only, if a person's orientation is not a choice, then the act is. We all become who we choose to be – at least on some levels. Behavior is always about choice. If I am prone to anger, the choices I make about its management will determine the quality of my life. Humans are not animals working by instincts. Humans make choices – good choices and bad choices.

What we understand from the Bible is that humans are subject to the full extent of the fall. While all sinners do not sin alike, we are all sinners and our choices reflect that.

Is Sexual Orientation a "Civil Right"?

Is sexual orientation the new black? The argument that makes this comparison takes the following form.

- Major premise: A sexual orientation is analogous to the category of race.
- Minor premise: Race is a category protected by anti-discrimination laws.
- Conclusion: Therefore, sexual orientation should have the same civil-rights protections as those afforded to race.

Is this a justice issue?

"Legal theorists and litigators began to argue that homosexuals were a class of citizens denied basic civil liberties, and that the courts should declare them to be a protected class, using civil rights precedents to force a moral and legal revolution."[19]

Biblical logic cannot accept the argument that homosexuality is an immutable characteristic, like the color of a person's skin.

Based on the misapplication of the Civil Rights Act, the LGBTQ mob has sued florists, bakers, and

---

[19] Dr. R. Albert Mohler, Jr, *Gay Marriage as a Civil right – Are Wrongs Right?* April 1, 2013.

photographers, who for religious reasons did not want to be a part of same-sex marriage celebrations.

Can LGBTQ human beings claim as a "right" what God has not given them?

Can Someone who is LGBTQ "Change"?

- No, say those in the LGBTQ world.
- Yes, say those in other worlds of thought.
- Why? say those who have been won over to the LGBTQ way of thinking.
- Possibly, say those who have open minds.
- Absolutely, say those who have given up the LGBTQ lifestyle.

Why Can't People be Free to Marry "Whomever They Love"?

In the 1960s, the Beatles sang, "All you need is love." The act of sex in and of itself is not always a loving act. Love must be both *defined* and morally *directed* and sometimes *deferred* as an expression of genuine *devotion*. Love is to "will the good of another." What, then, is "good"? Good is that which fulfills the purpose of its end and glorifies God.

Is Homosexuality "Natural"?

Homosexual behavior is against "nature" (Romans 1:26). Aberrant sexuality is defiance against the Creator. While the wrong end of a screwdriver may be used temporarily as a hammer, it is not a hammer and was not made to be a hammer. A bed sheet might temporarily serve as material for a sign, but it was not meant for that purpose. Complimentary plumbing cannot be dismissed. Sexually speaking, women were made for men and men were made for women.

Where Do Homosexual "Parents" Get Children to Raise?

Why isn't someone asking this question? "While attention has focused on sperm donors and surrogate mothers, thus far most of the children sought by aspiring homosexual parents are existing children whose ties to one or both of their real parents have been severed. Most often, this happens through divorce or cohabitation." Obviously, they do not produce children themselves. "Instead this pseudo-family can have children only by taking them from others."[20] They get them via the courts and social service bureaucracies that are sympathetic toward the modern LGBTQ family model.

The LGBTQ group Oppose the Bible

Matthew Vines, a homosexual, says, "It doesn't make a lot of sense to categorize this (homosexuality) as a sin when it's just a human difference." Feeling very strongly it became his goal "to systematically dismantle the religious argument against homosexuality." Vines started *The Reformation Project*, dedicated to changing church teaching on sexual orientation and gender identity and has thousands of followers on social media.

Leaving Bible-believing and Bible-teaching behind, the LGBTQ movement have created a religion of their own making – the "anything goes" religion. Romans chapter 1 says when people turn from the Creator, they become

---

[20] Stephen Baskerville, *The New Politics of Sex*, p. 95.

idolaters. In fact, idolatry is "self-worship." Sexuality has become the modernists' religion.

The Transgender Trend

The cover of *Time* magazine June 9, 2014 carried the headline, "The Transgender Tipping Point – America's Next Civil Rights Frontier" by Kathy Steinmaetz. It carried the story of Laverne Cox, the Netflix star of *Orange is the New Black,* who is one of a presumed 1.5 million Americans who identify as transgender and estimated 0.5 percent of the U.S. population. One transgender said, "Nature made a mistake which I have had corrected."

The UK's news service, *Mirror,* ran what was meant to be a shocking headline, "Transgender Man Gives Birth to Non-Binary Partner's baby with female Sperm Donor." It takes a few moments to understand, but the modern translation is two women (one claiming to be a man) had a baby with the contribution of a sperm donor.[21] They were celebrated as Britain's most modern family.

During the 2020 Covid-19 pandemic in the United States Pennsylvania's Secretary of Health was Dr. Rachel (previously Richard) Levine, who is also a professor of pediatrics and psychiatry at the Penn State College of Medicine. Dr. Levine stated, "Overall, our (LGBTQ) community is vulnerable in general, though, because of the stigma that sometimes we face. I think that there has been a lot of concerns about stigma in the health care community. And so when members of the

---

[21] Helen Whitehouse, *Mirror,* December 29, 2019.

LGBTQ community need health care, we worry about how we will be received….Hope is such an important thing. I think that we have to have hope for the future. I think we have to have hope for the future of our commonwealth in Pennsylvania, hope for the future of our nation. And in relation to some of the things we're talking about, hope for the future for the LGBTQ community. I firmly believe that we have made progress. We have been under challenges and faced a lot of challenges with this current administration. But hopefully, as I said, this will show us how we are all human. We're all in this together and we have to get past petty differences and prejudices that that tend to keep us apart."[22]

During a later interview, a reporter referred to Dr. Levine as "sir" three times, when he was corrected by the doctor, "Please don't misgender me," stating it was "really insulting."[23] To show support for the doctor, the mayor of Pittsburg Bill Peduto cancelled a previously scheduled interview with a radio station because of this incident.

Recently companies have begun weighing in with positive advertisement featuring transgenders.

- A Starbucks ad showed a transgender teenage girl finally being called by her preferred name as

[22] Daniel Reynolds, "Meet the Transgender Doctor Leading Pennsylvania's Covid-19 Response," Advocate, March 31, 2020

[23] Jeanna Wise, "'Please don't misgener me': Reported Calls Pa. health secretary 'sir' multiple times during interview," Pennsylvania Real-Time News, May 13, 2020.

a part of their *#whatsyourname* ad campaign premiering in the U.K.

- A Gillette commercial showed a man helping his transgender son shaving for the first time.[24]
- A 2019 Sprite soft-drink commercial that aired in Argentina highlighted this strange paradox well. In one scene, a mother is helping her adult child put makeup on and a grandmother is helping a young man dress in drag, and in another scene, a sibling or mother is helping a female put on a chest binder, so she can appear more male, a practice widely acknowledged to be harmful.
- A New Zealand feminine hygiene company yanked a controversial advertisement from the airwaves after many in the lesbian, gay, bisexual and transgender (LGBTQ) community objected to what some have deemed a "transphobic" message. The ad for Libra tampons depicts a showdown between two women in a ladies' restroom. Though it isn't clear if one of the characters is intended to be a transgender woman or a drag queen, her blonde opponent is depicted as "winning" the competition when she pulls out a tampon, alongside the tagline "Libra gets girls." The clip instantly sparked a bevy of complaints from the transgender community. "It's extremely offensive because it's pretty much saying the only way you can be a woman is to get your period," Cherise Witehira, president of Agender

---

[24] CNN, May 29, 2019.

NZ, told *The New Zealand Herald*. "Obviously we can't menstruate. However, we identify as female."

- Bud Light's socially progressive "Bud Light Party" campaign weighed in on the side of transgender rights. "Gender identity, it's really a spectrum and we don't need these labels," Amy Schumer says in a new spot that debuted in 2016. Her campaign co-star Seth Rogen added, "Beer should have labels, not people."
- Nike ran an ad during the 2016 Olympics featuring Chris Mosier, the first openly transgender athlete to compete on a U.S. men's national team.
- During December of 2019 Google ran an ad about everyone being a hero – one of which was a transgender student, Brandon Allen, 17, a student at White Station High School, Memphis, Tennessee. He was "Queen" of their homecoming, part of its royal court — with a gender-neutral title that the Memphis school instituted in 2019.

The media is working hard at creating a transgender-consciousness and it will only become more pervasive in the days ahead.

Transgender and Science

Pardon the repetition, but there are only two genders – male and female; not seventy-one which *Facebook* allows[25] or 112 allowed by *Tumblr,* also a social

[25] Facebook is not an expert in scientific gender issues.

networking site, who advertise, "Come for what you love, stay for what you discover."

When it comes to gender, males and females are clearly different in their physiological makeup.

- Males have one X and one Y chromosome, while females have two X chromosomes.
- Males have higher testosterone, while females have higher estrogen/progesterone.
- Males convert food into muscle, while females convert food into fat.
- Males have more red blood cells and clotting factors, while females have more white blood cells.

Gender is not "fluid." Rather, it is "fixed."

The LGBTQ crowd says, "One's sex is biological. One's gender is cultural." They like to say, "Sexual orientation determines who you go to bed with, gender identity determines what you want to go to bed as." This is all propaganda, not in any way factual.

Transgender and Self-Identifying

The illogical thing about transgenderism is that it is completely self-determined and arbitrary, rather than coherent. It is not clear what it means to "feel like" a woman or a man, or how "feeling like" something makes it so. Is a human free to create their own "reality" apart from facts?

The confusion can be laid at the feet of the behavior of lesbians, homosexuals, and bisexuals who have stated they are only doing what was natural for themselves – separating gender from sexuality. Here is how they state it. "Sex is a biological trait that is determined by the specific chromosomes... Gender, on the other hand, is socially, culturally, and personally defined."[26]

What about birth certificates, driver licenses, passports, and other legal documents that require sexual identification? This year it may be one thing, the next year it might be another. The transgender claim is they were born in a wrong body.

At the age of 75 can I now claim to be "trans-young"? I have found wearing skinny jeans and a sloppy sweater hasn't made me a day younger. Can my overweight friends self-declare they are "trans-slender"? Is there a skinny person inside them waiting to be discovered? Can I claim to be "trans-African" because I feel African? Former NAACP chapter President Rachel Dolezal claimed that she was African American for years but was finally outed in 2015 and dismissed from her job because of her dishonesty. I am thinking about declaring I am "feeling" I am "trans-wealthy." I am sure my banker would need more than my "feelings" in the matter.

In the not so distant past, "transgenderism" was a "Gender Disorder." Then it was changed to "Gender Dysphoria." There is something seriously delusional about this kind of thinking.

Radical feminist Gloria Steinem (1934-) gave her profound solution to the transgender debate. "We need

---

[26] Krista Conger, *Of Mice, Men and Women*, Sex, Gender and Medicine, Spring 2017.

to change society to suit the individual, not change the individual to suit the society."[27]

Transgender Children

The absolute saddest and sorriest aspect of transgenderism is its conversion of the thinking of some parents to its ideology regarding their children. Reflect on chapter 6 - "The Shameless Sexualization of Children." In 2013, there were only three gender clinics. By 2019 there are 41. These clinics report a 400 percent increase in children and teens identifying as transgender, no doubt, converts to the LGBTQ propaganda.

"Transgender activists' pressure both doctors and parents to consent to 'gender-affirming medical treatment' for children who otherwise likely would grow to accept their bodies. Such treatment typically starts with puberty blockers at age 8, cross-sex hormones at 14, and genital surgery for boys as young as 17. In one case, a 13-year-old girl was given a double mastectomy.

The detrimental side effects of hormones, such as increased depression, loss of bone density, and sterility, are well-known. Yet 15 states have banned counseling for gender-dysphoric children that would help them become comfortable with their biological sex.

The Equality Act, if passed, would make medical professionals liable to lawsuits for gender identity discrimination if they declined to do 'sex reassignment'

---

[27] Gloria Steinem, YouTube "On Feminism and Transgender Rights", Nov. 24, 2015.

procedures on children, regardless of conscientious objection or best medical judgment."[28]

Transgender and American Politics

When former Housing and Urban Development Secretary under President Obama and 2020 Democratic Presidential candidate, Julian Castro, was asked if his health-care plan would cover abortion if he became president he affirmed, "Yes, it would. I don't believe only in reproductive freedom. I believe in reproductive justice. And, you know, what that means is that just because a woman — or let's also not forget someone in the trans community, a trans female, is poor, doesn't mean they shouldn't have the right to exercise that right to choose. And so, I absolutely would cover the right to have an abortion."[29]

Transgender Reassignment

"Many trans people choose to use hormones and puberty blockers that can result in beards on biological females and breasts on biological males. Some go so far as to get facial feminization surgery or speech therapy, training a tenor voice to alto. According to one study, about two-thirds seek some form of medical treatment and about one-third seek surgery."[30]

---

28 Emilie Kao, *We Must Fight the Sexualization of Children by Adults*, The Heritage Foundation, Oct. 5, 2019.

29 https://www.nationalreview.com/corner/julian-castro-on-abortion-one-2020-democrat-hit-the-gas-pedal/

30 Kathy Steinmetz, *Time*, "The Transgender Tipping Point – America's Next Civil Rights Frontier" June 9, 2014.

Transgender Blowback

The path of incrementalism that the LGBTQ community have doggedly followed may have run into a roadblock - the "T" has been more than some can accommodate.

BATHROOM AND LOCKER ROOMS

"Bathroom Bill" is a term sometimes used by critics of laws making "gender identity" a protected status under civil rights laws. It refers to one implication of such laws—which is that transgender persons (who claim to be, and present themselves as the opposite of their biological sex) are entitled to use the restrooms, locker rooms and showers that correspond to their chosen "gender identity" rather than their inborn biological sex. And since people are not required to have sex reassignment surgery before adopting a new "gender identity," it would mean (for example) that women might be exposed to, or expose themselves to, someone who is fully biologically male.[31]

ATHLETIC COMPETITION

Dr. Georgia Purdom, writing on *The Biology of Gender* states,_"The distinctive anatomical and physiological differences between males and females have taken a front row seat in the current debate about transgender men (men identifying as women) participating in women's sports competitions. Basic biology cannot be denied because men have larger hearts, larger lungs, and more muscle mass (just to name a few differences) that

---

[31] Peter Sprigg, "'Gender Identity' Protections ('Bathroom Bills')," Family Research Council, July 2010. http://www.frc.org/onepagers/gender-identity-protections-bathroom-bills.

give them a distinct advantage over women. No matter how hard women train, they likely will not be able to beat men. So, including transgender men makes these sport competitions very unfair to women. The sexual revolution will now have to figure out how to deal with the outcomes of their wrong thinking."[32]

- 2018, two biologically male sophomores at different Connecticut high schools competed in female division of the state open track and field competition. They came in first and second place in the 100 and 200-meter dashes.
- July 2019, a transgender weightlifter won multiple gold medals at the 2019 Pacific Games in Samoa. Laurel Hubbard of New Zealand won two gold medals and a silver in the three heavyweight categories for women weighing more than 87 kilograms, or 192 pounds. Hubbard is physically male.

Because the Western world cowers before LGBTQ demands, no matter how unfair they are to women athletes, men who deem themselves female must be allowed to compete against women. They almost always win.

LESBIAN BLOWBACK

Some lesbians are breaking rank and speaking out against transgenderism. Lesbians who understand that they are female declare truthfully, transgender men and women are imposters. A transgender male only

---

[32] Dr. Georgia Purdom, *The Biology of Gender*, Answers in Genesis.com, January 14, 2019. https://answersingenesis .org/family/ gender/ biology-gender/

becomes a feminized male. A transgender female only becomes a masculinized woman.

TERF, an acronym for "Transgender Exclusionary Radical Feminist", insists that men who take on a female identity can never be a female. The TERF group have been excluded from the mainline LGBTQ movement and is accused of being transphobic and non-lesbian.

Julia Beck, a 26-year-old self-described radical lesbian feminist, was booted from a leadership post on Baltimore Mayor Catherine Pugh's LGBTQ Commission because she doesn't believe transgender women are really women. "If any man, any male person can call himself a woman or legally identify as female, then predatory men will do so to gain access to women's same-sex spaces," Beck said, "and this puts every woman and girl at risk."[33] Can it get any more strange? A lesbian believes gender is biological. How novel.

The creator of the "Harry Potter" series, J.K. Rowling, came under fire from LGBTQ groups after she took aim at an article that referred to "people who menstruate." Ms. Rowling wrote on Twitter, where she has 14.5 million followers: "'People who menstruate.' I'm sure there used to be a word for those people. Someone help me out. Wumben? Wimpund? Woomud?"

Ms. Rowling responded with messages relating to sex and to her support for transgender people but had a different view of gender. "If sex isn't real, there's no

---

[33] Jean Marbella, *Baltimore lesbian's view on Transgender Women Gets Her Kicked off LBGTQ Panel,* The Baltimore Sun, Feb. 14, 2019.

same-sex attraction," she wrote on Twitter. "If sex isn't real, the lived reality of women globally is erased. I know and love trans people, but erasing the concept of sex removes the ability of many to meaningfully discuss their lives. It isn't hate to speak the truth."[34] Boy, was she wrong. She was attacked by the LGBTQ mob for holding to obvious, scientific, biological truth.

"I refuse to bow down to a movement that I believe is doing demonstrable harm in seeking to erode 'woman' as a political and biological class and offering cover to predators like few before it. I stand alongside the brave women and men . . . standing up for freedom of speech and thought, and for the rights and safety of some of the most vulnerable in our society," Rowling said.[35]

In December 2019, Rowling had defended a British researcher, Maya Forstater, who lost her job last year at a think tank in London after posting messages on Twitter saying that transgender women cannot change their biological sex.[36]

The LGBTQ crowd were begging for this controversy when homosexuals feminized men and then lesbians masculinized women.

---

[34] Christs Carras, *Daniel Radcliffe on J.K. Rowling's anti-trans tweets: 'Transgender women are women'*, The Los Angeles Times, June 9, 2020.

[35] Brandon Showalte, *JK Rowling Explains Views on Transgenderism: 'I refuse to bow* down', The Christian Post, June 12, 2020.

[36] Jenny Gross, *Daniel Radcliffe Criticizes J.K. Rowling's Anti-Transgender Tweets*, The New York Times, June 7, 2020.

Transgender Disasters

Studies in Sweden show that men who had sex change surgery were 20 times more likely to attempt suicide. In 2016, the Southern Poverty Law Center (SPLC) announced a $250,000 settlement in its federal lawsuit on behalf of Ashley Diamond, a transgender woman denied proper medical care in a Georgia prison for males. Diamond had been taking female hormones for 17 years prior to her prison sentence beginning in 2012, the old policy meant that she was deprived of what the SPLC has called 'medically necessary care.' Her facial hair grew back, while her breasts disappeared, and voice dropped. She said she attempted suicide and self-castration.[37]

"The media wants to ignore all of the costs - not just the financial, but the physical, emotional and spiritual costs. They don't care about the damage being done to young people's bodies and minds—in fact, they celebrate it as a civil right.

- They don't care about the privacy and safety and equality of girls, when boys who identify as girls can share female-only spaces—like showers and locker rooms and bathrooms—and when boys who identify as girls win female athletic competitions.
- They don't care about the ability of doctors to practice good medicine, when bad medicine becomes mandated as a civil right, and good medicine becomes outlawed as a civil wrong.

---

[37] splc.org.

- And they don't care about the rights of parents to find the best care for their kids.

Sadly, some religious people give support to these narratives, when they agree to support 'gender identity' laws, provided they get a religious exemption. But bad public policy doesn't become good by exemptions for oneself that do nothing for the privacy, safety, equality, and liberty of others. 'Gender identity' ideology will impact everyone. Right and left. Conservative and liberal. Religious and secular."[38]

How much further can the national LGBTQ affirmation go? Is it too much to believe that in the perceivable future all restraints will be removed for polygamists? Why can't three or five or ten people be married if they "love" each other? Why can't pedophiles have the right to "be who they are" and be free to express their love if a 10-year old "consents" to sex with an adult? If marijuana can be legalized, why not child pornography?

If you believe this is a stretch, no one would have thought it would ever be legal to murder an unborn baby as an act of a woman's right and considered only a minor health procedure. Who believed twenty-years ago that lesbians and homosexuals would be allowed to marry by the decision of the United States Supreme Court? Who is to say the day might come when the

---

[38] Ryan T. Anderson, PhD, *The Left is Shunning Liberals with Concerns about Transgender Agenda,* The Heritage Foundation, Jan 29, 2019. https://www.heritage.org/gender/commentary/the-left-shunning-liberals-concerns-about-transgender-agenda

government would demand parents turn over their children to sex educators? Oh, it is already happening.

How Should Christians Minister To LGBTQ People?

In my experience, I have found three ranks among the followers of the LGBTQ agenda - mild, moderate and militant.

Some Christians are likely to be at the front of the line in believing and standing for the *right positions* regarding what the Bible says about LGBTQ matters. Sadly, the same people may be in the back of the line when it comes to the *right dispositions.*

On some occasions Christians have had bad cases of selective outrage. We have been outraged by open homosexuality, while being silent about fornication and adultery among heterosexuals who are fellow church members. We may be repulsed by the idea of same-sex marriage, but have gotten to the place that we accept couples living together who are unmarried and yawn at divorce as a fact of modern life. Heterosexual couples were the first to devalue purity and biblical marriage.

As church groups discuss and debate sexual issues which God has already addressed, they drift further and further away from God and drink the deadly poison of an anti-God culture.

Homosexuals and heterosexuals are the same – we are all humans. There is only one race, the human race. God "made of one blood all nations of men." (Acts 17:26). And we are all sinners (Romans 3:23) in need of the Savior, the Lord Jesus Christ (John 14:6; Acts

4:12; 1 Timothy 2:3-6).

As God's creation all people are created in the Maker's "image" and bear "His likeness" (Genesis 1:26-27). After the fall of Adam, all his offspring now also have Adam's marred "likeness... after his image" (Genesis 5:1-3). We are all "shapen in inquity," in sin our mothers conceive us (Psalm 51:5). **"The wicked are estranged from the womb: they go astray as soon as they are born, speaking lies."** (Psalm 58:3). All sinners do not sin alike, but all alike are sinners. All sinners may not be as bad as another sinner, but all sinners are as bad off.

While all humans are biologically the same, sexual behavior is not the same. All humans are equal, but all ideas and behaviors are not equal.

Homosexuals are vastly different in many ways from heterosexuals. It is only the biological sexual parts of males and females that were made by our Creator to work together. To put it another way, the anatomy of the male is made by God to perfectly fit the anatomy of the female. God created them "male and female" and declared all of His creation to be "very good." It is obvious that homosexual sexuality cannot reproduce another human apart from modern technology. Homosexuals should celebrate hetero-sexuals because *every* homosexual has physical life through a heterosexual couple or through the opposite-sex process.[39]

---

[39] Scriptures on gender, sexuality, homosexuality and marriage: Genesis 1:27-28; Genesis 2:18, 21-25; Matthew

What should our responses be toward LGBTQ people? In one or more ways, the following are how most people respond to the LGBTQ people privately or publicly.

- *Ignore them*...pretend they don't exist and that they don't matter.
- *Vilify them*...place them in our crosshairs and destroy them, if possible. It is hardly consistent to be giving it to LGBTQ people, while going along with fornicators and adulterers without a single word of disapproval.
- *Approve of them*...join their crowd and defend their decisions and behaviors. Believers cannot join the world's view that we are to support LGBTQ propaganda as if there is little or no spiritual or social consequences to their behavior.
- *Engage them*...openly discuss the biblical teaching about sin and the gospel of salvation, for them and anyone else. This doesn't mean they will accept God's truth about human sexuality; they may reject the truth and you. Don't view them as the opposition; view them as an opportunity to ask the hard questions and give the biblical answers.

19:3-6; Hebrews 13:4; Ephesians 5:22-25; 1 Corinthians 11:3; Matthew 5:27-28; Romans 1:24-28; 1 Corinthians 6:9-11; Genesis 9:20-24; Genesis 13:12-13; Genesis 19:4-11; Genesis 19:30-38; 2 Peter 2:6-8; Jude 7; 1 Corinthians 10:8: 1 Thessalonians 4:2-5; Leviticus 18:22, 27-30; Leviticus 20:13; Judges 19:22-23; Deuteronomy 22:5, Matthew 19:11-12; 1 Corinthians 7:6-7; 1 Timothy 1:10.

- *Love them...* God chose to love a whole world of sinners (John 3:16) and demonstrated His love when Christ died for all (Romans 5:8). That is what Jesus calls His followers to do – love people on all levels, even those who would believe they are our enemies. As Christians, we have a mandate to speak the truth, but we are called to speak the truth in love (Ephesians 4:15).

- 8 -

The Bible Had Human Sexuality Right All Along

A survey at the end of the 1960s revealed a quarter of men and two-thirds of women were virgins on their marriage night. If you were a single mother during that time, it was still very much stigmatized, and if you were cohabiting it was still called living in sin or "shacking up."

The seeds of immorality which were sown in the Sexual Revolution of the 1960s have resulted in many harvests that have come into their fulness over the decades that followed.

Time magazine said it all with its cover in July 11, 1968, "The Sex Explosion."

Religions Haven't Always Gotten Human Sexuality Right

If we pointed to world religions and their beliefs about human sexuality, many shocking things would be uncovered. But let's keep the conversation local – in America, among professed Christians. This is shocking enough.

The deepest and most profound divisions separating

professed Christians in American churches is not over worship styles, music preferences, how churches should do church, whether all spiritual gifts are still available or over the sovereignty of God and the responsibility of man. The most controversial and divisive issues are over what constitutes sin - currently sexual sins.

Many Christian church denominations are falling all over themselves to accommodate the current sexual culture. Small groups among Episcopalians, Presbyterians, and Methodists are doing what they can to resist the trends of immorality, but generally they are being overruled in their congregations on things God has already declared sexually immoral.

A recently appointed Church of England Archbishop of York, Stephen Cottrell, says the Bible must bend to modern sexual morality. Cottrell made his comments on the Bible in 2018 when he embraced the Archbishops of Canterbury and York's plea for a "radical new Christian inclusion." He said it would be wrong to ignore the "damage" that is done by rejecting Western society's current view of human sexuality. "But what we can do is recognize that what we know now about human development and human sexuality requires us to look again at those texts to see what they are actually saying to our situation, for what we know now is not what was known then."[1]

---

[1] https://www1.cbn.com/cbnnews/cwn/2019/ december/ church-of-englands-battle-over-sexual-morality-and-the-bible-continues

The Methodist church was positioned to officially "separate" (they preferred to not call it a "split") over the issue of homosexuality in May 2020, but the Covid-19 caused them to postpone their General Conference until 2021. Jan Lawrence, head of the pro-LGBTQ Reconciling Ministries Network, called the deal imperfect, but said it will "end the othering and marginalization of parts of God's creation."

CNN religious reporter, Daniel Burke, believes, "... the current breaks over homosexuality could be just the early tremors of an earthquake that will scatter the country's entire Christian landscape, (as) some scholars argue. In recent decades four of the seven traditional mainline Protestant denominations have split up over homosexuality or related issues, such as the interpretation of Scripture and frustrations over rehashing the same debate for decades. They read like an alphabet soup of American religion: The American Baptist Churches USA, the Episcopal Church, the Evangelical Lutheran Church in America and the Presbyterian Church USA. 'The mainline Protestants are like the shock troops,' said James Hudnut-Beumler, a professor of religious history at Vanderbilt University. 'They absorb the first body blows. But as the mainline goes, so more conservative and evangelical will go eventually.'"[2]

Less and less is the truth of mankind's sinfulness exposed because of the false assumption that people are

---

[2] Daniel Burke, "The Methodist Church Will Probably Split over Homosexuality, and that's bad for all of us," CNN, January 17, 2020.

basically good and it is not appropriate to make people feel bad over their shortcomings. If churches do not fearlessly call sin sin, the gospel of Jesus Christ becomes nothing more than "self-help" suggestions for people who only need a slight improvement of their lives here and there.

Governments Haven't Always Gotten Human Sexuality Right

Governments have seldom gotten much right at all, more especially when it comes to human sexuality. In matters that are the slightest bit controversial, leaders usually come down on the side of the things that will get them reelected. The government only decides what is legal, not necessarily what is right. And the more "help" the government gives, the more intrusion they take in our personal freedoms.

The German government, preceding and during World War II, was training doctors in "race hygiene." They were identifying and zealously reporting those in their communities who had any of the so-called genetic diseases and would be candidates for sterilization. The Nazis and Nazi doctors also were promoting the eugenics strategy of "selective breeding" to rebuild the nation's population, specifically its Aryan population.

In November 2013, China announced the decision to relax the one-child policy when they viewed human sexuality as a potential threat to their nation's economy due to overpopulation. Under the new policy, families could have two children if one parent, rather than both parents, was an only child.

China now has a one-child law because they view human sexuality as a potential threat to their nation's economy due to overpopulation.

Dr. Jennifer Morse believes our American government and wealthy donors, rather than impersonal historical forces or newly liberated women, propelled the Sexual Revolution. "The major planks of the Sexual Revolutionary platform were put in place through governmental action. The changes we now call the Sexual Revolution were initiated by elites, institutionalized through State power, and are sustained by a steady diet of propaganda and misinformation...The state bears the greatest responsibility for the toxic sexual culture in which we live."[3] There can be no denying, the United States government has interfered in the day-to-day lives of Americans in ways it was never meant to do and is responsible for much of our current national sexual condition.

- 1964 - Title VII of the Civil Rights Acts was first drafted without the inclusion of the word "sex." And in 1964 the word "sex" only meant "male" or "female," not sexual behavior.
- 1969 – President Richard Nixon signed the US Federal Hate Crime law which is still very ambiguous.
- 1993 – President Bill Clinton signed "Don't Ask, Don't Tell," which allowed gays and lesbians to

[3] Jennifer Morse, *The Sexual State*, pp. 54, 89.

privately serve in the military. "The strategy of the homosexual lobby was brilliant because in 1993 the image of homosexual men dressed in drag or in leather and chains wouldn't have changed any minds, but homosexual men in military uniform, with high-and-tight haircuts, only shortly removed from Operations Desert Shield and Desert Storm, now those are images that will win the nation's heart."[4]

- 1996 – President Clinton signed a "Defense of Marriage Act" identifying marriage only between a man and a woman. In 2013, President Clinton gave in to political pressure saying DOMA was discriminatory and should be overturned.
- 2003 – The Supreme Court struck down all Sodomy laws in the United States, yet it is still enforced when Sodomy is nonconsensual.
- 2004 – President George W. Bush endorsed "Civil Unions" for same-sex couples. His Vice President, Dick Chaney, who has a lesbian daughter, Mary, favored the right of states, rather than the federal government, to define marriage. He said, "Freedom means freedom for everyone" to enter "into any kind of relationship they want."
- 2009 – The Matthew Shepard Act expanded the 1969 Federal Hate Crime Law to include gender, sexual orientation, gender identity and disability.

---

[4] Travis Gilbert, sermon *Christian Clarity in the Midst of Culture Shift*, Faithful Men's Conference, October 8, 2019.

- 2011 The US Senate repealed "Don't Ask, Don't Tell" – allowing gays and lesbians to openly serve in the military.
- 2011 – President Barak Obama declared DOMA unconstitutional.
- 2012 – The headline on the cover of the May 21st *Newsweek* read, "The First Gay President," recognizing President Obama for his support of same-sex marriage. It had a picture of the president with a rainbow-colored halo. Politico reporter wrote, "It was the inevitable culmination of three years of work."[5]
- 2013 The United States Supreme Court ruled in a 5-4 decision that DOMA was unconstitutional.
- 2015 –The United States Supreme Court ignored the long-standing heterosexual stance of marriage when they legalized same-sex marriage on June 16, 2015 in the Obergefell v. Hodges case. The following is their legal decision. Carefully read their ruling.

> "No union is more profound than marriage, for it embodies the highest ideals of love, fidelity, devotion, sacrifice, and family. In forming a marital union, two people become something greater than once they were. As some of the petitioners in these cases demonstrate, marriage embodies a love that may endure even past death. It would misunderstand these men and women to say they disrespect the idea of marriage. Their plea is that they do respect it, respect it so deeply that they seek to find its fulfillment for themselves. Their hope is

[5] Dylan Byers, Politco, May 13, 2012.

> not to be condemned to live in loneliness, excluded from one of civilization's oldest institutions. They ask for equal dignity in the eyes of the law. The Constitution grants them that right."

- 2016 - President Obama allowed the Departments of Justice and Education to issue guidance regarding the use of bathrooms by transgenders.
- 2017 – President Trump revoked the order to allow transgenders to use the bathroom of their self-identified gender.

Simply because something is now legal in America does not make it moral. Man's law and God's law are often not the same.

Vance Havner was right in his appraisal and warning. "There is a universal moral law, whether we like it or not, and when we disregard it, we pull down the house on ourselves and our generation. The alternative to (personal…jdl) discipline is disaster."[6]

Parents Haven't Always Gotten Human Sexuality Right

Many parents are living down a divorce or two, so by default they don't demand of their children what they haven't abided by themselves. God allowed Moses to add the provision for divorce, but it was not God's plan. Jesus said it was "because of the hardness" of people's hearts, "but from the beginning it was not so."

---

[6] Vance Havner, *In Times Like These*, p. 23.

(Matthew 19:6)

Parents find themselves in a hard place when their son or daughter come out of the closet. I have seen the confusion of the whole family. Straight people generally don't know how to process these kinds of issues. Riding the fence isn't an option and wherever they land is uncomfortable!

Parents excuse some behavior by dismissively saying, "Boys will be boys." Mothers are afraid their daughters won't be part of the "in" group, so they go along with immodesty. Too many young girls are being sexualized by their parents, but at what cost?

The Medical Field Hasn't Always Gotten Human Sexuality Right

There is a reason the medical field calls what they do "practicing medicine," especially when it comes to the psychiatric field.

- In January 1966, the following statement was published which gave the culture's position on homosexuality.

> "Even in purely nonreligious terms, homosexuality represents a misuse of the sexual faculty and, in the words of one... educator, of 'human construction.' It is a pathetic little second-rate substitution for reality, a pitiable flight from life. As such it deserves fairness, compassion, understanding and, when possible, treatment. But it deserved no encouragement, no glamorization, no rationalization, no fake status as minority martyrdom."

Was that quote from *Christianity Today,* the magazine Billy Graham started in 1956? No, this wasn't in *CT*. Was that the opinion Dr. James Dobson of *Focus on the Family*? No, FOTF didn't show up until 1977. Was this the conviction of Pastor Jerry Falwell and *the Moral Majority*? No, the Moral Majority came around in 1979. This statement came from a feature story, "The Homosexuals in America," in the January 21,1966 non-religious *Time* magazine.[7] The article went on to say, "It (homosexuality...jdl) used to be 'the abominable crime not to be mentioned.' Today it is not only mentioned; it is freely discussed and widely analyzed. Yet the general attitude toward homosexuality is, if anything, more uncertain than before. Beset by inner conflicts, the homosexual is unsure of his position in society, ambivalent about his attitudes and identity—but he gains a certain amount of security through the fact that society is equally ambivalent about him. A vast majority of people retain a deep loathing toward him, but there is a growing mixture of tolerance, empathy..."

- As recently as 1972 the American Psychiatric Association (APA) treated homosexuality as a disorder deserving of psychiatric treatment. That would change.
- On December 23, 1973, *the Board of Trustees of the American Psychiatric Association (APA)* had another change of mind and *approved a revision in its official manual of psychiatric disorders.*

[7] *Time,* "The Homosexuals in America," January 21,1966.

"Homosexuality per se," the trustees voted, should no longer be considered a "psychiatric disorder"; it should be defined instead as a "sexual orientation disturbance." They had also affirmed that "...homosexuality per se is a normal and positive variation of human sexual orientation."

- In December of 2018, *the Board of Trustees of the American Psychiatric Association (APA) approved the following four guidelines.*
  1. APA reaffirms its recommendation that ethical practitioners refrain from attempts to change individuals' sexual orientation.
  2. APA recommends that ethical practitioners respect the identities of those with diverse gender expressions.
  3. APA encourages psychotherapies which affirm individuals' sexual orientations and gender identities.
  4. APA encourages legislation which would prohibit the practice of "reparative" or conversion therapies that are based on the a priori assumption that diverse sexual orientations and gender identities are mentally ill.
- The APA is now giving their full support to what they call "Transgender and Gender-Variant People." They want adequate medical treatment for transgenders and gender-variant people demanding all public and private insurers cover their reassignment treatments.
- ____,

I will leave a blank for you to fill in the next pronouncement that affirms and celebrates

> sexual deviance by the American Psychiatric Association. It is sure to come.

While all the afore mentioned groups have had sexuality wrong on some levels, the Bible has not been wrong about human sexuality.

The Bible Has Had Human Sexuality Right All Along

To the amazement of some, the Bible has had sexuality right all along. The Creator, the One who also inspired and supervised the writing of the Bible, knows what works best for those He created. Scan the chapters of the first book of the Bible, Genesis, and note how God had the ancient writer to record the good, the bad and the ugly of human sexuality. Even the old English translation, King James Version, seems very modern when it comes to candidly addressing sexuality.

Take a copy of God's Word and open it at the beginning. Look at each of the following scriptures and how they relate to sexuality.

Genesis 1:1
God is the Creator of all things, including humanity. Without the Creator and His self-revelation, human history would forever remain a mystery. Trying to discover ultimate origins without the Originator would be like taking a beautiful, powerful automobile and wondering how all the multiplied thousands of parts happened to inexplicably fall together to make it run so well. This is the beginning of faith. **"Now faith is the substance of things hoped for, the evidence of things**

not seen...Through faith we understand that the worlds were framed by the word of God, so that things which are seen were not made of things which do appear. ...he that cometh to God must believe that he is, and *that* he is a rewarder of them that diligently seek him." (Hebrews 11:1, 3, 6)

Genesis 1:27[8]
Those whom God created and their offspring bear "the image of God." "The image of God can be summed up by the word *personhood*. We are *persons*. Our lives involve relationships. We are capable of fellowship. We are able to love other persons in a Godlike sense. We understand communion. We have an amazing capacity for language. We have conversations. We know what it is to share thoughts, convey and discern attitudes, give and take friendship, perceive a sense of brotherhood, communicate ideas, and participate in experiences with others. Animals cannot do those things in the same sense people can."[9]

Genesis 1:27
These who were created were only 2 genders – male and female. This underscores the equality of the sexes.

Genesis 1:28
God's command to the male and female couple was, "Be fruitful, and multiply, and replenish the earth." "It is a unique and beautiful expression of God's love for

---

[8] Two accounts of creation are found in Genesis 1 & 2. Genesis 1 is general, affirming the equality of the sexes; Genesis 2 is particular, affirming the complementarity of the sexes.
[9] John MacArthur, *The Battle for the Beginning*, p. 164.

humanity, that He created us with the ability to procreate and thus produce more creatures made in His image. And not only did He want a world full of them, but He also designed men and women to partake in the joy of fulfilling that purpose. Children themselves are therefore a blessing from the Lord (Psalm 127:3)."[10]

Genesis 2:18
"God created us social beings. Since He is love, and made us in His own likeness, He has given us a capacity to love and to be loved. He intended for us to live in community, not in solitude."[11] Adam would find some of his need met in a female relationship. Adam's greatest need was God. God would give Adam a "help meet" for a human companion. This companion would be a *help* and not a *hindrance* to Adam.

Genesis 2:21
Adam in Hebrew is *Ish* and Eve is *Isha,* which means "from man." Eve was made *from* Adam and *for* Adam. Eve "was made neither out of nothing (the universe), nor out of 'the dust of the ground' (like Adam, v. 7), but out of Adam."[12] Eve was not an afterthought of God. Eve was a part of God's plan from the beginning. **"Known unto God are all his works from the beginning of the world."** (Acts 15:18) There was never any intent on the part of God to make all humans the same sex. From before the beginning of time, God had viewed those who would populate His world to be only male and female. Eve's "separate creation merely

[10] Ibid, pp. 169-170.
[11] John Stott, *Same Sex Relationships*, p. 36.
[12] Ibid, v. 37.

stresses the fact of how special she was – and how uniquely suited she was for compatibility with Adam."[13] In taking the rib from Adam and creating Eve, God would teach the generations following how the husband-wife relationship was to be viewed. Woman was made from the rib of a man...

- Not from his head to rule him.
- Not from his foot to be subjugated by him.
- But from his side to be equal to him,
- Under his arm to be protected by him,
- And near his heart to be loved by him.

Genesis 2:22
Marriage was established, not by Adam, but by the Creator. It would be both heterosexual and monogamous. This "affirms the complementarity of the sexes, which constitutes the basis for marriage being between people of the opposite sex."[14] Ivor Powell poetically said, "The wedding took place within the sacred precincts of God's open-air cathedral. God, the Father of the bride, gave her away; man's best Friend, the royal Surgeon, stood at the groom's side; and the Holy Spirit was the officiating minister. And when the service ended, the choirs of heaven sang their anthems. The honeymoon was spent within the restful tranquility of God's holiday home, and as the two lovers walked hand in hand, all creation acclaimed the wisdom of God."[15] It is God who created within all of us "the urge to merge." But there is to be no "merging" until there is

---

[13] John MacArthur, *The Battle for the Beginning,* p. 168.
[14] John Stott, *Same Sex Relationships,* p. 35.
[15] Ivor Powell, *Bible Pinnacles,* p. 2.

a "marriage."

Genesis 2:23

"Even the inattentive reader will be struck by the three references to 'flesh': 'This is...flesh of my flesh...they become one flesh'. We may be certain that this is deliberate, not accidental. It teaches that sexual intercourse in opposite-sex marriage is more than a union; it is a kind of reunion. It is not a union of alien persons who do not belong to one another and cannot appropriately become one flesh. On the contrary, it is the union of two persons who originally were one, were then separated from each other, and now in the sexual encounter of marriage come together again. Sexual intercourse within marriage is therefore much more than a union of bodies; it is a blending of complementary personalities through which the rich created oneness of human beings is experienced again. The complementarity of male and female sexual organs is a symbol at the physical level of a much deeper spiritual complementarity."[16]

Genesis 2:24-25

Here are the necessary elements that constitute biblical marriage.

- "...a man..." - The singular noun indicates that marriage is an exclusive union between two individuals.
- "...leave his father and mother..." – A degree of maturity is both expected and required for a man to take on the responsibilities of marriage. No one is ever fully ready for the changes that are

---

[16] John Stott, *Same Sex Relationships*, p. 37.

brought about by leaving. Also, there seems to be a public social occasion that is in view.[17]

- "…and shall cleave unto his wife…" – Marriage is a loving, cleaving commitment or covenant, which is heterosexual and permanent.
- "…and they become one flesh…" – Marriage must be consummated in sexual intercourse, which is a sign and seal of the marriage covenant.
- "…they were both naked…and were not ashamed." – In this sacred relationship there was no shame or embarrassment.[18] "The word *naked* implies more than nudity. It speaks of transparency, of having nothing to hide."[19]

This divine process is to be repeated over and over by every generation, in every culture, to populate the world.

Genesis 3:15
This verse is the first prophecy and promise of a Redeemer. Strangely, the Savior would be through the "seed" of a woman. This is significant language because normally, offspring are spoken of as the seed of the man. This was a distant reference to Jesus Christ's virgin conception. He was the offspring of the virgin Mary, with God being His only Father through the power and

---

17 Adam and Eve were the first parents to experience the "empty nest." They were the ones who had to learn to let go and encourage their children to marry and establish their own marriage relationships.

18 John Stott, *Same Sex Relationships*, Adapted, p. 38.

19 David Hocking, *The Rise and Fall of Civilization*, p. 85.

presence of the Holy Spirit (Luke 1:34-35). **"But when the fulness of the time was come, God sent forth his Son, made of a woman, made under the law, To redeem them that were under the law,…"** (Galatians 4:4-5) This seed of woman would be at enmity with Satan, suffer (Isaiah 53:5) and ultimately crush the Serpent's head (Revelation 12:9-11).

Genesis 3:16

Every childbirth, with its difficulty and anguish, is a witness to the fall of man, as is the dominance and tyranny of man. Female "sorrow" in this case "is in the area of woman's greatest fulfillment, in the bringing forth and in the bringing up of children."[20] Any fault or tension between the sexes isn't God's fault, but ours because of sin.

Genesis 4:1, 25

Procreation is one of God's reasons for sexuality in marriage. The Bible's statement that Adam "knew" Eve is an expression of sexual intimacy that resulted in the conception of a child.

Genesis 5:3

Prior to the fall, Adam bore God's image. After Adam's fall, his offspring also bore his fallen image, so all kind of deviance can be expected.

Genesis 9:20-25

Something improper, possibly a homosexual act, was carried out on Noah while he was drunk and naked. Whatever Ham did, the consequence resulted in a

---

[20] John Phillips, *Exploring Genesis*, p. 62.

severe punishment by a special requirement of servitude. and was recognized as a violation of innate morality,

Genesis 11:30
Barrenness, the physical inability of women to bear children, was a big deal to women in the Bible (Genesis 16:2; 30:1-2; 1 Samuel 1:2, 5, 11).

Genesis 16:1-4; 29:15-24
From the life stories of Abraham, Isaac, and Jacob, we see that polygamy has vast, enduring and negative consequences.[21]

Genesis 19:4-7
Homosexuality is deviant and recognized as "wicked." "Sodomy" gets its name from this passage.

Genesis 19:8
Lot's offering of his two daughters to this homosexual mob is beyond explanation. Pastor Mark Bradshaw adds, "The obligations of a host were one of the highest values and virtues in the ancient cultures. I believe the Greeks called it xenia. However the point could be made that in our attempts to be cordial and to 'get along' with our society, we must not forget the greater virtue of training up our children includes protecting them from evil (the evil one and his kingdom, demons and practitioners)."[22]

---

[21] While reading the Bible one needs to distinguish what the Bible "records as fact" as opposed to what the Bible "admonishes as principles to obey."

[22] Mark Bradshaw, Personal correspondence, June 10, 2020.

Genesis 19:24-25
Sodom and Gomorrah were destroyed by God because of their wicked lifestyle (Genesis 13:13; 2 Peter 2:6; Jude 7).

Genesis 19:30-38
Incest is an unimaginable wickedness. It would be unthinkable were it not in the Bible. Lot became the father of his own two grandsons, carried out by the plan of his two immorally minded daughters who had been educated in Sodom.

Genesis 26:34-35
Isaac's multiple wives were a "grief of mind" to him and to Rebekah.

Genesis 34:1-7
Rape is a brutal, criminal act.

Genesis 34:31; 38:15, 21-24
Prostitution is as old as the early generations of mankind.[23]

Genesis 38:6-10
God views male reproductive ability as a serious responsibility.

Genesis 38:13-30
Judah committed fornication with Tamar, his daughter-in-law, and she became pregnant resulting in her giving

---

[23] Rahab was a harlot - Joshua 6:17,25.

birth to twins, Zarah and Pharez.[24]

Genesis 39:7-10
Joseph showed sexual restraint, but he was still falsely accused of sexual assault by the wife of his boss and served an unjust imprisonment.

And this is just the first book of the Bible.

All truth in the Bible, including sexual truth, is....

- Transgenerational. Truth is not stuck in the past. Truth is not established by personal or public opinion. All truth is God's truth and God is eternal.
- Transcultural. God is creator of all segments of the world, so His truth is for all.
- Transformational. God's truth is redemptive. To the woman caught in adultery, Jesus said, "Neither do I condemn thee; go, and sin no more..." (John 8:11) God's grace had transformed many who became Christians in Corinth from lives of moral failure. To them Paul said, "Such were some of you..." (1 Corinthians 6:11).

How has the Bible had it right all along when it comes to sexuality?

Everything God created was "very good," and that included human sexuality since it was God's gift and design by His creation.

---

[24] Pharez was amazingly in the line of Messiah – Matthew 1:3.

Sex is "very good," but not the ultimate good. God is the ultimate good. Sex is a gift from our good God, but we should not elevate the gift of sex above the Giver of sex.

Sex is "very good" only when we observe it on God's terms – in a heterosexual, monogamous marriage. This involves purity outside of marriage by abstinence, and purity inside of marriage by fidelity. The male and female model of marriage is easy to understand and affirm biologically. Consult the "Creator's Manual" about built-in equipment if you have any questions. The institution of marriage did not originate with man, society, or government, but with God. After creating Eve, God brought her to Adam as his life partner (Genesis 2:22). If Eve had ever asked Adam, "Honey, do you love me?" the only answer he could have given was, "Who else?" Hebrews 13:4 says, **"Marriage *is* honourable in all, and the bed undefiled: but whoremongers and adulterers God will judge."** "The problem today is not gay couples wanting to get married," write Jonathan Rauch. "The threat to marriage is straight couples not wanting to get married or straight couples not staying married."[25] "The world of no-strings heterosexual hookups and 50% divorce rates preceded gay marriage."[26] It was heterosexuals that first devalued biblical marriage!

---

[25] Jonathan Rauch, "What I Learned at AEI," *The Public Interest 156*, p. 19).

[26] Andrew Sullivan, "Unveiled: The Case Against Same-Sex Marriage Crumbles," *New Republic*, August 13, 2001.

Sex is "very good" when biological opposite-sex parents conceive children after being married, and then nourish and care for them. Children are to be raised by both biological parents. "And Adam knew Eve his wife, and she conceived..." (Genesis 4:1) Parents are assigned by God with the principle authority and responsibility of their children.

Originally, marriage was understood as a permanent, "life-long" relationship. The Garden of Eden model was: one man, one woman, one lifetime. Biblical marriages are made in heaven, but so are thunder and lightning! It's like the boy's essay on Benjamin Franklin. He wrote, "Benjamin Franklin saw a pretty girl one day. And before long they were married, and he discovered electricity!" That's what I am writing about. Marriage has many electrifying challenges: gender differences, emotional differences and background differences. Each person and couple are unique.

Remarriage is only permissible after the death of a spouse (Romans 7:2-3), because of unfaithfulness (Matthew 19:9) or because an unbelieving spouse leaves a believer (1 Corinthians 7:15). God hates divorce (Malachi 2:16). Americans, many of them Christians, have become "serial polygamists." Rabbi Dr. Earl Grollman, a professional divorce lecturer and author, believes divorce can be more traumatic than death. He said, "The big difference is, death is a closure; it's over. With divorce, it's never over."[27] When it comes to divorce, everyone has their opinions. There is the opinion of the perpetrator; there is the opinion of the

---

[27] Charles Swindoll, *The Tale of the Tardy Oxcart*, p. 168.

victim; there is the opinion of the families of the perpetrators and the victims; there is the opinion of the community; there is the opinion of churches. What about God's opinion?

When God lays down certain prohibitions against some sexual acts, like "Flee fornication" (1 Corinthians 6:18) and "Thou shalt not commit adultery" (Exodus 20:14), He is not keeping you *from* sex; He is keeping you *for* sex. Sex is God's gift to be experienced and enjoyed in the Creator's context.

All kinds of deviant sexual behavior is possible by all people because all are fallen sinners (Romans 3:23; 5:12).

While you are free to choose to violate biblical patterns of sexuality, you are not free to choose the consequences of deviant sexual decisions. The Bible is littered with those who did not observe God's pattern for sexuality.

- Sexuality turned Samson from a *strong man* into a *weak man*. Samson was a "he-man" with a "wo-man" problem. He was physically stronger than any man in his day, but sexually he was a weakling.
- Sexuality turned David from a *great man* into an *ordinary man*. As a king, David had multiple wives, but it was his adultery with Bathsheba that ruined his royal status. Although he was for most of his life "a man after God's own heart" (Acts 13:22), it was this one sin that stained the memory of his

life (1 Kings 15:5).

- Sexuality turned Solomon from a *wise man* into a *foolish man*. Beyond all ability to calculate, King Solomon had 700 wives and 300 concubines, or "porcupines" as one little boy said (1 Kings 11:3). The Bible says these women "turned away his heart after other gods" (1 Kings 11:4).

"The issues of sex, marriage, and human relationships are rooted in the plan and purpose of God Himself. Many of us lack fulfillment and meaning in these areas because we have not consulted the God who made us and the only One who really knows what we are like and what we need. We stumble through life making a mess of these matters and then wonder what went wrong. We need to get back to the God of the Bible and commit ourselves and our future to Him. He is the God of origins, and His design and purpose is the only plan to follow for true happiness and peace of mind!"[28]

---

[28] David Hocking, *The Rise and Fall of Civilization*, p. 86.

- 9 -

Reclaiming Biblical Manhood in an Age of Radical Feminism

The Sexual Revolution of the 1960s is inseparably and undeniably tied to modern-day radical feminism. Former Solicitor General of the United States and United States Court of Appeals Judge Robert H. Bork (1927-) asserts, "Radical feminism is the most destructive and fanatical movement to come down to us from the Sixties. This is a revolutionary, not a reformist, movement, and it is meeting with considerable success. Totalitarian in spirit, it is deeply antagonistic to traditional Western culture and proposes the complete restructuring of society, morality, and human nature. Radical feminism is today's female counterpart of Sixties radicalism."[1]

The etymological meaning of the word "radical" is "of or relating to the root." Using the illustration of a tree, instead of feminists pruning the system which had existed for centuries, the new radicals have been going to the root of their problem – men.

What were the grievances against men by a small minority of the women in the liberation movement of the 1960s? It was the perceived inequities between men and women. It was the social domination of women by

[1] Robert H. Bork, *Slouching Toward Gomorrah*, p. 193.

men. In their words, it was the oppression of women and the privileges of men. It is the attempt to remove any social and economic barriers women might encounter because they are women.

The Toxic Age of Radical Feminism

Mothers of the Movement

In 1962, Helen Gurley Brown (1922-2012) - future editor-in-chief of *Cosmopolitan* magazine - published *Sex and the Single Girl.*

The following year, Betty Friedan (1921-2006) wrote *The Feminine Mystique.* Brown's book glamorized sex outside of marriage and financial independence, while Friedan explored women's supposed dissatisfaction with being mere mothers and housewives. "A culture that forced women to seek relief in the medicine cabinet (think Rolling Stones' "Mother's Little Helper") drove Friedan and others to gather women, liberals, and intellectuals into the National Organization for Women, which advocated for contraception and safe abortion, equal pay, more open workplaces, and women's studies in college."[2] In her notes from the Second Year of Women's Liberation, we find Friedan's revealing comments: "We must destroy love…love promotes vulnerability, dependence, possessiveness, susceptibility to pain, and prevents the full development of woman's human potential by directing all her

[2] A & E History Channel, *The 1960s - The Decade that Changed a Nation,* p. 24.

energies outward in the interests of others."[3] It seems that would fall under the heading of "radical."

Gloria Steinem (1934-) an American feminist, journalist, and social political activist, became nationally recognized as a leader and a spokeswoman for the American feminist movement in the late 1960s and early 1970s. Steinem, a columnist for *New York* magazine and a co-founder of *Ms. Magazine,* is famous for saying, "For the sake of those who wish to live in equal partnership, we have to abolish and reform the institution of legal marriage."[4]

Dr. Mary Jo Bane (1942-), Associate Director of the Center for Research on Women at Harvard University states, "Marriage has existed for the benefit of men and has been a legally sanctioned method of control over women ... the end of the institution of marriage is a necessary condition for the liberation of women. Therefore, it is important for us to encourage women to leave their husbands and not to live individually with men... we must work to destroy (marriage)... All of history must be re-written in terms of oppression of women. We must go back to ancient female religions like witchcraft."[5] She further believes, "We really don't know how to raise children... the fact that children are raised in families means there's no equality. In order to

---

[3] Angela Howard & Sasha Ranae Adams Tarrant, *Reaction to the Modern Women's Movement - 1963 to the Present.*

[4] Gillian Swanson, *Antifeminism in America: A Historical Readers,* p. 328.

[5] Mary Jo Bane, *Declaration of Feminism,* November 1971.

raise children with equality, we must take them from families and raise them."[6]

Organizations and Lobbyists of the Movement

The *National Organization for Women* (NOW) was founded in 1966, and is headquartered in Washington D.C., with 50 state offices and 600 local chapters. Its founders were Betty Friedan, Shirley Chisholm, Pauli Murray, and Muriel Fox. NOW is a 501(c)(4) non-profit, with annual revenues above $3.3 million. With the associated organizations which include the following, additional millions are added to their coffers: *Legal Momentum (Non-profit) National Organization for Women Foundation (NOW), National Organization for Women PAC (Political Party/527)* and *Hollywood NOW (Non-profit),* a child organization. Obviously, the financial numbers for NOW are much higher.

Discover the Networks also indicates that NOW has received funding from the American Express Foundation, the Baker Street Foundation, the California Endowment, the ChevronTexaco Foundation, the Community Foundation of Greater Memphis, the Fannie Mae Foundation, the Ford Foundation, the Hilton Family Foundation, the Jessie Smith Noyes Foundation, the Philadelphia Foundation, the New World Foundation, the New York Community Trust, the New York Times Company Foundation, the

[6] Bane was a mentor to Hillary Rodham while she was a student at Wellesley College.

Rockefeller Family Fund, the Shefa Fund, the Target Foundation, and the Vanguard Public Foundation.[7]

On the official NOW website, they clearly state what they endorse for women. 1. Reproductive rights and justice. 2. Economic justice. 3. Ending violence against women. 4. Radical justice. 5. LQBTQIA+ rights. 6. Constitutional equality.

"NOW is a grassroots arm of the women's movement. NOW's purpose is to promote feminists' ideals, lead societal change, eliminate discrimination and achieve and protect equal rights for all women and girls in all aspect of social, political, and economic life."[8]

NOW has not been entirely consistent by defending President Bill Clinton after he was accused of sexual harassment and deeming Sen. Ted Kennedy (D-Massachusetts) a "champion" despite an incident in which he killed a woman while allegedly driving negligently.[9]

---

[7] Discover the Networks: National Organization for Women." Undated. Accessed November 3, 2017. http://www.discoverthenetworks.org

[8] www.now.org

[9] Jackson, Robert. *"NOW Won't Back Paula Jones, Cites Her Backers." LA Times.* April 23, 1998. November 3, 2017. http://articles.latimes.com/1998/apr/23/news/mn-42260; *"In Memoriam: NOW Mourns Loss of Women's Rights Champion Senator Ted Kennedy."* NOW.org. August 26, 2009. Accessed November 3, 2017. https://now.org/media-center/press-release/in-memoriam-now-mourns-loss-of-womens-rights-champion-senator-ted-kennedy/.

Working alongside of NOW is *Planned Parenthood Federation of America.* It was originally founded in 1923 by Margaret Sanger (1879-1966) as the "American Birth Control League." She was a proponent of "eugenics" - the science of improving a human population by controlled breeding to increase the occurrence of desirable heritable characteristics. It fell into disfavor only after the perversion of its doctrines by the Nazis. While touting themselves as "providing women's health needs," PPFA's 800 plus clinics have been the largest federally funded "abortion mills," performing one of every three abortions in the United States. PPFA advocates for federally funded abortions. In 2009-2010, PPFA received $487,400,000 from the U.S. government. Moreover, the organization's total net assets topped $1 billion for the first time.[10] By 2018 Planned Parenthood's net assets had jumped to 1.9 billion.[11]

Message of the Movement

Feminism isn't about giving a woman the freedom to choose her own path. It's about all women following the radical feminist's path.

The gender neutrality movement by radical feminists is the idea that policies, language, and other social institutions (social structures, gender roles, or gender identity) should avoid distinguishing roles according to people's sex or gender, in order to avoid discrimination

---

10 Discover the Networks: Planned Parenthood Federation of America.

11 https://www.heritage.org/life/commentary/planned-parenthoods-annual-report-out-heres-what-you-need-know

arising from the impression that there are social roles for which one gender is more suited than another. Robert H. Bork, in his book *Slouching Toward Gomorrah,* helps us understand the feminists' message. "In feminine jargon, 'sex' is merely biological while 'gender' refers to roles and is claimed to be 'socially constructed,' which means that everything about men and women, other than their reproductive organs, can be altered by changes in the social and cultural environment. One of the major implications of this view is that human sexuality has no natural form but is culturally conditioned. Radical feminists concede that there are two sexes, but they usually claim there are five genders. Though the list varies somewhat, a common classification is men, women, lesbians, gays, and bisexuals. Thus, heterosexuality, being socially constructed, is no more 'natural' or desirable than homosexuality... Changes in the social and cultural environment to make the roles of men and women identical are what the feminists intend."[12]

Betsy Cario is a reproductive biologist who owns the only sperm bank in Colorado, directs a non-profit that specializes in reproductive health education and teaches a class at the University of Northern Colorado called "Human Sexuality." She addressed the TEDx Mile High Women Conference on December 14, 2016. Her talk was entitled, "Why I Am Not a Feminist." That sounds encouraging, but it's not what you think. She says she is not a feminist because the word "feminist" frames sexuality in male and female binary and does not include those who are other. Her personal goal is to

---

[12] Robert H. Bork, *Slouching Toward Gomorrah,* p. 197.

phase out language that offends, so she isn't a "feminist," she is an "equalist."[13]

Don't get too excited to read only one-fifth of Americans identify as feminists, according to a new HuffPost/YouGov poll. According to the survey, just 20 percent of Americans — including 23 percent of women and 16 percent of men — consider themselves feminists. Another 8 percent consider themselves anti-feminists, while 63 percent said they are neither.[14] Modern-day feminists are still feminists, but some of them now prefer to be called "equalists" in order to include all their LGBTQ allies. Without getting distracted, where are the 16 percent of men who consider themselves feminists. What does that mean?

So, looking back over the past sixty years of this remaking of gender identity and gender roles, how is it working out? People, families and the nation are falling apart as you read these words. I was born just a few months before the Boomers came along and they have lived up to their name – they have blown up, exploded, and self-destructed. Neither individuals, families, nor the nation have recovered from the Sexual Revolution of the sixties.

At the core of America's greatest modern failure is the failure of men. Stu Weber says we can trace this disaster

---

[13] Betsy Cario, TEDx Talks, YouTube, Dec. 14, 2016.

[14] Emily Swanson, *Poll: Few Identify as Feminists, But Most Believe in Equality of Sexes*, Huffpost, Dec. 6, 2017. https://www.huffpost.com/entry/feminism-poll_n_3094917

to failure in high office. Not the presidency of the United States or the presidency of any international conglomerate or the chairman of a board, but "the greatest position a man can hold is his office as head of the home... In God's economy, a man will never get any higher, never have any greater influence, never wield any greater power than he does as the head of his own home. To fail at home is to have failed everywhere. And that's where men are made. I believe America shudders and is wracked with pain today because men have failed to be men."[15]

A Biblical Understanding of Male and Female

"These gender battles in the cultural wars are not 'faddish.' They are not a 'minor distraction' or a 'cultural hiccup' to be lightly regarded or blandly accommodated. Hear me, please, when I say that these issues represent a rock-bottom, down-in-the-trenches, gut-tearing attack on our society's vital organs. To tinker with the image of God, represented in male and female, is to slap God in the face. This is something more than politics, economics, social studies, or some bleeding-heart, feel-good crusade for 'equality.' This is a culture-killing disease. It also represents an ancient, long-simmering attack on the very person of God, and His loving intentions for His children."[16]

Although feminists do not have a high view of the Bible, they do have an opinion of it.

---

[15] Stu Weber, *Four Pillars of a Man's Heart*, pp. 26-27.
[16] Ibid, p. 36.

Radical Feminists view the Bible as Outdated, Misogynistic and Sexist

Let's examine our "outdated" Bible and see what it says about men and women.

How are Men and Women the Same?

Men and women are not simply interchangeable, but rather complement each other in mutually enriching ways for the glory of their Maker. Men need women and women need men. So, in what ways can we say men and women are the same?

- They were both created by God (Genesis 1:27). God doesn't make any inferior products. God didn't mess up when He made Adam and correct His flaws on the second go-round when He made Eve. God didn't make Eve less glorious than Adam. Neither were superior or inferior to the other.

- They both bear the image of God. Bearing the image of God "means *to be like God* and *to represent God*. No other creatures in all of creation, not even the powerful angels, are said to be in the image of God. It is a privilege given only to us as men and women."[17]

- They both have equal value and dignity before God. Males and females are both important to God, yet

[17] Wayne Grudem, *Biblical Foundation for Manhood and Womanhood*, p. 19.

for centuries some cultures have long preferred boy babies over girl babies. "Inexpensive blood tests that can determine the sex of a fetus as early as seven weeks have been developed. And countries around the world have imported ultrasound equipment. 'Ultrasound is available even in very poor countries,' says Valerie Hudson, professor in the Department of International Affairs at Texas A&M University. 'The Chinese government actually imported ultrasound machines mounted on carts in the 20th century, so that even the most remote village would have access to this technology."[18] Asia, Southeastern Europe, the Middle East and some parts of Africa are also aborting girl babies for this reason. The result of sex-selective abortions, infanticide and neglect of baby girls, according to the *United Nations Population Fund,* is that there are more than 117 million "missing" females in Asia alone, and many more around the world.[19] Neither males nor females have any worth apart from God. We have no inherent value – Adam was made from dirt and Eve was made from a rib. Our only value is that we can both freely bring glory to God. In Christ, both males and females are what they are by the grace of God (1 Corinthians 15:10). "If there is anything of significance, anything of importance, anything of relevance in our lives, it is attributable to the undeserved intervention of God."[20]

---

[18] Susan Brink, *Selecting Boys Over Girls is a Trend in More and More Countries,* NPR, August 26, 2015)

[19] https://www.unfpa.org/gender-biased-sex-selection

[20] Stuart Briscoe, *Holy Living in a Hostile World,* p. 118.

- They both need and have the same provision of salvation (Galatians 3:26-27). "...male and female...are all one in Christ Jesus." Males are not forgiven for their sins in one way, while females are forgiven in another way. "God so loved the world...that whosoever..." (John 3:16). Jesus didn't die for us because we are valuable; we are valuable because Jesus died for us. Our value is based on the price of Jesus' blood that was freely given for our redemption. "...for the same Lord over all is rich unto all that call upon him." (Romans 10:12)

- Males and females can be intellectually equal. All people are not created with the same intellectual abilities, but we can presume there are as many intelligent women as there are very smart men. Men, if you ever think of taking an IQ test, don't do it. It's better not knowing.

- In Christian growth, biblical character traits and expectations are not gender-specific (1 Corinthians 13; Galatians 5:22-23; Romans 12:9-21). Men and women alike can bear the full fruit of the Spirit and grow in grace and in the knowledge of our Lord and Savior Jesus Christ (2 Peter 3:18). The common trend is there is more spirituality and dedication among women than among men.

- In marriage, the roles of husband and wife complement each other. Men and women aren't in marriage to *outdo* or *undo* their partner. Both are to be team players, *finding* and *filling* their place to the glory of their Maker.

- In marriage, the husband and wife care equally for each other.

- In marriage, the husband and wife surrender exclusively to each other. Faithfulness is expected of both marriage partners.

- In marriage, the husband and wife are equally accountable to each other.

- In marriage, the husband and wife should honor their spouse in private and in public (1 Peter 3:7; Ephesians 5:33). Authors Gary Smalley and John Trent define the word "honor" well in their book *The Gift of Honor*. "In ancient writing, something of honor was something of substance (literally, heavy), valuable, costly, even priceless. For Homer, the Greek scholar, 'The greater the cost of the gift, the more the honor.' ... Not only does it signify something or someone who is a priceless treasure, but it is also used for someone who occupies a highly respected position in our lives, someone high on our priority list."[21]

- In family life, both the father and the mother are to be obeyed and honored as parents by their children (Exodus 20:12; Ephesians 6:1-2). Obedience for a

---

[21] Gary Smalley and John Trent, *The Gift of Honor*, pp. 23, 24-25.

child is not optional and often it must be unpleasantly enforced by the parents. It is unlikely children will voluntarily honor their parents when they are grown unless they have been required to obey them when they were young.

- In church life, both men and women are admitted into church membership the same way – upon profession of their personal faith in Jesus Christ, followed by the same act of baptism (Acts 2:41; 1 Peter 3:21). There is not one kind of baptism for men and a different baptism for women.

How are Men and Women Different?

It should be obvious to all that men and women are different. What we need to see is not so much the differences *from* each other, but the differences *for* each other.

Warning: If you dare to hold these views publicly prepare for some major blow-back from the pro-feminist-influenced culture.

- Physically, men and women are different in many ways. In our day of foolishness, men and women have been thrown into a gender blender. This social experiment will not work because men and women are different. There, I've said it for all to read. It will probably keep me from being elected to high public office. Anatomically and physiologically, men and women are different. The Bible says women in some ways are "the weaker vessel" (1 Peter 3:7). Males in general are bigger than females.

Males have more muscle mass, longer limbs, bigger bones and internal organs, and, on average, are taller. But don't take that "weaker" stuff too far. As mentioned in chapter 2, my great-grandmother, Mary Carolyn Locke (1835-1897), a pioneer woman in the early days of Texas, the mother of 11, the grandmother of 64, could hardly be called a weak woman.

- Reproductively, men and women are different. Males are able to father a child, but only women can conceive, carry, give birth and feed a child.

- Regarding life-assignments, men and women differ.

- In marriage, Christ is the head of the man and the husband is the head of the wife (1 Corinthians 11:3; Ephesians 5:23). God's chain of command in marriage, in the home and in the church is through the man, who is to be the spiritual leader. A home with two heads is a monster and a home with no head is dead. Even in biblically sound, conservative churches, when this truth is advanced, you can sometimes feel the tension that results in the hearts of some women against this truth because of the influence of modern-day radical feminism. When I have dared to show respect to some modern women in the public, I do not know whether they will be pleased or angered. On a recent trip with my wife, an airport shuttle tram was taking us toward our baggage. When it arrived, I allowed my wife and a lady who was behind me to exit first. After exiting, the lady turned and said, "Thank you, there are not many gentlemen left." (I asked Susan to repeat what the lady said so she would remember!) When the word "head" is used here as a metaphor, it doesn't refer to anatomy, but to authority. Women are not "headless" without men. They have plenty of brains on their own. Jesus understood well His divine equality in the Godhead. He said, "I, and my Father, are one." (John 10:30) Jesus would eventually be crucified because He made Himself "equal with God." (John 5:18; 10:33; 19:7) Yet, while God of very God, when Christ was on this earth, His head (authority) was God. Jesus was on the earth to do the Father's will (John 4:34).[22] While Jesus was on this earth, He voluntarily consented to temporarily take a lower position than God the Father (Philippians 2:5-8). Headship, when properly understood, does not mean domination, rather a condition of voluntary commitment carried out in obedience to God's will. "The man is answerable for his actions, ultimately and inescapably, to Christ. By the same token the woman is answerable to the man...This is God's ordained order and state of affairs. No amount of argument is going to change it. All attempts to defy it can only lead to breakdown and chaos...The feminist lobby, for all its noise, anger, organization, and resentment, is not going to change the way things are."[23]

- In marriage, men lead by providing (1 Timothy 3:8) and protecting, while women are supportive and receive the loving care of their husbands. In much

[22] John 7:16; 8:28; 10:37-38; 12:49; 14:10; 17:8
[23] John Phillips, *Exploring 1 Corinthians*, pp. 232-233.

of the Bible these responses are not demanded, but simply assumed privileges. When you don't teach men to protect and value women, you get men who will violate and victimized women. When you don't teach women to value relationships with men who are responsible and good, you get men who are incentivized to irresponsibility and bad behavior. Here is a great test for unmarried women who are open to a relationship with a man. Observe how a young man treats his mother and sister, it is a good indicator of how he will treat his wife.

Three guys were bragging at work about how much control they had over their wives. One said, "My wife never says 'no' to me." The second one said, "My wife always says 'yes' to me." After a while they turned to the third guy and says, "Well, what about you? What sort of control do you have over your wife?" The third fellow says "I'll tell you. Just the other night I had a big argument with my wife and before it was over I had her on her hands and knees." The two guys were amazed. "Really? What happened then?" the guys asked. His answer was, "She said, 'Get out from under the bed you chicken and fight like a man!'"

- In marriage, men are called to love their wives sacrificially and selflessly, while wives are called to joyful submission (Ephesians 5:21-35). The Bible does not command a husband to *control* his wife, but it does speak about *caring* about her at the deepest level. Husbands are to love their wives as Christ loved the church and gave Himself for it (Ephesians

5:25). Real Christian marriage is not made up of two partners struggling to do their best, but three; with Christ doing His work together with the husband and wife.

- In church, only men are to serve as pastors (1 Timothy 3:2; Titus 1:6).[24] Women are not to teach men or exercise authority over men (1 Timothy 2:12). Older women are to be godly examples to young women, teaching them to "love their husbands, to love their children, *To be* discreet, chaste, keepers at home, good, obedient to their own husbands, that the word of God be not blasphemed." (Titus 2:4-5) Some years ago a man I was mentoring was shocked to find out our church did not ordain women. He asked, "Isn't the church supposed to be an 'equal employment opportunity' business, like where I work?"

	Errors of Passivity	Biblical Ideal	Errors of Aggressiveness
Husband	Wimp	Loving, humble Headship	Tyrant
Wife	Doormat	Joyful, intelligent submission	Usurper

[25]

Restoring Biblical Manhood

When it comes to spirituality, too many men are standing silently in the shadows.

---

[24] As a side note it would be interesting to study the influence women have had in creating false religions who refused this restriction.

[25] Wayne Grudem, *Biblical Foundations for Manhood and Womanhood*, p.38.

"Let the woman learn in silence with all subjection. But I suffer not a woman to teach, nor to usurp authority over the man, but to be in silence. For Adam was first formed, then Eve. And Adam was not deceived, but the woman being deceived was in the transgression. Notwithstanding she shall be saved in childbearing, if they continue in faith and charity and holiness with sobriety." (1 Timothy 2:11-15) It is very possible that many have based their understanding of the history of the fall of the human race from this passage and have laid the blame on Eve. The idea is that Eve and the serpent were in the garden, Eve fell victim to the serpent's deception, she then ate, and then went and found Adam and he willfully disobeyed.

But what if Adam was silently standing in the shadows, physically observing, but not willing to step up and take charge? Here are how the events read in Genesis. **"And when the woman saw that the tree *was* good for food, and that it *was* pleasant to the eyes, and a tree to be desired to make *one* wise, she took of the fruit thereof, and did eat, and gave also unto her husband <u>with her</u>; and he did eat."** (my underline; Genesis 3:6) The Hebrew for "with" is the Hebrew "*'im*" which means "close association and physical proximity." This preposition is used in the word "Immanuel," "God with us." Adam was right there with Eve, we could say. Nothing in the narrative suggests a lapse of time between Eve's eating the fruit and her offering it to Adam. Adam was passive about his role of protecting his wife. Silence was not golden – it ended up being deadly for the whole human family.[26]

We could say Adam's first failing was in not being a man. Like Adam, men in ages following have too many times stood by in silence and just let things happen.

In 2019 my wife and I were privileged to visit the city and campus of Oxford University on a ministry trip to England. There is a huge monument in the center of the town that was completed in 1843 in honor of three Anglican priests who were tried for heresy by Catholic Queen Mary. Hugh Latimer and Nicholas Ridley were burned at the stake on October 16, 1555. Thomas Cranmer would die in the same manner five months later, March 21, 1556. They died just outside the city walls to the north, where Broad Street is now located.

What would they have been thinking? In the moment of martyrdom Latimer said to Ridley as they were about to be burned at the stake, "Play the man, Master Ridley; we shall this day light such a candle, by God's grace, in England, as I trust shall never be put out."
"Play the man!"

---

26 Dr. Larry Crabb, *The Silence of Adam*, pp. 87-99.

How would that go over in our day of radical feminism?

Actually, that statement did not originate with Hugh Latimer. Latimer had evidently read the account of the second-century martyr named Polycarp (69-156). When given the opportunity to renounce his faith in Jesus Christ, Polycarp, who was a student of John the Apostle said, "86 years have I served him, and he has done me no wrong. How can I blaspheme my King and my Savior?" As Polycarp was being taken into the arena, it is said a voice came to him from heaven: "Be strong, Polycarp and play the man!" No one saw who had spoken, but some who were there heard the voice. Whether that is true or not, it is recorded in the lore of Polycarp.

"Play the man." The phrase states an understanding that when certain situations arise, those of the male gender are to stand up and take responsibility. In the days of the wild west, it might have been "Buck up, brother." I am sure the old cowboy didn't have any idea that it was an intransitive verb that meant "be encouraged, to brace up."

The Apostle Paul's challenge was, **"Watch ye, stand fast in the faith quit you like men, be strong."** (1 Corinthians 16:13), which means "to conduct oneself in a manly or courageous way, to be brave, to display courage… .the imperfect imperative calls for an habitual action."[27] They were to be "ready to take up the right."

---

[27] Cleon L Rogers Jr & III, *The New Linguistic and Exegetical Key to the Greek New Testament*, p. 390.

Paul's earlier complaint was they were behaving like children (1 Corinthians 3:1). It is time for men to grow up and take their God-given responsibilities.

True manhood has clearly observable qualities and expectations. The dying words of King David to his son, Solomon, who would be the new king, was, "**...be thou strong therefore, and shew thyself a man;...**" (1 Kings 2:2).

Masculinity Requires a Relationship with God

Authentic masculinity comes from a genuine, personal, growing relationship with the living God. This is the first step in becoming a true male. At the first, it took God to make a man; and it still does! Usually, men are all about assignments and achievements. The only way that can be pulled off is by God accomplishing His work *for* us, *in* us and *through* us. Instead of seeing life as a project, we need to see it as a relationship. God has taken the initiative to pursue a relationship with mankind. God sent His Son, Jesus Christ, to earth to be our Savior by being crucified in our place. Look closely at the following Scriptures.

- **"For God so loved the world, that he gave his only begotten Son, that whosoever believeth in him should not perish, but have everlasting life. For God sent not his Son into the world to condemn the world; but that the world through him might be saved. He that believeth on him is not condemned: but he that believeth not is condemned already, because he hath not believed in the name of**

the only begotten Son of God." (John 3:16-18)

- **"For when we were yet without strength, in due time Christ died for the ungodly. For scarcely for a righteous man will one die: yet peradventure for a good man some would even dare to die. But God commendeth his love toward us, in that, while we were yet sinners, Christ died for us. Much more then, being now justified by his blood, we shall be saved from wrath through him. For if, when we were enemies, we were reconciled to God by the death of his Son, much more, being reconciled, we shall be saved by his life.** (Romans 5:6-10)
- **"For Christ also hath once suffered for sins, the just for the unjust, that he might bring us to God, being put to death in the flesh, but quickened by the Spirit:"** (1 Peter 3:18)
- **"To wit, that God was in Christ, reconciling the world unto himself, not imputing their trespasses unto them; and hath committed unto us the word of reconciliation. Now then we are ambassadors for Christ, as though God did beseech *you* by us: we pray *you* in Christ's stead, be ye reconciled to God. For he hath made him *to be* sin for us, who knew no sin; that we might be made the righteousness of God in him."** (2 Corinthians 5:19-21)
- **"He was in the world, and the world was made by him, and the world knew him not. He came unto his own, and his own received him**

not. But as many as received him, to them gave he power to become the sons of God, *even* to them that believe on his name: Which were born, not of blood, nor of the will of the flesh, nor of the will of man, but of God." (John 1:10-13)

- **For by grace are ye saved through faith; and that not of yourselves: *it is* the gift of God: Not of works, lest any man should boast."** (Ephesians 2:8-9)
- **"Not by works of righteousness which we have done, but according to his mercy he saved us, by the washing of regeneration,..."** (Titus 2:5)

Have you entrusted your eternal soul into God's care? Have you placed your trust in Christ alone, understanding that He has done all that is necessary for you to be welcomed by God? A man who was preparing to commit suicide asked a Christian, **"Sirs, what must I do to be saved? And they said, Believe on the Lord Jesus Christ, and thou shalt be saved, and thy house." (Acts 16:30-31)**

Masculinity Has a Model to Emulate

The model for masculinity is Jesus Christ, the consummate man. Jesus is the only perfect model of a man. Other men were marked with great feats, but also with great failures. Only Jesus was without a single sin. Jesus always did those things that pleased His Father (John 8:29). Instead of creating our own personal checkoff list of dos and don'ts, what we need to do is become more and more like Jesus. Everything He was, we need to become.

- **"For whom he did foreknow, he also did predestinate *to be* conformed to the image of his Son, that he might be the firstborn among many brethren."** (Romans 8:29)
- **"But we all, with open face beholding as in a glass the glory of the Lord, are changed into the same image from glory to glory, *even* as by the Spirit of the Lord."** (2 Corinthians 3:18)

As a purely physical standard, Jesus was a man's man. Most likely, following his foster father Joseph's vocation, Jesus would have spent the first 25 years of his life learning about carpentry in the days before power tools. He was a workman, aware of the method of building. His frequent references to building, houses, agriculture, nature, mountains, and wildlife make it abundantly clear that he was a man's man, and not a cultured academic. He was not raised in Jerusalem, studying in the Temple all day long. He understood the challenges and hardships known by most men of his day. Consider Jesus' physical manliness.

- The toughness He demonstrated to walk up and down the land of Israel was amazing.
- His hands were rough from more than a couple of decades of hard, physical work.
- He was fit and trim from his constant activity of carpentry.
- His hair must have been brittle and coarse from the sun and climate.
- His skin would have been leathery from working and walking in the sun.

- He must have had incredible physical stamina and endurance to live through his beating and survive as long as He did on the cross. A weak man would have collapsed under the weight of the cross and the cruelty of the punishment long before Jesus did.[28]

Jesus, also, taught us by word or example what the qualities of an authentic man are.

- Salvation is only in Him (John 14:6).
- Without Him we can do nothing (John 15:5).
- God's Word is our life-sustaining substance (Matthew 4:4).
- Prayer is something we should do all the time (Luke 18:1).
- Humility is required when we are true servants (John 13:4-5, 12-15).
- Material success can be dangerous (Matthew 13:22; 19:16-26).
- Worry about stuff doesn't make any sense (Matthew 6:25-34).
- Seeking earthly status is detestable to God (Luke 16:15).
- By losing your life you will gain life (Luke 9:24).
- Service to others is our mission (Matthew 20:28).
- Obedience is costly but ultimately rewarding (Philippians 2:8-11).

Who are you going to follow – Christ or the culture?

---

28 Paul Barreca, *Jesus, the Ultimate Man*, October 5, 2014.

As Joshua faced the daunting task of replacing Moses, he must have had all kinds of questions going through his mind. Who could ever replace the great Moses? How will I ever know how to overcome the enemies we will face? Will I become a huge failure?

Look closely at the words of Major W. Ian Thomas (1914-2007), in his book, *The Saving Life of Christ.* "Joshua went out to make a reconnaissance of the walled city of Jericho and to draw up plans for tackling the first major task that confronted him, but as he did so he became strangely aware of the presence of a Man – a Man with His sword drawn in His hand – and in so many words, he said, "Whose side are you on? Are you on our side or are you on their side? **'And he said, Nay; but *as* captain of the host of the LORD am I now come.'** Joshua 5:13-14a) The man with the sword in His hand said, in effect, 'I am neither on your side nor am I on their side. I have come as Captain of the host of the Lord. I have not come to take side – I have come to take over!'"[29]

Masculinity Requires Absolute Surrender

"And Joshua fell on his face to the earth, and did worship, and said unto him, What saith my lord unto his servant? And the captain of the LORD'S host said unto Joshua, Loose thy shoe from off thy foot; for the place whereon thou standest *is* holy. And Joshua did so." (Joshua 5:14b-15)

---

[29] Major W. Ian Thomas, *The Saving Life of Christ*, pp. 137-138.

While we sometimes ascribe some men as extraordinary, all men are really only very ordinary. Study closely the men of the Bible and you will clearly see the only extraordinary thing about them was their extraordinary God. Of two very ordinary men, it was said, **"Now when they saw the boldness of Peter and John, and perceived that they were unlearned and ignorant men, they marvelled; and they took knowledge of them, that they had been with Jesus."** (Acts 4:13) What made these world-changing apostles different was their extraordinary Savior, Jesus Christ – "...they had been with Jesus."

"When I was a child, I spake as a child, I understood as a child, I thought as a child: but when I became a man, I put away childish things." (1 Corinthians 13:11)

Thirty years after Joshua had made his initial surrender to God, as he approached the end of his life, he challenged others to make a similar surrender. **"And if it seem evil unto you to serve the LORD, choose you this day whom ye will serve; whether the gods which your fathers served that *were* on the other side of the flood, or the gods of the Amorites, in whose land ye dwell: but as for me and my house, we will serve the LORD."** (Joshua 24:15)

By virtue of who Jesus is and what He did by His birth, life, death, resurrection, ascension and promised return, and my surrender to Him, allow me to share my Family Constitution.

The Locke Family Constitution

- We are the Lord's people. Through no merit of our own we have been bought with a price; thus, we are eternally secure. It is well with our souls.
- What we have is the Lord's. We are not owners, but managers of God's vast resources and as we have the resources and opportunities, we will willingly be generous.
- We intend to love God first. Jesus is our Lord; we are His servants.
- We honor the biblical model of marriage between a man and a woman and believe all sex outside of marriage is sinful.
- We intentionally serve God as a Baptist people through a unique family history. We are Christians by spiritual birth. We are Baptists by conviction.
- Our whole family has been set apart to serve God and it becomes the commitment of each person to personally and individually live to the glory of God.
- We will not financially or emotionally support life-styles contrary to Scripture.
- We will continue to reinvest in others what those before us have poured into us. We are the product of many loving and faithful friends.
- We have transferred our treasures to heaven by a lifetime of financial giving.

- 10 -

Living a "G" Rated Life in an "X" Rated World

From the moment a person becomes a Christian they are involved in a constant conflict. We are at war! In this conflict there are no conscientious objectors, no draft dodgers, and no armchair generals. From day one, every bit of ground we gain in the Christian life is against opposition and resistance.

The Bible identified for us three enemies against which we must fight, or we will be taken prisoner:
the world, the devil and the flesh.

- The world is our external enemy.
- The devil is our infernal enemy.
- The flesh is our internal enemy.

The World

It has been well established in the previous chapters that ours is now an "X" rated world. There is no denying that! The only other possibility would be to say that our world is rapidly moving toward a "XXX" rated world.

Since the fall of Adam, the world in which we have been born has never been conducive to living a God-honoring, holy life. It has been and remains enemy territory against which we must constantly contend. The world is a big negative. We are instructed to:

- Not *court* the world. (James 4:4)
- Not be *contaminated* by the world. (James 1:17)
- Not be *conformed* to the world. (Romans 12:2)
- Not *care* about the things of the world. (1 John 2:15-17)
- Not be *condemned* with the world. (1 Corinthians 11:32)

Instead of the wickedness of the world being an incentive to be like them, it should be like a thorn reminding us that we are "pilgrims and strangers" in this world.

The Devil

Another enemy of the Christian living the "G" rated life is the devil. The existence of Satan is doubted or denied in our day of science and sophistication. "It is not popular today to believe in a literal, personal devil even among professed Christians. The devil is increasingly seen as being somewhere between a figment of our imagination and a useful device to coerce obedience."[1] Yet the Bible clearly presents Satan as a real, supernatural intruder.[2] Satan is "the god of this world." (2 Corinthians 4:4) "Evil angels are employed in the execution of Satan's purposes, which are diametrically opposed to those of God, and have to do with the

[1] John MacArthur, *Daily Readings from the Life of Christ*, January 12.

[2] Clarification: Satan is not omnipresent, omnipotent, or omniscient, but he oversees countless demons who do his evil work throughout the world.

hindrance and harm of the spiritual life and well-being of God's people."[3]

The Flesh

When a person is saved, God gives them a new nature, which is great news. The bad news is we do not lose the old nature – the flesh. There is a part of the believer, the old part, that looks at the world and listens to the voice of Satan and is tempted to silence the voice of the Holy Spirit and disobey the teachings of the Word of God.

An easy way to understand what the "flesh" means is to drop the "h" and spell it backward – "self."

The "flesh" is our "self-life" that must wait to be redeemed when we will receive a glorified body at Jesus' return. Until then, the only way it is redeemed is by progressive sanctification as we are filled by the Holy Spirit as we yield ourselves to the Lordship of Jesus Christ.

- The flesh is unhelpful for sanctification (John 6:63; Romans 7:18).
- The flesh is antagonistic to sanctification (Romans 8:7).

Vulnerable to Sexual Sins

No matter how different each person is from others, we all struggle with temptation. In one way or another, from one enemy or from all three, we are regularly provided opportunities to disregard God and do our own thing.

---

[3] Emery H. Bancroft, D.D, *Elemental Theology*, 1977.

It was somewhat surprising to me that even the American Psychological Association posts information on their website on "Overcoming Temptation." Of course, they deny any belief or need for divine intervention while they address various addictions as things with which people must deal and overcome.

Let's settle in on this idea of "temptation." Do you give much thought to your vulnerability to its possibility and reality? Previous generations understood the threat temptations potentially pose to the Christian's life and took temptation seriously. They even put it in songs to be sung in weekly church services as reminders of every person's vulnerability to sins.

Oh, to grace how great a debtor
Daily I'm constrained to be
Let Thy goodness like a fetter
Bind my wandering heart to Thee
Prone to wander, Lord, I feel it
Prone to leave the God I love
Here's my heart, oh, take and seal it
Seal it for Thy courts above.

Come Thou Fount,
Robert Robinson, 1758

Yield not to temptation, for yielding is sin
Each victory will help you some others to win
Fight manfully onward, dark passions subdue
Look ever to Jesus and He'll carry you through
Just ask the Savior to help you
To comfort, strengthen and keep you
He is willing to aid you
And He will carry you through

Yield Not to Temptation,
Horatio R. Palmer, 1868

I need Thee every hour,
Stay Thou near by;
Temptations lose their power,
When Thou art nigh.
I need Thee, O I need Thee;
Every hour I need Thee!
O bless me now, my Savior,
I come to Thee.

I Need Thee Every Hour,
Annie Sherwood Hawks, 1872

Tempted and tried, we're oft made to wonder
Why it should be thus all the day long;
While there are others living about us,
Never molested, though in the wrong.
Farther along we'll know more about it,
Farther along we'll understand why;
Cheer up, my brother, live in the sunshine,
We'll understand it all by and by.

Farther Along,
W. B. Stevens, 1938

It is foolish to presume that 21st Century Christians are not vulnerable to temptation when there are so many scriptural warnings. **"The whole world lieth in wickedness."** (1 John 5:19) **"Be sober, be vigilant; because your adversary the devil as a roaring lion, walketh about, seeking whom he may devour."** (1 Peter 5:8). **"The spirit indeed is willing, but the flesh is weak."** (Matthew 26:41)

"Our human design is such that all 'parts' are intertwined: body, soul and spirit (1 Thessalonians 5:23). A problem in one 'part' affects the other parts too."[4]

The Apostle Paul, considered by many to be one of the greatest Christians to ever live, understood his vulnerability to the yielding to temptations that leads to devastating consequences. Look closely at his personal concerns and direction.

- **"But I keep under my body, and bring *it* into subjection: lest that by any means, when I have preached to others, I myself should be a castaway."** (1 Corinthians 9:27)
- **"Wherefore let him that thinketh he standeth take heed lest he fall."** (1 Corinthians 10:12)
- **"Brethren, if a man be overtaken in a fault, ye which are spiritual, restore such an one in the spirit of meekness; considering thyself, lest thou also be tempted."** (Galatians 6:1)

---

[4] Darrell W. Sparks, *Taking Temptation Seriously*, p. 19.

Vice-President Mike Pence, since becoming a Christian, refuses to dine with a woman who is not his wife. For that stance, the Vice President has been attacked as misogynistic. If he eats alone with a woman, that woman is only his wife, Karen Pence; if he attends an event where alcohol is served and "people are being loose," he prefers that his wife be present and standing close to him. Matt Walsh, a conservative Christian blogger, asked, "Seriously what's the appropriate reason for a married person to go out for a meal alone with a member of the other sex (outside of family)?" Erick Erickson, also a conservative Christian blogger, replied, with apparent seriousness, "planning your spouse's surprise party or funeral and that is it." The jokes came quickly: "Honey it's not what you think- we were planning your surprise funeral," one person wrote.[5]

This practice does not charge every woman as a temptress, but it does underscore the potential remaking of something that seems innocent into something that is devastating – the loss of one's reputation, marriage, and family.

Violators of Sexual Standards

One reason we can have great confidence in the inspiration and truthfulness of the Bible is that it does not gloss over the sins and failures of those who were pronounced "righteous."

---

[5] Jia Tolentino, *Mike Pence's Marriage and the Beliefs That Keep Women from Power*, The New Yorker, March 31, 2017.

Samson

One such violator of sexual impropriety was Samson. While being recognized as one of the strongest men with great physical abilities, Samson was among the weakest when it came to restraining his sexual desires. While Samson is listed among the heroes and heroines of the faith in Hebrews 11, he was far from being faithful to God's purpose as a judge over Israel. His sexual violations began by trying to marry a daughter of the Philistines (Judges 14:20), followed by having sexual relations with a "harlot" (Judges 16:1) and ultimately being betrayed by the money-grubbing Delilah (Judges 16:4-21). Sin had so darkened his heart, the Bible says, "...he wist (knew) not that the LORD was departed from him." (Judges 16:20) Samson could have lived as a champion long celebrated by others for his supernatural feats but squandered his calling and died as a clown remembered for his carnal failures.

David

Another well-known violator of purity was King David and his adulterous relationship with Bathsheba (2 Samuel 12:2-4. **"And it came to pass in an eveningtide, that David arose from off his bed, and walked upon the roof of the king's house: and from the roof he saw a woman washing herself; and the woman *was* very beautiful to look upon. And David sent and enquired after the woman. And *one* said, *Is* not this Bathsheba, the daughter of Eliam, the wife of Uriah the Hittite? And David sent messengers, and took her; and she came in unto him, and he lay with her; for she was purified from her uncleanness: and she returned unto her house."**

A one verse commentary of David is given in 1 Kings 15:5. **"...David did *that which was* right in the eyes of the LORD, and turned not aside from any *thing* that he commanded him all the days of his life, save only in the matter of Uriah the Hittite."**

"The comprehensive nature of David's sin appears only on closer examination. It has been pointed out that the breaking of the tenth commandment, coveting his neighbor's wife, led to his breaking the seventh and committing adultery. Soon, in order to break the eighth, stealing what did not belong to him, he broke the sixth and committed murder. He broke the ninth by bearing false witness against his neighbor. He brought dishonor on his parents and thus broke the fifth. Thus, he broke all the commandments which refer to loving one's neighbor as one's self. And of course, in its very nature, his sin dishonored God as well. There is no such thing as a simple sin. Sin is always complicated."[6]

Gomer

The Old Testament prophet Hosea married a woman by the name of – wait for it - Gomer. Surprise! Surprise! Surprise! Now that is love! Any man who could get up in the morning and say, "Gomer, I love you," is a man who knows something about love. Seriously, there may be no match to Hosea's love for Gomer anywhere in the entire Bible. Hosea's love was not some kind of fleeting flash of emotion. You may have heard about the husband who asked his wife, "I don't get it. How can you be so beautiful and so clueless at the same time?"

---

[6] J. Oswald Sanders, *Bible Men of Faith,* p. 123.

She answered, "I am beautiful so that you would love me. I am clueless so that I can love you!"

Hosea and Gomer began having babies. That is what most married people do. What is interesting is God named every one of their children.

- The first child God named *Jezreel,* meaning "may God scatter." Jezreel was the valley where the army of Israel was to be defeated. God was going to scatter the ten tribes and sow them among the nations. Jezreel's name prophesied of Israel's defeat.
- The second child was a girl. God named her *Lo-ru-ha'-mah.* "Lo" is the Hebrew negative. "Not to be pitied." Imagine people asking Hosea what his pretty baby girl's name was and him answering, "No Pity."
- The third child was a boy God named *Lo-am'mi.* It meant, "Not of my people." By this time Hosea was sure he was not the father.

One morning it happened - there was no breakfast on the table and Gomer was not to be found. She left Hosea and her children and became unfaithful - more than a mere adulteress - she became a harlot, a prostitute. Hosea remembered what God had said. "Go, take unto thee a wife of whoredoms and children of whoredoms:..." Hosea 1:2.

Life between chapters one and two seems to involve some considerable time. The children were now old enough to understand their mother's situation. It was not the fault of these children that their mother had left. Instead of Hosea taking out his disappointment on the little girl and the last boy, he loved them as his own. Hosea dropped the "lo" calling them "Ammi" and "Ruhamah" meaning "mine" and "pitied." Hosea wraps those unfortunate children in his loving arms. He would be the only parent they would know for years.

Later, in desperation, Hosea turned to his then grown children, **"Plead with your mother, plead: for she *is* not my wife, neither *am* I her husband: let her therefore put away her whoredoms out of her sight, and her adulteries from between her breasts;"** (Hosea 2:2)

From the story line it seems that Gomer had completely thrown her life away. By this time, she had been with many "lovers" (Hosea 2:5). She was living it up with her lovers (Hosea 2:5b). She was enjoying her "hey day." But remember this: for every "hey day" there is a "payday."

Eventually she was "used" up. Finally, in desperation, she "sold" herself as a slave to the man with whom she was living. Here is how life went for Gomer. At first, she had given herself to "strangers." Then she found a "friend" (Hosea 3:1). Gomer had given up all pretense of decency and was living with her new "friend." This "friend" must have "lost that loving feeling" because He would eventually become Gomer's "master."

Under Mosaic law, Hosea had several options in response to Gomer's despicable behavior. The prophet could have...

- *Deserted* her...In the bitterness of his heart, Hosea could have thrown her away and gone on with his life. "Good riddance," he might have said.
- *Divorced* her...This was allowed under Mosaic law. Just put her on the curb with the other garbage.
- Brought about her *Death*... Gomer's adultery was a sin which was punishable by death.
- *Disgraced* her... Instead of killing a woman like this, they would humiliate her by selling her like a piece of damaged property. She would be brought to the "city gate," the public square, stripped to the waist and then auctioned off as a slave.

In the lowest moment of Gomer's life, Hosea was told by the Lord, **"Go yet, love a woman beloved of *her* friend, yet an adulteress, according to the love of the LORD toward the children of Israel, who look to other gods, and love flagons of wine."** (Hosea 3:1)

Somehow word had gotten to Hosea that Gomer was going to be auctioned off in some nearby city. We are not told how the bidding went, but when it was all over Hosea was awarded his "prize." "Sold to the man in the back." **"So I bought her to me for fifteen *pieces* of silver, and *for* an homer of barley, and an half homer of barley:..."** (Hosea 3:2). This was not a large sum. It was "silver" not gold; it was some "barley," a grain of the cheapest sort. She brought only half the price of a good slave. No one really wanted her but Hosea.

This may be how the next events unfolded. Gomer was shoved off the block like an animal, pushed into the dirt on her face - bruised, broken, weeping. She probably wished she were dead. Then Hosea walked through the curious crowd, knelt down beside the abused body of Gomer, took her face in his hand and turned her toward him. It was the first time Hosea had touched Gomer in years. She looked up and it was, of all people, Hosea. Shamed, fearful, tears blurring her vision, her mind was filled with uncertainty.

Gomer may have broken the silence by saying, "Hosea, I'm so sorry. Thank you for saving me today from these awful people. I know I don't deserve it. I'm sorry. Hosea, I want to make you this promise—I'll be your slave for the rest of my life."

Hosea might have taken off his clean coat, covering the shame of Gomer's nakedness and wiping off some of her dirt with his prophetic mantel. As he gently lifted her up, spoke softly, "Gomer, let's go home! I don't need a slave; what I need is a wife. Our children do not need a servant; they need a mother. I still love you."

And of all things, in that moment of mercy and grace, possibly on their way home, Hosea renews His vows to Gomer. **"And I said unto her, Thou shalt abide for me many days; thou shalt not play the harlot, and thou shalt not be for *another* man: so *will* I also *be* for thee."** (Hosea 3:3) "Gomer, you don't need to ask me a thousand times after this. My coming to you means I have forgiven you. The past is past. Let's go on with our lives now."

Do you know who this story is about? It is about us. This is a parallel of our unfaithfulness to God and His jealous love that pursues us.

"This is the debt I pay
Just for one riotous day,
Years of regret and grief,
Sorrow without relief...
Slight was the thing I bought,
Small was the debt I thought,
Poor was the debt at best –
God! But the interest!

Paul Dunbar[7]

When I was researching and writing this chapter I wept again and again when I thought about those who have served as Christian pastors/leaders who violated God's standards of sexual morality. As I pondered my fifty plus years of ministry, name after name came to my mind of men who, for moments of sexual pleasure, violated what they said they believed. There isn't any need to think about other Christian denominations whose leaders have fallen like Jim Bakker, Jimmy Swaggart, Ted Haggard, Bill Gothard, Bill Hybel and Mark Driscoll.

Baptists have their own sad stories. Bill Weber, the founding pastor of Prestonwood Baptist Church, Plano, Texas, was dismissed in 1988 for multiple adulteries with female church members. Webber's ministry had

---

[7] Quoted by David Roper, *Out of the Ordinary,* p.106.

been bankrolled by millionaires like Mary Kay Ash, founder of Mary Kay Cosmetics company.[8] He believed his own press releases and thought he could defy God's laws.

An outstanding young black pastor, Darrell Gilyard, a friend of Jerry Farwell, ran in the highest circles of Southern Baptists. Yet Gilyard committed sex crimes against two teenage girls in the church he pastored, fathering a child by one who accused him of raping her in 2004. In 2007, he was arrested on charges of lewd and lascivious conduct. In 2009, he pled guilty to two counts, was sentenced to prison and the state designated him a sex offender. He served three years in a state prison until he was released in December 2017, on probation. "Right now I'm doing well," said Gilyard, "I have this label as a leper of society, but that label is not me... Of course I believe I have changed," he said, "but time will tell everyone if I have changed."[9]

Ollin Collins started a Baptist church in north Fort Worth with nine members which grew in 20 years to 2,000 members. The church had a multi-million, 3,150-seat auditorium, as well as a school through grade 12, a day care center and gymnasium/ family life center. All was well until he was fired for having sex with ladies who had come to him for counseling.

---

[8] Glenna Whitley, *The Second Coming of Billy Weber*, D Magazine, July 1989.

[9] https://www.firstcoastnews.com/article/news/local/pastor-darrell-gilyard-breaks-silence-on-his-fall-from-grace/271089581

Pastor Jack Schaap of First Baptist Church, Hammond, Indiana, son-in-law of famed Jack Hyles, is presently in prison for carrying a 16-year-old across state lines and having sex with her. Schaap was sentenced to 12 years in federal prison and is due for release in 2025. His testimony was, "I became a fool."[10]

There are three possible explanations for the fall of these well-known, successful Baptist pastors.

Frontline Casualties

Dr. Lewis Sperry Chafter (1871-1952) believed that "committed Christians are placed on the front lines of the battle. It's the place where the enemy's fiercest pressure is felt, but it also offers the best view of his crushing defeat."[11] No doubt Satan targets leaders because when one leader falls, thousands are injured with the defeat. Anyone who volunteers for Christian ministry is entering enemy territory.

Delusional

C.W. Brister (1926-2008), was a professor of pastoral counseling at Southwestern Baptist Theological

---

[10] Anyone can be forgiven of consensual or criminal sexual acts if they humbly confess them to God through Jesus Christ. Being forgiven does not mean the consequences will be removed or lessened. In the case of a pastor, he can be forgiven by God, but has disqualified himself from serving a church in the future as their leader. A bank president can be forgiven of embezzlement, but you do not put him back in charge of the vault. Church discipline should be carried out if there is a refusal to repent (1 Corinthians 5).

[11] Quoted by David Jeremiah, *Slaying the Giants in Your Life*, p. 92.

Seminary in Fort Worth. How could enormously successful leaders, he asks, get involved in such paradoxical behavior? Brister describes a phenomenon known as the "rapture of the deep," a feeling of euphoria experienced by deep-sea divers who inhale too much nitrogen. The initial intoxicating effect masks the fact that their minds cannot think or react clearly. In the disorienting "rapture," divers have been known to pull off their life-giving air supply, or swim the wrong way, toward a beautiful underwater mirage that is certain death. There is inherently something stupid about sin and its results.

Deceived and Destroyed by Pride

Some people read their own press releases, develop a life-long love affair with themselves, and believe they are above and beyond the basic responsibilities required of others. They are the exception to the rule. The Bible's clear commands become suggestions or options. Adrian Rogers gives us the answer. "Have you ever been around people who absolutely 'reek' with conceit? Some astute observer has expressed it: 'Conceit is a disease that makes everybody sick except the one who has it.' But the conceited person is the sickest of all. Intoxicated with self-importance and blinded to his own prideful sin, the conceited person thinks that by all his pompous pride and attention-getting actions, he is somehow going to gain the admiration of people – yet, he loses what he most wants, the honor of others."[12] "Pride cometh before destruction…" (Proverbs 16:18). "A man's pride shall bring him low…" (Proverbs

---

[12] Adrian Rogers, *God's Way to Health, Wealth and Wisdom,* p. 150.

29:23). Jerry Vines (1937-) adds, "The soul and the spirit are so close together only the Word of God can distinguish between the two (Hebrews 4:12). Talent emanating from a man's soulish nature can easily be mistaken for spiritual power."[13]

Two Dangers

1. Believing you will never yield to temptation.
2. Believing you cannot help but yield to temptation.

Victors Over Sexual Temptation

J. Oswald Sanders believed, "Sex attraction is perhaps the strongest lure of mankind."[14]

We all are living in a society that is saturated with sex. Sexual messages are included in the majority of commercials. Sexual products and services are common. Young people are engaging in sex early in their teen years like it is a game.

The best marriage, the best parents, the best friends, the best counselors, the best pastor, the best church, the best youth group cannot build a wall high enough to shut out this temptation.

---

[13] Jerry Vines, *Vines – My Life and Ministry*, p.224.
[14] J. Oswald Sanders, *Bible Men of Faith*, p. 39.

Since our present world is so saturated with sexual temptation, some have given in and given up. That should not be the response of a Christian.

"The Lord knoweth how to deliver the godly out of temptations..." (2 Peter 3:9)

"There hath no temptation taken you but such as is common to man: but God *is* faithful, who will not suffer you to be tempted above that ye are able; but will with the temptation also make a way to escape, that ye may be able to bear *it*." (1 Corinthians 10:13)

People must know what to do about sexual temptation *before* it happens, so when it does happen, they will know how to honor God. It is too late to make decisions *in* the temptation.

Joseph

As a young man of age twenty-seven in the first book of the Bible, Joseph, shows us that we can be victors over sexual temptation. We do not have to give in. We do not have to go along. We do not have to be overcome. We can be overcomers.

After having been sold into slavery in Egypt, Joseph's master had an aggressive wife who began to sexually pursue him. There are people who would drag us down to their level if we allowed them. Just like God uses people to *direct* us in His ways, so the devil uses people to *destroy* people by his ways.

Think about Joseph's temptation. It surfaced totally

unexpectedly. Everything was going as well as it could when out of nowhere this temptation came. That is what makes temptation a temptation—it catches us unexpectedly. It is like lightening when it strikes.

The temptation Joseph faced may have seemed irresistible. Surely, we must assume that Mrs. Potiphar was an attractive woman. If she was a worn-out, overweight, ugly hag, where would the temptation be? The temptation went on and on as she spoke to Joseph "day by day" (Genesis 39:10).

How did Joseph handle his hormones? How did Joseph withstand the tremendous pressure to "go with the flow" and when in "Egypt to do what the Egyptians do"?

There was clearly a strategy.

- Joseph *"refused"* (Genesis 39:8a). Joseph immediately said "no" to temptation.
- Joseph *reflected* about the consequences such behavior would have on his master and his Maker (Genesis 39:8b-9). Though he was only a young man, Joseph was wise enough to see the difference between lust and love. "...how can I do this great wickedness?" he asked. Joseph knew sin not only involved people, but ultimately all sin is against God. Even though Joseph had stood his ground the first time openly and verbally, temptation kept coming (Genesis 39:10). But Joseph made a big mistake. He was not as cautious as he should have been (Genesis 39:11). One day he found

himself in a compromising situation—he was in the house alone with Potiphar's wife. This was her opportunity. She caught Joseph by his garment and insisted that he carry out her wishes. Some people find themselves in compromising situations and then give in, only to regret it.

- Joseph *removed* himself (Genesis 39:12). As soon as Joseph saw what was about to happen, he "left...fled...got out." Now that says it all! Way to go, Joe! Joseph was determined to practice "safe sex" - no sex before marriage.

The full story of Joseph is he was falsely accused of sexual assault and spent two years in prison on a false charge. It is better to be in prison while maintaining one's sexual integrity and purity, than to be free having fallen to temptation.

Vigilant Against Sexual Temptation

You have heard it said, "An ounce of prevention is better than a pound of cure." This is an old English phrase that means it is better and easier to stop a problem from happening than to contain or correct it after it has started.

We practice prevention all the time. To provide the safest possible place for our families, we shut windows, lock doors, turn on alarms and remove valuables from the reach of those who would take them.

Doctors prescribe medications and treatments for their patients who have potentially debilitating and deathly physical conditions.

Mechanics suggest regular maintenance on vehicles to avoid being broken down on some lonely road.

One of the most outstanding preachers of the past was R. G. Lee (1886-1978), long-time pastor of Bellevue Baptist Church in Memphis, Tennessee. Dr. Lee compiled this outstanding record:

- 24,071 joined the church during his tenure, including 7,649 by baptism.
- The church grew from 1,430 members to 9,421.
- Lee taught his 400-member Bible class an average of 44 Sundays a year for nearly 38 years.

After retiring as pastor, he traveled some 100,000 miles a year preaching from Alaska to Australia to Asia, "night and day to bring the Gospel to as many people as possible." Dr. Lee preached his most famous sermon, "Pay Day, Some Day," 1,275 times, with an estimated three million hearing this great classic, resulting in some 8,000 professions of faith. Dr. Lee said that much of the time he travelled by himself. He made it a habit, while he was away from home, that in the late evening he would drink a glass of buttermilk and eat an onion sandwich. He said, "I drink the buttermilk so I can sleep. I eat the onion sandwich to make sure I sleep alone."

Everyone who desires to honor God must be similarly vigilant.

Slow down and look closely to the following ways we can protect ourselves against sexual sins and build a life of true holiness. Take a Bible and turn to the scriptures that are referenced.

- No neglect of salvation, Hebrews 2:3; Philippians 2:12-13.[15]
- No person is exempted, 1 Corinthians 10:12-13.
- No resistance to the Holy Spirit, Ephesians 4:30; 1 Thessalonians 5:19.
- No sin normalized, Proverbs 8:13, Proverbs 14:9; Ephesians 5:3-4, 8-12.
- No sex outside of marriage, Hebrews 13:4, Ephesians 5:3; Proverbs 6:32.
- No hesitancy to leave a sex-based non-marital relationship, 1 Corinthians 6:18; 2 Timothy 2:22; 1 Thessalonians 4:3.
- No life unrecoverable, John 8:3-11; 1 John 2:1-2.
- No sin covered, Proverbs 28:13; Hebrews 4:13.
- No transgression unconfessed, 1 John 1:9; Psalm 32, 38, 51.
- No mind unrenewed, Romans 12:2.
- No Bible unread, Job 23:12; Psalm 119:9-11; Matthew 4:1-11.
- No bending of the rules, Titus 2:11-12; Hebrews 12:14.

---

[15] If you are a Christian, "justification" has been secured for your past and "glorification" is assured for your future, the only salvation area left is present-day, on-going "sanctification."

- No thought unchallenged, 2 Corinthians 10:4-5, Philippians 4:8-9; Proverbs 23:7.
- No sight unguarded, Job 31:1; Matthew 5:28.
- No prayer unspoken, Luke 18:1; 1 Thessalonians 5:17.[16]
- No lack of church attendance, Hebrews 10:25; Ephesians 5:25; Acts 20:28, Ephesians 3:21.
- No confidence in the flesh, Philippians 3:3; Matthew 26:41; Romans 7:18.
- No place for the devil, Ephesians 4:27; James 4:7.
- No appearance of evil, 1 Thessalonians 5:22; Proverbs 4:14-15.
- No questionable friends, 1 Corinthians 15:33; 2 Samuel 13:3.
- No suggestive flattering, Proverbs 26:28
- No besetting sin tolerated, Hebrews 12:1.
- No warning sign ignored, Hebrews 3:7-8.
- No time unaccounted, Psalm 90:12.
- No part not surrendered, Exodus 21:5-6.

Does this list overwhelm you? Everybody wants solutions that are simple, easy to follow and taken care of in a few minutes. "Three easy ways….Four foolproof ways... Seven steps to... "

I hope your response is, "There is no way I can do all of these things all of the time!" Precisely, living a "G" rated life in an "X" rated world is impossible apart from God consuming your entire life – your spiritual life, your

[16] God's 24-hour emergency hotline is open: Psalm 50:15; Jeremiah 33:3.

emotional life, your physical life, your family life, your relational life, your work life, your recreational life – all of it.

God's Sovereign Position

As you go about your life from day to day remember this: while God is more than willing to assist you, He is not your assistant. Honor Him today as your Sovereign while you take your place as His servant. He is high and holy. He is majestic and mighty. He rules and reigns. His kingdom has no end. God claims us with greater power than all the governments of the world put together.

God's Saving Purchase

"What? know ye not that your body is the temple of the Holy Ghost *which is* in you, which ye have of God, and ye are not your own? For ye are bought with a price: therefore glorify God in your body, and in your spirit, which are God's." (1 Corinthians 6:19-20) God claims us with a greater price than all the gold and silver in the world. We are redeemed by the precious, priceless blood of Christ. We belong to God.

God's Sanctifying Purpose

God's purpose of salvation is not only to keep you out of hell, it is to get heaven into your life. It is "Christ in you the hope of glory" (Colossians 1:27), not "Christ and you." He alone is worthy of all praise. "Bring forth the royal diadem and crown Him Lord of all!" God wants us. God wants all of us. God wants all of us all of the time.

- *Surrender all your life.*
- *Surrender all that you have in life.*
- *Surrender all along the way to the very end of life.*

Part III: Looking Ahead

- 11 -

Coming to a Church Near You

The signs of the days to come for Christians and churches in America made an appearance during the Covid-19 pandemic in early 2020.

When the Bill of Rights was adopted by America's founding fathers on March 4, 1789, they recognized in the first line of the first amendment that our Republic would be a free religious people.

> Amendment 1: Congress shall make no law respecting an establishment of religion or prohibiting the free exercise thereof, or abridging the freedom of speech or of the press, or the right of the people peaceably to assemble and to petition the government for a redress of grievances.

America was founded to be a free people, freedom given by the Creator, not the government. Twenty-first century America is more and more trending toward secularism - the philosophy whose aim is to keep faith-based/religious ideology out of public life and policy.

Interestingly, during the pandemic abortion clinics, take-out restaurants, liquor stores, marijuana shops,

Walmart and Home Depot were considered "essential" and were allowed to stay open, but church assemblies were "non-essential" and were ordered closed.

Early in the requirement for "social distancing," Kentucky Governor Andy Beshear ordered that there be no churches assembling. He said if people show up at their church the state police would record attendees' license plates and notify them it is a misdemeanor violation of orders issued by state health officials. The governor went on to say, "Local health officials then will contact the people associated with those vehicles and require them to self-quarantine for 14 days. This is the only way we can ensure that your decision doesn't kill someone else."[1]

Being good citizens and understanding the danger of the pandemic to fellow Americans, churches accommodated and "live-streamed" services. So far so good.

As churches began preparing for Easter services many innovated by having drive-in services - gathering in the church's parking lot while listening on FM radio in their cars at a safe distance from other cars and with their windows rolled up.

Louisville, Kentucky, Mayor Greg Fischer said "no" to drive-in services in his city. He said he could not allow

---

1 Faith Karimi, Mallika Kallingal and Rebekah Riess, CNN, *Kentucky will take down License Plates of people Attending Easter services and order them to Quarantine,* April 11, 2020.

"hundreds of thousands" of people to be out when they needed to be home.

Thankfully, a circuit judge stepped in and overruled these actions as unconstitutional.[2]

Here is the point. The very *idea* that state or city officials would articulate and desire to initiate such unconstitutional actions is unthinkable. That they would even *suggest* such measures is a statement of what it will be like in the future. These are only some of many attempts that are likely to occur to remake America in the future.

"When the righteous are in authority, the people rejoice; but when the wicked beareth rule, the people mourn." (Proverbs 29:2)

Back in 1989, pollster George Gallup, Jr. said that sex-related issues would dominate the culture, and thus be a prominent issue for churches, in the foreseeable future. He was right.[3]

Stephen Baskerville believes "the greatest threat to religious freedom – and therefore to freedom generally – in the West today is sexual radicalism. Sexual radicalism is now on a direct collision course with the Christian faith. As predicted by a lesbian attorney in

---

[2] Andrew Wolfson, *Judge Rejects Louisville Mayor's Claim he was 'suggesting' Drive-through Services were Banned,* Louisville Courier Journal, April 14, 2020.

[3] *Christianity Today,* November 17, 1989. https://www.christianitytoday.com/ct/1989/november-17/tracking-americas-soul-our-nations-most-famous-pollster.html

1997, 'the legal struggle for queer rights will one day be a showdown between freedom of religion versus sexual orientation.' Today, when the two come into direct confrontation, freedom of religion almost always loses."[4]

Some Churches Are Capitulating to the LGBTQ Culture

The truth is, most churches have not just given up on basic morality, they are now accommodating open immorality. More and more churches are falling all over themselves, bowing to the pressure of the LGBTQ propaganda.

The United-Methodist as a denomination were not able to live up to their name. In May of 2021, it will become the divided-Methodist church, with a major number in the denomination separating over LGBTQ issues – officiating same-sex marriages and ordination of gay and lesbian ministers.

In 2016, Wilshire Baptist Church, Dallas, who separated from the Southern Baptist Convention and joined the Cooperative Baptist Fellowship, did so over the LGBTQ agenda. They ended up losing almost 400 members as a result of this decision. They now advertise themselves as an "inclusive" congregation, code for being open to the LGBTQ community. In 1991, they began ordaining women for ministry which also marks their liberal path. In 2018, they joined with Congregation Beth Torah and the Church of Jesus

[4] Stephen Baskerville, *The New Politics of Sex*, p. 216-217.

Christ of Latter-Day Saints who made up the small group *Dialogue Institute Dallas* to host a Ramadan dinner for those who practice Islam.

A.A. Davis (1900-1978), the pastor who preached the charge at my father's ordination in 1943 and was a lecturer on Baptist history, spoke about preaching on the Trail of Blood where his friend Dr. W. R. White (1892-1977) pastored at the First Baptist Church of Austin. Today, FBC Austin has become a "gay friendly" congregation, stating it "welcomes and wants people of every race, gender, sexual orientation, marital status, age, physical and mental ability, nationality, and economic station to thrive in the full life of our community." The pastor Rev. Dr. Griff Martin proudly says, "We have ordained gay deacons. We have done gay weddings. We are celebrating children of gay couples."

Calvary Baptist Church, in Washington D.C., is a 157-year-old congregation that was founded by abolitionists. In 2017, the church called Rev. Maria Swearingen and Rev. Sally Sarratt, a married lesbian couple, as co-pastors. The church is affiliated with the Cooperative Baptist Fellowship.

All three of the above-mentioned churches would serve the blood-bought Baptist name well by removing it from their identity.

Confusion reigns because many Christian groups fail to stand firmly on a solid scriptural doctrinal position which compels them to separate from those who choose to be in noncompliance.

The buildings known as the Church of the Holy Sepulcher in Jerusalem has a unique story. It has been occupied simultaneously by five Christian groups — Greek Orthodox, Roman Catholic, Arminian, Coptic and Ethiopian. These groups live under the same roof but hold separate worship services. They do so, not as a matter of respect, but as a matter of avoidance. Each claim ownership of the building. Their internal relationships are so combative that they cannot trust one another even to hold the keys to their presumed holiest sites. They are instead held by two Muslim families who have the responsibility every day of unlocking the door for a waiting public. This habit has gone on since the 11th century.

Conservative Churches Will More and More Be Targeted by the LGBTQ Culture

"Christians should accustom themselves to the thought that the American state no longer supports, in any meaningful sense, the laws of God, and prepare themselves spiritually for the prospect that it may one day formally repudiate them and turn against those who seek to live by them."[5]

As one of my preacher friends reminded me recently, "All the Christians' games are now away games."

We are among those whom sociologist Peter Berger called *"cognitive minorities"* - those who hold views

---

[5] Andrew Hartman, *A War for the Soul of America: A History of the Cultural Wars*, p. 215.

dissonant with wider society.[6]

> Allow a moment to make a necessary clarification in our confused world. When I use the word "church" I am referring to a "local, visible congregation of baptized believers in Jesus Christ who assemble for worship and minister under divine authority to obey the commission to carry the gospel to the ends of the world." Enough of this Protestant "invisible, universal church" foolishness that is *promoted* as the one "true Church," (e.g. C.I. Scofield, Charles Ryrie, etc.), while local congregations are *demoted* as only an expression or a miniature of the true church. The "invisible, universal church" teaching that it is the body of Christ is a coverup for the conflicting doctrines in different religious groups. All saved people are in the "family of God." Each New Testament church is a complete, fully operating "body of Christ" over which Jesus is the authoritative Head (1 Corinthians 12:27). Satan has his churches and preachers (2 Corinthians 11:14-15; Matthew 13:24-30, 36-43), as does God (1 Timothy 3:15; Acts 20:28). They are not compatible (2 Corinthians 6:14-18). That which distinguishes them is their teachings and order which are derived from an accurate understanding of Scripture, which is their sole and final authority. In all matters one must ask, in what way is truth being upheld or denied in our conclusions?

The New York City Commission on Human Rights released new guidelines in December 2015, regarding discrimination based on gender identity or expression. "Far too often, transgender and gender non-conforming individuals suffer discrimination, harassment, and

---

[6] Glynn Harrison, *The Sexual Revolution's Long Shadow*, www.bethinking.org

violence on a scale many cannot imagine," said Carmelyn P. Malalis, New York City Human Rights Commissioner. "New York City does not and will not tolerate discrimination on the basis of gender identity or gender expression. Today's guidance makes it abundantly clear what the City considers to be discrimination under the law and the Commission will continue to aggressively enforce protections to make that promise a reality. Every New Yorker deserves to live freely and safely, free from discrimination."[7] Most individuals and many transgender people use female or male pronouns and titles. Some transgender and gender non-conforming people prefer to use pronouns other than he/him/his or she/her/hers, such as they/them/theirs or ze/hir. Many transgender and gender non-conforming people choose to use a different name than the one they were given at birth. The intentional or repeated refusal to use an individual's preferred name, pronoun or title, repeatedly calling a transgender woman "him" or "Mr." after she has made clear which pronouns and title she uses can result in fines in New York City of up to $250,000, but these fines won't be handed out for accidentally misusing pronouns. According to the new guidelines, the commission can impose civil penalties of up to $125,000 for violations of the law and (in extreme circumstances) of up to $250,000 for violations that are the result of "willful, wanton, or malicious" conduct.

A *Washington Post* headline of October 29, 2019, was

---

[7] https://www1.nyc.gov/office-of-the-mayor/news/961-15/nyc-commission-human-rights-strong-protections-city-s-transgender-gender

clear, "Why America Needs Hate Speech Law." Yet, there is no agreement on the definition of what hate speech is and who gets to decide. The same media that insists on "freedom for all" does not seem to really mean it. "Tolerance" is another word that is tossed about freely. You have surely noticed, the more radical always demand that they are on the receiving end of the "tolerance," but are never expected to be on the giving end. At one time "tolerance" meant you can have your point and I can have mine, and if we can't come to a common conclusion we can agree to disagree. But today "tolerance" means you must accept, approve and celebrate other people's opinions and if you don't, you are bigoted, unintelligent, and intolerant. The same people who say there is no absolute truth, believe their position is absolutely better than yours...end of conversation.

Silenced

"So far, 80 cities and states have passed unconstitutional and ungodly laws banning people from receiving Christian counseling to fight unwanted same-sex attractions and dysphoric gender identities. In *Otto v. Boca Raton*, that Florida city has chosen to bow to the anti-science, anti-God LGBTQ agenda which seeks to silence anything – even the very Word of God – that might be used to dispel the LGBTQ lie. Not only has the city chosen to silence Christian counselors, they went so far as to mandate that even if patients want Christian counseling, they are not legally allowed to receive it. While on the surface this case appears to deal with only homosexuality, if allowed to stand, these counseling bans will be used as a precedent to ban other forms of Christian counseling as well as Christian speech itself. If we lose, this case will help set the legal precedent to apply Christian counseling bans across sectors of counseling – marriage, child rearing, social behavior and even God's order for the family and home. In short, this ban is a key strike in attempting to remove God's Word from the public square by preventing people from seeking godly counsel."[8]

How long will it be before the official government position is, "Christians are free to worship inside their facilities, but you must keep your so-called Bible principles to yourself." By law, Christians may be silenced, or they could be jailed.

Shamed

U.S. Department of Justice Attorney General William P. Barr told law students at Notre Dame, "We keep an eye out for cases or events around the country where states are misapplying the establishment clause in a way that discriminates against people of faith... The law is being used as a battering ram to break down traditional moral values and to establish moral relativism as a new orthodoxy."[9]

On March 27, 2020, during the Covid-19 pandemic, New York City Mayor Bill de Blasio singled out Christian and Jewish congregations and threatened that agents would shut down their houses of worship if they

---

[8] Mat Staver, Liberty Counsel, Quoted in *Sword of the Lord*, April 3, 2020, p. 18.

[9] William P. Barr, Attorney General, Remarks to the Law School and the de Nicola Center for Ethics and Culture at the University of Notre Dame, October 1, 2019.

held in-person services. "A small number of religious communities, specific churches and specific synagogues are unfortunately not paying attention to this guidance even though it's so widespread," de Blasio said. The Democrat mayor further warned that if the congregations refuse to disperse, the city would "take additional action up to the point of fines and potentially closing the building permanently."[10]

I will grant it that in moments of pressure and passion we are all capable of misspeaking. We have all done that. But that Mayor de Blasio even said it speaks volumes. Jesus said, "...out of the abundance of the heart the mouth speaketh." (Matthew 12:34)

It is not surprising that Mayor de Blasio has described himself as "spiritual but not religious." When you ask, "What does that mean?" you have arrived at your answer. It means anything and nothing.

Slammed

An op-ed writer for *The New York Times* blames evangelicals for the spread of the coronavirus in America — and that would mean white evangelicals, to be sure. The Times headline was bold and provocative: "The Road to Coronavirus Hell Was Paved by Evangelicals." Yes, "Trump's response to the pandemic has been haunted by the science denialism of his ultraconservative religious allies." According to Katherine Stewart, the author of the article, "Donald

---

[10] Samuel Smith, *Evangelicals slam NYC's Threat to 'permanently' Close Churches that Defy Coronavirus Order*, Christian Post, April 2, 2020.

Trump rose to power with the determined assistance of a movement that denies science, bashes government and prioritizes loyalty over professional expertise. In the current crisis, we are all reaping what that movement has sown."[11] Being an op-ed article doesn't require truthfulness, only opinion.

Shut Down

The real intent of some of those in government slipped out in the 2020 Democratic President campaign. CNN and the Human Rights Campaign Foundation hosted a town hall with nine Democratic presidential candidates on October 10, 2019, presenting their views on LGBTQ issues. Beto O'Rourke was asked whether he thought that "religious institutions like colleges, churches, charities should lose their tax-exempt status if they oppose same-sex marriage?"

In his typical blunt way, the former El Paso congressman answered: "Yes, there can be no reward, no benefit, no tax break for anyone or any institution, any organization in America that denies the full human rights and the full civil rights of every single one of us. And so as president, we're going to make that a priority and we are going to stop those who are infringing upon the human rights of our fellow Americans."[12]

However what is worse than a church losing their tax-exemption is losing the presence of the Lord. In the account of the Laodicean church in Revelation, chapter

---

[11] Katherine Stewart, *The New York* Times, March 27, 2020.

[12] Benjy Sarlin, *O'Rourke says Churches Against Gay Marriage, Should Lose their Tax Benefits, Draws Backlash,* NBC News, Oct 11, 2019.

three, you see a missing attendee. Jesus is on the outside knocking and asking for someone to open the door and allow Him to come in.

God's Churches Should be Models and Megaphones for Basic Morality

Rather than faulting the culture for its lack of basic morality, God's people and God's churches need to step forward and take at least part of the blame for the culture's immoral condition because we have failed to set a consistent biblical standard.

A mother was at her wit's end. Her two boys were totally out of control, terrorizing the whole neighborhood. One day the mom was next door at her friend's and poured out her woes. The friend offered a solution. She once had a similar problem with her little boy, and she took him to the nearby church and made him talk to the preacher. That took care of the problem. The distraught mother was desperate and decided to do the same thing. They were not a church-going family, but it was worth a try. She marched her boys down to the church and turned them over to the preacher. The preacher took the oldest boy into his office and said, "Young man, where is God?" The boy was petrified and didn't say a word. The preacher repeated the question, "Young man, where is God?" No response. A third time the preacher raised his voice, "Young man, where is God!" The boy jumped up, slipped past the preacher, grabbed his little brother in the next room and said, "Bubba, we've got to get out of here. They've lost God and they're trying to pin it on us!"

No one can question the fact that our American society has lost God. It is in the arena of morality that we will discover both what is missing and what is necessary.

The Reality of God has been Lost and Needs to be Found

While we may discuss and debate the existence of God, all reality begins with the reality of God. "...he that cometh unto God must believe that he is..." (Hebrews 11:6). A lack of that belief places a person in the category of a "fool." (Psalm 14:1) Maybe a clarification needs to be made here. God doesn't cease to exist because someone doesn't believe in His reality. God exists without anyone's permission. This is the point. Hebrews 11:6 says, "...he that cometh unto God must believe that he is, and *that* he is a rewarder of them that diligently seek him." The benefits of the reality of God only come to those who affirm His reality. When someone does not embrace the reality of God, they lose the rewards which come out of that reality. So, what else do they lose?

The Holiness of God has been Lost and Needs to be Found

When someone does not embrace the reality of God, he loses the reality of truth and what God is – God is a holy God. The holiness of God has been described as His "otherness" – His distance and difference from mankind. Everything about God sets Him apart from man. God's name is "holy." (Isaiah 57:15) The angels worship Him by crying, "Holy, holy, holy, is the Lord of hosts." (Isaiah 6:3) The Godhead is holy – the "Holy Father" (John 17:11), Jesus is "the Holy One of God" (Mark 1:24), and the Comforter is "the Holy Spirit"

(Luke 11:13). "God commands those whom he has separated from other people to be his people, that they should separate themselves from all that displeases him and is contrary to his will. Holiness of life is what he requires of all those whom he has brought into fellowship with himself."[13]

By way of cultural application, since this book is about the sexual consequences of decades past, it is impossible for God to make....

- An intellectual mistake because of His omniscience.
- A moral mistake because of His holiness.
- A mistake in judgment regarding man's behavior because of His justice.

The Fear of God has been Lost and Needs to be Found

When someone does not embrace the reality of God, he loses an understanding of the holiness of God, and subsequently then loses the fear of God. Think about how these are connected. The Bible says, "The fear of the Lord is the beginning of knowledge...and the beginning of wisdom." (Proverbs 1:7; 9:10)

"When you do not fear God, you will not fear sin. There is a direct relationship between a high view of God and a high view of sin. A low view of God will bring a low view of sin. When there is no fear of God there is no fear of sin."[14] **"Because sentence against an evil work is not executed speedily, therefore the heart of the sons**

---

[13] J. I. Packer, *God's Words – Studies of Key Bible Themes*, p. 173.

[14] Henry Blackaby, *Holiness*, p. 9.

of men is fully set in them to do evil. Though a sinner do evil an hundred times, and his *days* be prolonged, yet surely I know that it shall be well with them that fear God, which fear before him: But it shall not be well with the wicked, neither shall he prolong *his* days, *which are* as a shadow; because he feareth not before God." (Ecclesiastes 8:11-13) People often believe that if they do not feel or see any immediate consequences for their sin then everything is okay.

"If you lose the fear of God, there is nothing to restrain you."[15] ***"It is* a fearful thing to fall into the hands of the living God."** (Hebrews 10:31)

The Law of God has been Lost and Needs to be Found
God revealed Himself to Adam with a law that was to be obeyed (Genesis 2:16-17), with disobedience bringing death (immediate, progressive and ultimate). Since we are the offspring of our original parents, like them Adam's race does not appreciate imposed codes of duty and behavior. **"Whosoever committeth sin transgresseth also the law: for sin is the transgression of the law."** (1 John 3:4) Sin, at its root, is lawlessness. God's law knows no plea bargains, out of court settlements, or manipulating the system. It is God's law, which is perfect, on which we are reflecting, not man's law which is imperfect.

All these matters are tied together: the reality of God, His holiness, His appropriate reverence, His eternal moral law. Together these truths challenge modern, misguided views.

---

[15] Ibid, p. 15.

- All human life has value – pre-birth, end of life and everything in between.
- Sexuality that is not divinely ordered is deviant and destructive.
- Marriage is heterosexual, not homosexual.

Apart from the divine law of God we are only left with relativism where we pick and choose what we think is right or wrong.

Henry Blackaby (1935-) make a connection for us. "If I were to attempt to find the beginning of what I believe is a national neglect of God, I would return to the early 1960s. It seems as though God removed the hedge of protection from around America in that decade. We began to see unrestrained things take place from the '60s to this present day. There seems to have been nothing to hold back the tide of injustice in society. A deep departure from God in the churches has continued since that decade. It is as if the hedge of His protection has been broken down, and God is letting us experience the consequences of our own sin."[16]

The major problem of our culture is not in the *White House,* as bad as that can sometimes be. The major problem is in the *church houses,* the congregations of God-professing people. **"For the time *is come* that judgment must begin at the house of God: and if *it* first *begin* at us, what shall the end *be* of them that obey not the gospel of God?"** (1 Peter 4:17)

- Is it too much to ask of those who profess to

[16] Ibid, p. 20.

know and love Jesus Christ to live morally pure lives, and when they sin that they confess it humbly to Him?

"Submit yourselves therefore to God. Resist the devil, and he will flee from you. Draw nigh to God, and he will draw nigh to you. Cleanse *your* hands, *ye* sinners; and purify *your* hearts, *ye* double minded. Be afflicted, and mourn, and weep: let your laughter be turned to mourning, and *your* joy to heaviness. Humble yourselves in the sight of the Lord, and he shall lift you up." (James 4:7-10)

- Is it also unrealistic to expect that churches are to operate morally in distinction to the world's immorality?

  "Be ye not unequally yoked together with unbelievers: for what fellowship hath righteousness with unrighteousness? and what communion hath light with darkness? And what concord hath Christ with Belial? or what part hath he that believeth with an infidel? And what agreement hath the temple of God with idols? for ye are the temple of the living God; as God hath said, I will dwell in them, and walk in *them;* and I will be their God, and they shall be my people. Wherefore come out from among them, and be ye separate, saith the Lord, and touch not the unclean *thing;* and I will receive you, And will be a Father unto you, and ye shall be my sons and daughters, saith the Lord Almighty." (2 Corinthians 6:14-18)

- Is it beyond reason that churches should remove from their membership those who are openly living in sin and refuse to repent for their scandalous behavior?

  "I wrote unto you in an epistle not to company with fornicators: Yet not altogether with the fornicators of this world, or with the covetous, or extortioners, or with idolaters; for then must ye needs go out of the world. But now I have written unto you not to keep company, if any man that is called a brother be a fornicator, or covetous, or an idolater, or a railer, or a drunkard, or an extortioner; with such an one no not to eat." (1 Corinthians 5:9-11)

- How can we bear influence on our world if we have lost our moral zeal and maintain an attitude of noninvolvement?

  "Ye are the salt of the earth: but if the salt have lost his savour, wherewith shall it be salted? it is thenceforth good for nothing, but to be cast out, and to be trodden under foot of men. Ye are the light of the world. A city that is set on an hill cannot be hid. Neither do men light a candle, and put it under a bushel, but on a candlestick; and it giveth light unto all that are in the house. Let your light so shine before men, that they may see your good works, and glorify your Father which is in heaven." (Matthew 5:13-16) What good is salt

> if it has lost its flavor? It is good for nothing! Or what good is our light if it is under a basket?

The balance of humility and helpfulness is difficult, but not impossible. **"Create in me a clean heart, O God; and renew a right spirit within me... Restore unto me the joy of thy salvation; and uphold me *with thy* free spirit. *Then* will I teach transgressors thy ways; and sinners shall be converted unto thee."** (Psalm 51;10, 12-13)

Here is another difficult balance: not being judgmental while exhibiting reasonable judgment. It is not wrong to identify false doctrine and expose standards that are clearly unscriptural. We become judgmental when we assign people to utter condemnation. Ultimate judgment belongs to God alone (John 5:22; Acts 17:31). Eternal vengeance is God's prerogative (Romans 12:19). None of us should try to be God in these matters.

God's Churches are Agents of Hope As they Proclaim the Gospel

People in America don't need cleaning up. They need more than soap. Vance Havner (1901-1986) noted, "If they had a social gospel in the days of the prodigal son, somebody would have given him a bed and a sandwich, and he never would have gone home."

The need of the people of America is a radical change of mind and heart. Most people have not connected the dots: the majority of Americans do not share our morals because they do not share our Savior.

Most of the world believes the Christian message is understanding and obeying a demanding list of "dos" and "don'ts." In fact, it is a message of "done." God has already "done" everything that is necessary to forgive, deliver and transform any sinner who is willing to repent and trust what Jesus Christ has already "done" by His death and resurrection.

While the world can offer the pleasures of sin that only last for a season (Hebrews 11:25), God offers pleasures forevermore (Psalm 16:11).

Despite the aggressive nature of our current culture against Christians in America, we still have tremendous opportunity and influence wherever we are because of the hope-filled Gospel of Jesus Christ. The powerful message of God's love through His Son's death, burial and resurrection is still soul-saving, life-changing, and nation-altering.

Evangelist Bailey Smith (1939-2019) challenged Christians, "Change must start in your own heart, in your home, in your church – and spread out into your community, your city, your state, and across the length and breadth of this land. Too many followers of our supernatural Lord have acted as though there's nothing that can be done, as if the almighty, sovereign God cannot counter the wickedness all around us. What's more, many Christians have fallen back on the 'lite gospel,' fearful that if they speak out against sin they will become unacceptable and be considered politically incorrect. Instead of sounding the trumpet of light, we are tooting the piccolos of lite religion. Often what's being tooted is not worthy of being called Christianity.

We cannot continue to follow the line of least resistance!"[17]

Have we lost the will to fight against this revolution?

Studied Up

What are Christians to do? It is apparent and obvious – we can't hide from the intrusion of modern influence. It is everywhere. We are very much "in" the world (John 17:11), but we are not "of" the world (John 17:14, 16), yet we are sent "into" the world (John 17:18). What we can do is sharpen our biblical understanding and hold to its standards. It is that balance of "separation" with "engagement" that requires constant attention on our part. While understanding the danger and intrusion of the culture, we must arm ourselves with truth which sets us and others free (John 8:32).

Stirred Up

Peter wrote his second epistle with the intent to "stir up" his readers to the challenge they were facing (2 Peter 3:1). In Paul's final epistle he challenged the young preacher Timothy that he "stir up the gift of God" which he had received at his commissioning (2 Timothy 1:6). The idea of those words is to rekindle the fire that burned in his soul. A fire must be constantly stirred up lest it die out. At a time in Jeremiah's life when he was ready to give up, God's word was in his heart like a fire shut up in his bones and he could not quit (Jeremiah 19:9).

---

[17] Baily Smith, *Taking Back the Gospel*, p. 173.

Stand Up

Stand up, stand up for Jesus, Ye soldiers of the cross;
Lift high his royal banner, It must not suffer loss.
From victory unto victory His army shall he lead,
Till every foe is vanquished, And Christ is Lord indeed.
Stand up, stand up for Jesus, Stand in his strength alone;
The arm of flesh will fail you, Ye dare not trust your own.

Put on the gospel armor, Each piece put on with prayer;
Where duty calls or danger, Be never wanting there.
Stand up, stand up for Jesus, The strife will not be long;
This day the noise of battle, The next the victor's song.
To them that overcometh, A crown of life shall be;
They with the King of Glory Shall reign eternally.
George Duffield (1818-1888)

Our spiritual heroes were at one time "jail birds" because they stood up and stood openly for God.

- Joseph spent time in prison on a trumped-up charge of sexual assault (Genesis 39).
- John the Baptist was arrested and imprisoned for speaking out against King Herod's unlawful marriage, and ultimately beheaded (Matthew 14).
- Jeremiah was arrested and put in prison in Jerusalem during the Babylonian captivity because he was perceived as not being patriotic (Jeremiah 32).
- Paul and Silas were jailed at Philippi because they cast a demon out of a young lady whose owners were making money from her divination (Acts 16).

- Jesus, our Lord and Savior, was arrested, tortured and died the death of a Roman criminal for no sin of His own, but for ours.

Years ago, I was having Bible studies with a couple who had recently come to faith in Christ. She spoke about how being a Baptist was not a favored status. She was surprised she had encountered "internet ridicule." How will that compare to our Baptist forbearers who died by the millions as anabaptists because they stood against false doctrine and immorality.

Speak Up

"And they called them, and commanded them not to speak at all nor teach in the name of Jesus. But Peter and John answered and said unto them, Whether it be right in the sight of God to hearken unto you more than unto God, judge ye. For we cannot but speak the things which we have seen and heard." (Acts 4:18-20) **"... and when they had called the apostles, and beaten *them,* they commanded that they should not speak in the name of Jesus, and let them go. And they departed from the presence of the council, rejoicing that they were counted worthy to suffer shame for his name. And daily in the temple, and in every house, they ceased not to teach and preach Jesus Christ."** (Acts 5:40-42)

According to Ephesians 4:15 it is possible to speak the "truth in love." When we speak, we need to do so with clarity and charity; conviction with compassion; having the correct position with a corresponding correct disposition. Jesus was "... full of grace and truth" (John

1:14) and we can strive toward that lofty standard.

"But sanctify the Lord God in your hearts: and *be* ready always to *give* an answer to every man that asketh you a reason of the hope that is in you with meekness and fear:" (1 Peter 3:15)

"Holding fast the faithful word as he hath been taught, that he may be able by sound doctrine both to exhort and to convince the gainsayers. For there are many unruly and vain talkers and deceivers, specially they of the circumcision: Whose mouths must be stopped, who subvert whole houses, teaching things which they ought not, for filthy lucre's sake." (Titus 1:9-11)

"Keep yourselves in the love of God, looking for the mercy of our Lord Jesus Christ unto eternal life. And of some have compassion, making a difference: And others save with fear, pulling *them* out of the fire; hating even the garment spotted by the flesh." (Jude 21-23)

In Chuck Swindoll's book on preaching, *Saying It Well,* he told of being in chapel as a first-year student at Dallas Theological Seminary.

> "Dr. Dwight Pentecost spoke that morning. He made it his purpose to encourage us, to refuel our tanks, to help us keep going through the difficulties of living in tiny, uncomfortable spaces, eating on a shoestring budget, and studying late into the night only to get up early the next morning. The central theme of his

> message was simple: it's worth it.
>
> He closed his message with a personal story of his own trek through seminary. He and his wife, Dorothy (to whom he was married for sixty-two years before her death), had come to Dallas in the latter years of the Great Depression, just before the start of World War II. They lived in a makeshift trailer parked next to the seminary, since student housing didn't yet exist and few could afford apartments. To say 'times were tough" was an understatement.
>
> One night during supper, his wife said something that changed his perspective, and he wanted to share it with us. She said, 'Dwight, I've decided I'm no longer going to be discouraged. I've decided that as long as we live here, while we're preparing for ministry, we're going to live an abnormal life."
>
> Swindoll went on to write, "I don't know why, but those words completely shifted my paradigm. I realized that, sometimes, life takes on the 'abnormal' when you're in transition, when you're moving between one kind of 'normal' to another. Accepting and embracing 'abnormal' helps you do what needs to be done without losing heart."[18]

It is very likely we are going to live abnormal lives in America until Jesus returns. Let's embrace it with joyful submission and optimistic anticipation!

---

[18] Charles R. Swindoll, *Saying It Well*, pp. 239-240.

- 12 -

Things Aren't Coming Apart, They're Coming Together

If things are as bad as the previous chapters have laid out, why doesn't God step in and do something about it? What is God doing in our days? Is God doing anything at all?

There have been times in human history when God was silent. The prophet Habakkuk was complaining about what was going on in his nation and that God wasn't doing anything about it. God gave an answer to the prophet for why He was silent. **"Behold ye among the heathen, and regard, and wonder marvellously: for *I* will work a work in your days, *which* ye will not believe, though it be told *you*."** (Habakkuk 1:5). "Sometimes God allows us to live in the tension of His silence for a while."[1] The period between the Old Testament and New Testament was a time of 400 years of silence – there was not a word from any of God's prophets.

In our day, God is still speaking. Man is He speaking! **"See that ye refuse not him that speaketh. For if they escaped not who refused him that spake on earth, much more *shall not* we *escape*, if we turn away from him that *speaketh* from heaven: Whose voice then**

[1] Steve Farrar, *Get in the Ark*, p. 141.

shook the earth: but now he hath promised, saying, Yet once more I shake not the earth only, but also heaven. And this *word,* Yet once more, signifieth the removing of those things that are shaken, as of things that are made, that those things which cannot be shaken may remain. Wherefore we receiving a kingdom which cannot be moved, let us have grace, whereby we may serve God acceptably with reverence and godly fear: For our God *is* a consuming fire." (Hebrews 12:25-29)

God is speaking. The problem isn't that God is not speaking; the problem is that people act as though they are not listening. In fact, people often do not like what they hear God saying to them. This was the reaction of the Jewish people just before the city of Jerusalem was destroyed and they were taken away captive to Babylon. **"Moreover all the chief of the priests, and the people, transgressed very much after all the abominations of the heathen; and polluted the house of the LORD which he had hallowed in Jerusalem. And the LORD God of their fathers sent to them by his messengers, rising up betimes, and sending; because he had compassion on his people, and on his dwelling place: But they mocked the messengers of God, and despised his words, and misused his prophets, until the wrath of the LORD arose against his people, till *there was* no remedy."** (2 Chronicles 36:14-16)

God broke His silence as the New Testament begins, by sending John the Baptist. The people were not impressed with John's wardrobe or his diet, and especially not his style or his message.

If God is speaking to us today, what is He saying? God is saying, "The world is through *without* Jesus, but the world is not through *with* Jesus! Jesus is coming again!"

There are 318 references to Jesus' second coming in the 216 chapters of the New Testament. Read just a few of them.

- John 14:3 Jesus said, **"I will come again and receive you unto myself..."**
- Acts 1:11 The angels said, **"This same Jesus shall so come as ye have seen Him go..."**
- Hebrews 9: 28 affirms, **"So Christ was once offering to bear the sins of many; and unto them that look for him shall he appear the second time without sin unto salvation."**
- Hebrews 10:25 **"Not forsaking the assembling of ourselves together, as the manner of some is; but exhorting one another; and so much the more as ye see the day approaching."**
- Revelation 22:20 **"He which testified these things saith...."** Who is that? Jesus. **"...Surely I come quickly."** John cannot contain himself. **"Amen. Even so come, Lord Jesus."**

As you see the pieces of the prophetic puzzle coming together, you should be encouraged to understand that so many things are pointing to His coming. The curtain call is soon.

Have you given any thought to the possibility that we may be the generation that is living when the Lord Jesus returns?

When is Christ returning? Well, He could come at any moment. Jesus' instruction to us was not to "keep time," but to "keep watch."

With every passing day our "**...salvation is nearer than when we believed.**" (Romans 13:11)
Speaking of His second coming Jesus challenges us, "**Know that it is near, even at the door.**" (Matthew 24:33)

Jesus clearly said we "**...know not the day or the hour your Lord doth come,**" (Matthew 24:42), but it does not mean we should not concern ourselves with His coming. Many of the present-day false messiahs and cults, like the Seventh Day Adventists and the Jehovah's Witnesses, made predictions about the date of Jesus' return years ago...and not surprisingly, they were all wrong. In 1988 a man wrote a widely circulated paper giving "88 Reasons Why Jesus was Coming Again in 1988." He was wrong 88 times!

No one knows the time so don't waste your time, or anyone else's time, trying to guess the time.

Since Hebrews 9: 28 reminds us to "look" for Christ's return and 2 Timothy 4:8 promises a crown of righteousness unto all that "love" His appearing, we should be ready at any moment for Jesus to return.

Adrian Rogers believed, "We should be living as though Jesus died yesterday, rose this morning, and is coming back this afternoon."[2]

---

[2] Adrian Rogers, *The Comfort of His Coming*, p. 3.

Why should we believe Jesus' coming could be at any moment?

By searching the events of the day on the internet and by studying your Bible, you can understand a great deal about what is going on in the world. As a matter of fact, if you are paying close attention, you will likely know more than the President's top advisers!

Every year in March or April the world around us begins to change. Flowers begin to bud and bloom. Birds rediscover their songs. Spring is arriving. Then, months later you see geese honking their way south. You know fall and winter are on the way.

Jesus said certain events and calamities that will come at the end of this age are like labor pains that precede childbirth. He said those events were "the beginning of sorrows..." (Matthew 24:8) This word translated "sorrows" in Matthew 24 is translated in Galatians 4:19 as "travail in birth." The stages of "sorrows" are like birth pains.

In fact, since our original parents, Adam and Eve, fell in sin in the Garden of Eden, "the whole creation groaneth and travaileth in pain together until now." (Romans 8:22)

While modern medical achievements have altered some things, it has not changed the pain of childbirth. Mothers know how it goes. The baby starts kicking around months before he or she arrives. As the time of birth gets closer, there are mild indications that someone is on the way, but then the discomfort goes away. When "it's time," the pains are relentless. They are harder. They are faster. They are distressful beyond any man's understanding. Only women can inform us about this. Then the delivery pains come worse than the birth pains.

"For when they shall say, Peace and safety; then sudden destruction cometh upon them, as travail upon a woman with child; and they shall not escape." (1 Thessalonians 5:3).

> "We can ignore even pleasure. But pain insists upon being attended to. God whispers to us in our pleasures, speaks in our conscience, but shouts in our pains: it is His megaphone to rouse a deaf world…No doubt pain as God's megaphone is a terrible instrument; it may lead to final and unrepented rebellion. But it gives the only opportunity the bad man can have for amendment. it removes the veil; it plants the flag of truth within the fortress of the rebel soul."
>
> C.S. Lewis, *The Problem of Pain*[3]

Pain has always been one of God's greatest preachers, but more so at the end of this age.

The context of Matthew 24 indicates "signs" of the judgments will occur during the Tribulation era. The world we are living in is being set up for the seven years of Tribulation predicted in the Bible. Before the

---

[3] http://www.cslewisinstitute.org/C_S_Lewis_on_the_Problem_of_Pain_page3.

Tribulation begins, the rapture of God's saints will occur, which is the first phase of Jesus' second coming. There are two phases of Jesus' second coming.

The Second Coming of Jesus

Phase One: *Rapture*	Phase Two: *Revelation*
• In the air • "For" His saints • Comes as a Thief in the night • Rewards believers • Blessed hope	• To the earth • "With" His saints • Every eye shall see Him • Judges unbelievers • Glorious appearance

Things aren't coming apart; they are coming together!

Charles H. Dyer advises, "No one will know exactly when God's prophetic clock will begin ticking, but we should expect God to begin arranging the stage for the final act of his drama. The stage may yet be empty of actors, but if all the props are in place and the house lights begin to dim, you can be sure the final act is soon to begin."[4]

Israel is in Place in Her Homeland

The nation of Israel has been in her homeland since 1948. The tiny country of Israel is the geographic center of the earth. "This is Jerusalem: I have set thee in the midst of the nations and countries round about her." (Ezekiel 5:5) Zechariah 12:2 and 3 predicted, **"Behold, I will make Jerusalem a cup of trembling unto all the people round about, when they shall be**

[4] Charles H. Dyer, *The Rise of Babylon,* p. 207.

in the siege both against Judah *and* against Jerusalem. And in that day will I make Jerusalem a burdensome stone for all people: all that burden themselves with it shall be cut in pieces, though all the people of the earth be gathered together against it." The more trouble there is in Israel the closer we are to the second coming.

The Nations are Gathering for the Last Days

Jesus said the time before His return will be marked by "wars and rumors of wars." (Matthew 24:6). A study of human history is basically a study of wars. A "rumor" of war breaks out on the other side of the world and it is now covered immediately on satellite television. Any cessation in wars among people only means they are reloading for the next war.

Russia and Iran

The Russian ("the king of the north") and Iranian (Persia) alliance is in place as predicted in Ezekiel 38:5. These are strange bedfellows – communists partnering with Islamists. Without going into detail, look at this comment made by C.I. Scofield (1843-1921). "That the primary reference is to the northern (European) powers, headed up by Russia, all agree. The whole passage should be read in connection with 'Magog,' his land. The reference to Meshech and Tubal (Moscow and Todolsk) is a clear mark of identification. Russia and the northern powers have been the latest persecutors of dispersed Israel, and it is congruous both with divine justice and with the covenants (e.g. Gen. 15:18, note; Deut. 30:3, note) that destruction should fall at the climax of the last made attempt to exterminate the remnant of Israel in Jerusalem."[5]

Keep in mind, Dr. Scofield wrote this in 1909 when Israel had not become a nation. They were still a "dispersed" people. Also, it was a time at the end of the Russian Czars and just before the country's civil war broke out in 1918. Scofield could not know Russia would later become a world power apart from the Bible.

The Asian Nations

The global threat from the east is predicted for the last days. Revelation 16:12-16 predicts "kings of the east," which could include China, North and South Korea, Japan and India, will muster a mammoth army. Hal Lindsey calls this army "the yellow peril."[6] Revelation 9:16 speaks of a 100-million-man army that will come against Israel. The actors are in place. The stage is set. All that remains is for God to lift the curtain and for this dreadful drama to begin. In the second phase of Jesus' return He will reveal Himself as "the King of kings and Lord of lords" at the great battle of Armageddon (Revelation 19:11-18).

Unprecedented Natural Disasters Are Occurring

Natural disasters, which aren't so natural, will mark the time before Christ returns. **"And there shall be signs in the sun, and in the moon, and in the stars; and upon the earth distress of nations, with perplexity; the sea and the waves roaring; Men's hearts failing them for**

---

[5] C. I. Scofield, *Scofield Reference Bible*, p. 883.
[6] Hal Lindsey, *The Late Great Planet Earth*, p. 70.

fear, and for looking after those things which are coming on the earth: for the powers of heaven shall be shaken." (Luke 21:25-26) Jesus said, **"...there shall be famines, and pestilences, and earthquakes, in divers places."** (Matthew 24:7)

Pestilences

The word "pestilences" in Matthew 24:7 means "plagues" and is only one of several cosmic catastrophes. We can now add to the Spanish flu, smallpox, polio, Asian flu, Legionnaires disease, Swine flu, influenza, malaria, AIDS, SARS, Ebola, the recent Covid-19 pandemic of 2020. Covid-19 reached 210 countries worldwide with in excess of 12.5 million cases and 560,000 recorded deaths as of July 2020. Unlike some diseases before, one of the factors for the rapid and far-reaching spread was modern travel – airplanes, subways, buses and cruise ships.

Beyond the epidemics and pandemics, those of us who are last days people have our own unique diseases – heart disease, cancer, high blood pressure, diabetes... on and on. The pressure and pace of modern life is killing all of us slowly, but surely.

Famines

As the Covid-19 virus was spreading over the globe, East African countries, including Sudan, South Sudan, Ethiopia, Yemen, Uganda, Somalia, Kenya and Tanzania, were battling swarms of locusts. The headlines read, "Along with climate shocks, conflict and acute food insecurity, the East Africa region now faces a hunger threat from Desert Locust. This is a scourge of biblical proportions." These locusts eat their weight daily. An estimated 20.2 million people are now facing severe acute food insecurity."[7]

Look at what is ahead for those who will live during the Tribulation because they have refused to receive Christ into their lives. **"And the fifth angel sounded, and I saw a star fall from heaven unto the earth: and to him was given the key of the bottomless pit. And he opened the bottomless pit; and there arose a smoke out of the pit, as the smoke of a great furnace; and the sun and the air were darkened by reason of the smoke of the pit. And there came out of the smoke locusts upon the earth: and unto them was given power, as the scorpions of the earth have power. And it was commanded them that they should not hurt the grass of the earth, neither any green thing, neither any tree; but only those men which have not the seal of God in their foreheads. And to them it was given that they should not kill them, but that they should be tormented five months: and their torment *was* as the torment of a scorpion, when he striketh a man. And in those days shall men seek death, and shall not find it; and shall desire to die, and death shall flee from them. And the shapes of the locusts *were* like unto horses prepared unto battle; and on their heads *were* as it were crowns like gold, and their faces *were* as the faces of men. And they had hair as the hair of women, and their teeth were as *the teeth* of lions. And they**

[7] Christopher Carbone, *Coronavirus Makes It Hard to Battle Swarms of Locusts Ravaging Africa*, Fox News, March 31, 2020) https://www.foxnews.com/science/coronavirus-makes-it-harder-to-battle-swarms-of-locusts-ravaging-africa

had breastplates, as it were breastplates of iron; and the sound of their wings *was* as the sound of chariots of many horses running to battle. And they had tails like unto scorpions, and there were stings in their tails: and their power *was* to hurt men five months. And they had a king over them, *which is* the angel of the bottomless pit, whose name in the Hebrew tongue *is* Abaddon, but in the Greek tongue hath *his* name Apollyon. One woe is past; *and,* behold, there come two woes more hereafter." (Revelation 9:1-12)

Earthquakes

While the world was dealing with the Covid-19 virus and famine in East Africa, the Croatian capital, Zagreb, was hit by a 5.4 magnitude earthquake, its biggest in 140 years, causing damage and injury. Jesus said in the last days there would be **"earthquakes in divers** (different) **places..."** (Matthew 24:7) Luke's gospel adds, "great earthquakes." (Luke 21:11)

John MacArthur says, "The global increase in disease, hunger, and natural disasters will torment humanity. It will seem as if the world itself is beginning to disintegrate."[8]

Moral Collapse

We are living in a morally mixed up world. Jesus pointed to the "days of Noah" and the "days of Lot" as typifying the conditions of the days prior to His return. The biblical account of Noah's days is found in Genesis 4-6.

---

[8] John F. MacArthur, *The Second Coming*, p. 93.

"And GOD saw that the wickedness of man *was* great in the earth, and *that* every imagination of the thoughts of his heart *was* only evil continually. And it repented the LORD that he had made man on the earth, and it grieved him at his heart." (Genesis 6:5-6)

Jesus also said of the last days, "Iniquity shall abound," (Matthew 24:12). The word "iniquity" here means "lawlessness." This lawlessness doesn't seem to be only that of human anarchy, although we have seen in 2020 rioting and looting in America. I am wondering if this refers to personal and national "defiance against God's laws." Sin is no longer hidden – it is now given special status, protection under civil rights law, and is publicly celebrated. Don't be deceived. Things that human governments have declared legal do not make them lawful in the eyes of God.

See for yourself how far we have gone in the wrong direction morally: fornication, adultery, divorce, abortion and same-sex marriage hardly gather any attention anymore.

One-World Government, Economy and Religion is Staging

The idea of a one-world government is being advanced by many world leaders. On March 26, 2020, former UK Prime Minister Gordon Brown called for a "temporary" global government to fight the impact of Covid-19. This would be an international taskforce to distribute medicine, equipment and built multilateral cooperation. It would be led by the G20 and the United Nations.[9]

Brown had previously spoken at the G20 Summit in 2009, stating, "I think the new world order is emerging and with it the foundations of a new and progressive era of international cooperation."[10]

The one-world government of the Tribulation period that follows the rapture will be coupled with a one-world economic system (the Mark of the Beast - Revelation 13) and a one-world religious system (the Great Whore – Revelation 17-18).

.

"Technology has brought our world together. In addition, many religious organizations (the World Council of Churches, the United Religions, the Parliament of the World's Religions, and the InterFaith Movement, for examples) are working hard to bring about a one-world reality."[11]

The Anti-Christ is on the Scene

The anti-Christ is already on the scene. Did you know that?

---

[9] www.independent.co.uk, March 26, 2020. https://www.independent.co.uk/news/uk/home-news/coronavirus-gordon-brown-global-government-un-g20-covid-19 a9427376.html?fbclid=IwAR150w6FtJKrJNoDGiYyntHAlkKJp0327XFj_4L3VptRNxoQZB2QfG2V028

[10] https://beholdisrael.org/former-british-prime-minister-gordon-brown-voices-support-of-one-world-government/

[11] Wayne Grudem Editor, *Biblical Foundations for Manhood and Womanhood,* Peter R. Jones p. 261.

- **"Little children, it is the last time: and as ye have heard that antichrist shall come, even now are there many antichrists; whereby we know that it is the last time."** (1 John 2:18)
- **"And every spirit that confesseth not that Jesus Christ is come in the flesh is not of God: and this is that *spirit* of antichrist, whereof ye have heard that it should come; and even now already is it in the world."** (1 John 4:3)
- **"The mystery of iniquity doth already work...and then shall that Wicked be revealed..."** (2 Thessalonians 2:7-8).

There have been men who would qualify as the Antichrist since the days of the apostles. The Antichrist cannot come until the authentic Christ has returned at the rapture. The Antichrist cannot come until the restrainer, the Holy Spirit and God's churches and Christians, have been removed (2 Thessalonians 2:6-7; Matthew 5:13-14).

- We're not looking for the antichrist; we are looking for the authentic Christ.
- We're not looking for the undertaker; we should be looking for the upper taker!

The Bible never encourages us to attempt to identify "who" the antichrist will be - Nero, Napoleon, Hitler, Stalin, Henry Kissinger, Bill Clinton, Al Gore, George W. Bush, Barack Obama, or Donald Trump. You don't need to figure out who the antichrist is, because if you do you will have been left behind and that's bad news for you!

Antichrist will rule a world-government. He will allow and establish a world-religion with multiple beliefs, a spiritual stew, finally declaring himself to be god.

There will be Increasing Hostility toward Christ and His People in the World

"Then shall they deliver you up to be afflicted, and shall kill you: and ye shall be hated of all nations for my name's sake. And then shall many be offended, and shall betray one another, and shall hate one another." (Matthew 24:9-10).

As previously noted, "As Christians, all our games are away games." We no longer have a "home-field" advantage. **"Yea, and all that will live godly in Christ Jesus shall suffer persecution. But evil men and seducers shall wax worse and worse, deceiving, and being deceived."** (2 Timothy 3:12-13)

The Days Prior to Jesus' Return will be Marked by Spiritual Apostasy

"Now the Spirit speaketh expressly, that in the latter times some shall depart from the faith, giving heed to seducing spirits, and doctrines of devils; Speaking lies in hypocrisy; having their conscience seared with a hot iron; Forbidding to marry, *and commanding* to abstain from meats,..." (1 Timothy 4:1-3) **"For the time will come when they will not endure sound doctrine; but after their own lusts shall they heap to themselves teachers, having itching ears; And they shall turn away *their* ears from the truth, and shall be turned unto fables."** (2

Timothy 4:3-4)

Jesus said of the last days, **"And because iniquity shall abound, the love of many shall wax cold."** (Matthew 24:12). A "falling away," an apostasy will separate those who only profess a belief in Christ but have never been born again. (2 Thessalonians 2:2-3). Our times qualify as the "falling away" before Christ returns in His glory.

"Apostasy is something that doesn't happen overnight. It happens over an extended period of time, as a person's faith becomes eroded, weakened, damaged, and then destroyed."[12]

Many churches are becoming exactly what the Bible declares of the Laodicean church. They are neither hot nor cold – they are lukewarm (Revelation 3:15). And where was Jesus? He was outside their assembly, standing at the door, knocking, pleading for any individual to open and allow Him to come in (Revelation 3:20).

The Gospel of Jesus Christ will Go Out to All Nations

Even in the worst of times God has a remnant who will be going about to do His work. Jesus both prophesied and promised, **"And this gospel of the kingdom shall be preached in all the world for a witness unto all nations; and then shall the end come."** (Matthew 24:14)

Jesus mentioned the faithfulness of Noah in Matthew

---

[12] Greg Laurie, *The Great Compromise*, p. 5.

24:37-39. God's warning of judgment by Noah had been ignored. While Noah was a boat-builder, 2 Peter 2:5 says he was also a "preacher of righteousness." J. Dwight Pentecost remarked, "Noah preached the longest sermon in history, a one-hundred-year sermon, but the only converts he had were his own family. The rest, occupied with routine activities, were indifferent to the warning."[13]

Things are not coming unraveled – they are unfolding. They are not collapsing – they are coming together.

Of this we can be certain.

- God alone knows all the future.
- God alone controls all the future.
- God alone can be trusted with your future.

God is still on the throne,
and He will remember His own:
Tho' trials may press us and burden distress us,
He will remember His own:
His promises are true, He will not forget you,
God is still on the throne!

What is the world coming to? It is ultimately coming to Jesus.

"Wherefore God also hath highly exalted him, and given him a name which is above every name: That at the name of Jesus every knee should bow, of *things* in heaven, and *things* in earth, and *things* under the earth; And *that* every tongue should confess that

[13] J. Dwight Pentecost, *Prophecy for Today*, p. 190.

Jesus Christ *is* Lord, to the glory of God the Father." (Philippians 2:9-11)

Every cult, every creature, every celebrity, every celestial being will gather before Jesus, bend their knee and confess with their tongue, "Jesus Christ is Lord, to the glory of God the Father."

"...The kingdoms of this world are become *the kingdoms* of our Lord, and of his Christ; and he shall reign for ever and ever." (Revelation 11:15)

"Bring forth the royal diadem and crown Him Lord of all."

"Until the trumpet sounds or death comes to usher us into eternity, we are to keep our eyes on the Savior (Hebrews 12:2). **"And when these things begin to come to pass, then look up, and lift up your heads; for your redemption draweth nigh."** (Luke 21:28) Whatever else is coming in the future, we can rest assured that Jesus is coming again!"[14]

---

[14]Ed Hindson, *The Popular Encyclopedia of Bible* Prophecy, p. 365.

Bibliography

Tim Adler, *Deadline,* October 5, 2011.

Kerby Anderson, *Point of View Radio Talk Show,* January 22, 2016. https://pointofview.net/viewpoints/absolute-truth/

Ryan T. Anderson, PhD, *The Left is Shunning Liberals with Concerns about Transgender Agenda,* The Heritage Foundation, Jan 29, 2019. https://www.heritage.org/gender/commentary/the-left-shunning-liberals-concerns-about-transgender-agenda

Andy Andrews, *How Do You Kill 11 Million People?* Thomas Nelson, Nashville, TN, 2011.

A & E History Channel, *The 1960s - The Decade that Changed a Nation,* Waterbury Publications, Inc., New York, NY, 2019.

Deborah Anapol, Ph,D, *Whatever Happened to the Sexual Revolution,* www.psychologytoday.com August 15, 2012.

Answers in Genesis, *Social Issues,* Hebron, KY, 2009.

Francesca Bacardi, *Miley Cyrus Talks Coming Out as Pansexual,* ENews, October 11, 2016.

Emery H. Bancroft, D.D. (1877-1944), *Elemental Theology,* Zondervan Publishing, Grand Rapids, MI, 1977.

George Barna, *The Frog in the Kettle* Regal Books, Ventura, CA, 1990.

BBC News, https://www.bbc.com/news/health-51676020.

William P. Barr, Attorney General, The United States Department of Justice, Remarks to the Law School and the de Nicola Center for Ethics and Culture at the University of Notre Dame, October 1, 2019.

Paul Barreca, *Jesus, the Ultimate Man,* Sermon Central, October 5, 2014.

Stephen Baskerville, *The New Politics of Sex,* Angelico Press, Kettering, OH, 2017.

Henry Blackaby, *Holiness,* Thomas Nelson, Nashville, TN, 2003.

Max Blau, *STAT forecast:* Opioids could kill nearly 500,000 Americans in the next decade," June 27, 2017. https://bit.ly/2OQVCAY

Martin and Deidre Bobgan, *Psychology's Influence in the Sexual Revolution,* midnightcall.com.

Robert H. Bork, *Slouching Toward Gomorrah,* Regan Books/HarperCollins, New York, NY, 1996.

Mark Bradshaw, Personal correspondence, June 10, 2020.

Dave Breese, *Seven Men who Rule the World from the Grave,* Moody Press, Chicago, Il, 1990.

Jerry Bridges, *The Practice of Godliness,* Navpress, Colorado Springs, CO, 1983.

Susan Brink, *Selecting Boys Over Girls is a Trend in More and More Countries,* National Public Radio, August 26, 2015.

D. Stuart Briscoe, *Holy Living in a Hostile World,* Harold Shaw Publishers, Wheaton, IL, 1982.

D. Stuart Briscoe, *The Communicator's Commentary,* Word, Waco, TX, 1982.

Daniel Burke, *The Methodist Church Will Probably Split over Homosexuality, and that's bad for all of us,* CNN, January 17, 2020.

Michael W. Chapman, *Dr. Fauci on Tinder Hookups During COVID-19: 'If You Want to Go More Intimate ... That's Your Choice'*, CNS News.com, April 17, 2020.

Christopher Caldwell, *The Age of Entitlement,* Simon & Schuster, New York, NY, 2020.

Christopher Carbone, *Coronavirus Makes It Hard to Battle Swarms of Locusts Ravaging Africa,* Fox News, March 31, 2020. https://www.foxnews.com/science/coronavirus-makes-it-harder-to-battle-swarms-of-locusts-ravaging-africa

Christs Carras, *Daniel Radcliffe on J.K. Rowling's anti-trans tweets: 'Transgender women are women'*, The Los Angeles Times, June 9, 2020.

Francis Collins, Director of the National Institute of Health, quoted by Adam Mabry, *Life and Doctrine,* Altheia Resources, Cambridge, MA, 2014.

Rebecca L. Collins, Victor C. Strasburger, Jane D. Brown, Edward Donnerstein, Amanda Lenhart and L. Monique Ward, *Sexual Media and Childhood Well-being and Health,* American Academy of Pediatrics, November 2017.

Krista Conger, *Of Mice, Men and Women,* Sex, Gender and Medicine, Spring 2017.

Dr. Larry Crabb, *The Silence of Adam,* Zondervan Publishing, Grand Rapids, MI, 1995.

Rene Denfeld, *The New Victorians,* Simon and Schuster, London, 1995.

Lilian Diarra, *The Culture Trip,* January 24, 2017. https://theculturetrip.com/africa/ghana/ articles/ghana-s-slave-castles-the-shocking-story-of-the-ghanaian-cape-coast/

Johnny Diaz, *Pixar Short Film 'Out' Features Studio's First Gay Main Character,* New York Times, May 24, 2020.

Ryan Dobson, *Be Intolerant,* Multnomah Publishers, Sisters, OR, 2003.

Charles H. Dyer, *The Rise of Babylon,* Tyndale House Publishers, Inc, Wheaton, IL, 1991.

Bob Dylan, The Times They are a-Changin', Song Lyrics, 1963.

Stephanie Ebbert, *Sex Work or Sexual Abuse?* Boston Globe, Dec. 16, 2019.

Mary Eberstadt, *How the West Lost God,* Templeton Press, West Conshohocken, PA, 2013.

Mary Eberstadt, *The Elephant in the Sacristy,* Weekly Standard, June 17, 2002.

Jonathan Elliot, Debates of the Adoption of the Federal Constitution – Vol. 5, 1787, J. B. Lippincott Co, Philadelphia, PA, 1845.

Zachary Evans, *National Review,* February 19, 2020.

Familylife.com, *Casualties of the Sexual Revolution.*

Steve Farrar, *Get in the Ark,* Thomas Nelson Publishers, Nashville, TN, 2000.

https://www.firstcoastnews.com/article/news/local/pastor-darrell-gilyard-breaks-silence-on-his-fall-from-grace/271089581

Vin Gallo, *State's Kid Governor is Making Her Mark,* Journal Inquirer, September 12, 2019.

Travis Gilbert, sermon *Christian Clarity in the Midst of Culture Shift*, Faithful Men's Conference, October 8, 2019.

Andre Goncalves, *Should We Stop Having Children in Order to be Truly Sustainable and Save the Planet?* September 19, 2018. www.youmatter.world.

Billy Graham Evangelistic Association, *The High Cost of Free Love,* Decision magazine, Feb. 2, 2017.

Jenny Gross, *Daniel Radcliffe Criticizes J.K. Rowling's Anti-Transgender Tweets,* The New York Times, June 7, 2020.

Wayne Grudem, *Biblical Foundations for Manhood and Womanhood,* Crossway Books, Wheaton, IL, 2002.

Amy Gunia, *Time* magazine, April 9, 2020.

Rich Harris, *The National Center for Missing and Exploited Children.*

Andrew Hartman, *A War for the Soul of America: A History of the Cultural Wars,* University Press, Chicago, IL, 2015.

Marie Hartwell-Walker, Ed.D., *Children Who are Home Alone,* pyschcenteral.com, Oct. 8, 2018.

https://psychcentral.com/lib/children-who-are-home-alone/

Vance Havner, *In Times Like These,* Fleming H Revell Company, Old Tappan, NJ, 1969.

Healthline.com, Everything You Need to Know About Pornography 'Addiction'

https://www.healthline.com/health/pornography-addiction

Healthline.com, *Here's What to Know About Having a Baby Who Is Intersex.*

https://www.healthline.com/health/baby/what-does-intersex-look-like#considerations

Daniel R. Heimbach, *True Sexual Morality*, crossway Books, Wheaton, IL, 2004.

Howard G. Hendricks, *Heaven Help the Home*, Victor Books, Wheaton, IL, 1985.

https://www.heritage.org/life/commentary/planned-parenthoods-annual-report-out-heres-what-you-need-know

Roy Hession, *Forgotten Factors*, Christian Literature Crusade, Fort Washington, PA, 1976.

Ed Hindson, *The Popular Encyclopedia of Bible* Prophecy, Harvest House Publishers, Eugene, OR, 2004.

David Hocking, *The Rise and Fall of Civilization*, Multnomah, Portland, OR, 1989.

Dominic Holden, *Most LGBTQ Americans Actually Love Having Cops And Corporations In Pride Parades*, Buzzfeed, June 24, 2019.

Angela Howard & Sasha Ranae Adams Tarrant, *Reaction to the Modern Women's Movement - 1963 to the Present*, Routledge Publishing, New York, NY, 1997.

Richard H. Howe, Southern Evangelical Seminar Video Series.

Huffpost, *Deadnaming a Trans Person is Violence*, March 17, 2017.

Emily Jacob, *New York Post*, February 24, 2020.

Robert Jeffress, *Hell? Yes!* Waterbrook Press, Colorado Springs, CO, 2004.

David Jeremiah, *I Never Thought I'd See the Day*, FaithWords, New York, NY, 2011.

David Jeremiah, *Slaying the Giants in Your Life*, W Publishing Group, Nashville, TN, 2001.

Fred Kaeser Ed.D., Psychology Today, Sept 23, 2011.

Emilie Kao, The Heritage Foundation, January 15, 2019.

Emilie Kao, *We Must Fight the Sexualization of Children by Adults*, The Heritage Foundation, October 5, 2019. https://www.heritage.org/marriage-and-family/commentary/we-must-fight-the-sexualization-children-adults

Shelia Kaplan. C.D.C. Reports a Record Jump in Drug Overdose Deaths Last Year, *New York Times*, Nov. 3, 2017.

Faith Karimi, Mallika Kallingal and Rebekah Riess, CNN, *Kentucky will take down License Plates of people Attending Easter services and order them to Quarantine*, April 11, 2020

Shannon Keaton, *Polls Find Lesbians Are Only 16 Percent of the LGBTQ Population in America*, BuzzFeed, June 15, 2018.

Michael H. Keller and Gabriel J.X. Dance, *The New York Times*, September 29, 2019.

Emily Larsen, *Elizabeth Warren Claps as CNN Invites 9-year-old Transgender Boy to Ask Her a Question*, Washington Examiner, October 10, 2019.

Greg Laurie, *The Great Compromise*, Word Publishers, Dallas, TX, 1994.

C.S. Lewis, *Joyful Christian*, Simon and Schuster, New York, NY, 1977.

Liberty Council, https://lc.org/sandra2

Hal Lindsey, *Satan is Alive and Well on Planet Earth,* Zondervan Publishing House, Grand Rapids, MI, 1972.

Taylor Lorenz, *The Atlantic,* June 22, 2018.

James Love, personal correspondence.

John MacArthur, *The MacArthur New Testament Commentary - Matthew 1-7,* Moody Press, Chicago, IL, 1985.

John MacArthur, *Daily Readings from the Life of Christ,* Moody Press, Chicago, IL, 2008.

John MacArthur, *The Battle for the Beginning,* W Publishing Group, Nashville, TN, 2001.

John F. MacArthur, *The Second Coming,* Crossway Books, Wheaton, IL, 1999.

John MacArthur, *The Vanishing Conscience,* Word Publishing, Dallas, TX, 1994.

J.W. MacGorman, *Romans: Everyman's Gospel,* Convention Press, Nashville, TN, 1976.

Samantha McLaren, *15 Gender Identity Terms You Need to Know to Build an Inclusive Workplace,* LinkedIn Talent Blog, May 20, 2019.

https://www.merriam-webster.com/dictionary/pornography

Albert Mohler, Jr., *Southern Seminary Winter 2014,* Vol. 82, No. 1.

Albert Mohler, Jr., *Answers in Genesis* Magazine, April 1, 2013.

Elizabeth McDade-Montez, PhD, *New Media, Old Themes: Sexualization in Children's TV Shows,* March 18, 2017.

Leon Morris, *The Apostolic Preaching of the Cross,* Baker Books, Grand Rapids, MI, 1968.

Jennifer R. Morse, *The Sexual State,* TAN Books, Charlotte, SC, 2018.

www.nationalreview.com/corner/julian-castro-on-abortion-one-2020-democrat-hit-the-gas-pedal/

nbcdfw.com, February 25, 2020.

David A. Noebel, *Understand the Times,* Summit Press, Manitou Springs, CO, 2006.

OHCHR Report on Sexual Orientation and Gender Identity, Family Watch International, 2011.

John Owen, *Sin and Temptation,* Sovereign Grace Publication, Inc, Lafayette, IN, 2001.

J. I. Packer, *God's Words – Studies of Key Bible* Themes, Baker Book House Company, Grand Rapids, MI, 1989.

PBS, *The Pill and the Sexual Revolution,* https://www.pbs.org/wgbh/americanexperience/features/pill-and-sexual-revolution/

J. Dwight Pentecost, *Prophecy for Today,* Discovery House Publishers, Grand Rapids, MI, 1989.

John Phillips, *Exploring 1 Corinthians,* Kregel Publishing, Grand Rapids, MI, 2002.

John Phillips, *Exploring Genesis,* Kregel Publishing, Grand Rapids, MI, 1980.

John Phillips, *Exploring Romans,* Kregel Publishing, Grand Rapids, MI, 1969.

Ivor Powell, *Bible Pinnacles*, Kregel Publications, Grand Rapids, MI, 1985.

Nelson L. Price, *The Emmanuel Factor*, Broadman, Nashville, TN, 1987.

Dr. Georgia Purdom, *The Biology of Gender*, Answers in Genesis.com, January 14, 2019.

Todd S. Purdum, staff writer, *The Atlantic, April 26, 2019.*

Jonathan Rauch, "What I Learned at AEI," *The Public Interest 156*, Summer 2004.

President Ronald Reagan in a speech on Socialized Medicine in 1961.
https://www.youtube.com/watch?time_continue=82&v=AYrlDlrLDSQ&feature=emb_title

Wilhelm Reich, *The Sexual Revolution*, The Noonday Press, New York, NY, 1962.

Daniel Reynolds, *"Meet the Transgender Doctor Leading Pennsylvania's Covid-19 Response,"* Advocate, March 31, 2020.

Bradford Richardson, *The Washington Times,* June 14, 2016.

Roy Riffle, *Sesame Street Announces New Transgender Character*. Gish Gallop. https://www.gishgallop.com/sesame-street-announces-new-transgender-character/

Adrian Rogers, *God's Way to Health, Wealth and Wisdom*, Broadman, Nashville, TN, 1987.

Adrian Rogers, *The Comfort of His Coming,* Booklet, Love Worth Finding Ministries, Memphis, TN.

Cleon L. Rogers Jr & Cleon L. Rogers III, *The New Linguistic and Exegetical Key to the Greek New Testament,* Zondervan Publishing House, Grand Rapids, MI, 1998.

David Roper, *Out of the Ordinary,* Discovery House Publishers, Grand Rapids, MI, 2003.

Robert Royal, *Transgenderism and Perfect Freedom,* www.thecatholicthing,org, June 17, 2019.

Melian Sally, Smithsonian Magazine, June 3, 2019. https://www.smithsonianmag.com/smart-news/new-york-city-monument-will-honor-transgender-activists-marsha-p-johnson-and-sylvia-rivera-180972326/

J. Oswald Sanders, *Bible Men of Faith,* Moody Press, Chicago, IL, 1974.

Benjy Sarlin, NBC News, *O'Rourke says Churches Against Gay Marriage, Should Lose their Tax Benefits, Draws Backlash,* Oct 11, 2019.

Francis and Edith Schaeffer, *Everybody Can Know,* Tyndale House Publisher, Wheaton, IL, 1973.

Francis A. Schaeffer, *The God Who is There,* Inter-Varsity, Downers Grove, IL, 1968.

Francis A. Schaeffer, *The Great Evangelical Disaster,* Crossway Books, Westchester, IL, 1984.

Brandon Showalters, *The Christian Post,* March 3, 2020.

Brandon Showalte, *JK Rowling Explains Views on Transgenderism: 'I refuse to bow down',* The Christian Post, June 12, 2020.

Chris Sikich, *Indianapolis Star,* March 1, 2020.

SimilarWeb, March 1, 2020.

Gary Smalley and John Trent, *The Gift of Honor*, Thomas Nelson, Nashville, TN, 1987.

Baily Smith, *Taking Back the Gospel*, Harvest House Publishers, Eugene, OR, 1999.

Zachary Smith, Hyperallergic.com, May 30, 2019. https://hyperallergic.com/502763/marsha-p-johnson-and-sylvia-rivera-are-getting-a-permanent-monument-in-new-york-city/

Darrell W. Sparks, *Taking Temptation Seriously*, Theophilus Publishers, Aurora, IN, 2016.

Peter Sprigg, "'Gender Identity' Protections ('Bathroom Bills')," Family Research Council, July 2010. http://www.frc.org/onepagers/gender-identity-protections-bathroom-bills.

R. C. Sproul, *The Revolution That Enslaves*, www.ligonier.org/learn/articles/revolution-enslaves/ January 1, 2017.

Todd Starnes, Oct 29, 2019, https://patriotpost.us/opinion/66420-texas-school-district-mandates-teaching-kids-how-to-have-anal-sex-2019-10-29

Mat Staver, Liberty Counsel, Quoted in *Sword of the Lord*, April 3, 2020.

Gloria Steinem, On Feminism and Transgender Rights, YouTube, Nov. 24, 2015. https://www.youtube.com/watch?v=cEBckvXs-u8

Kathy Steinmetz, "The Transgender Tipping Point – America's Next Civil Rights Frontier" Time magazine, June 9, 2014.

Jarrett Stepman, *The Left's Long War on Parents Over Schooling Their Kids*, The Daily Signal, April 23, 2020.

John Stott, *Same-Sex Relationships*, The Good Book Company, North America, 2017.

Lee Strobel, *God's Outrageous Claims*, Zondervan, Grand Rapids, MI, 2005.

Andrew Sullivan, *Unveiled: The Case Against Same-Sex Marriage Crumbles*, New Republic, August 13, 2001.

Gillian Swanson, *Antifeminism in America: A Historical Readers*, Editors Angela Howard & Sasha Rames Adams Tarrant. Routledge, Abingdon, OX, 2009,

Charles R. Swindoll, *Saying It Well*, Faith Works, New York, NY, 2012.

Charles Swindoll, *The Tale of the Tardy Oxcart*, Word, Nashville, TN, 1998.

Jack R. Taylor, *After the Spirit Comes*, Broadman Press, Nashville, TN, 1978.

The Heritage Foundation, *We Must Fight the Sexualization of Children by Adults*, Oct 5, 2019.

Major W. Ian Thomas, *The Saving Life of Christ*, Zondervan Publishing Co, Grand Rapids, MI, 1977.

Jia Tolentino, *Mike Pence's Marriage and the Beliefs That Keep Women From Power*, The New Yorker, March 31, 2017.

Elmer Towns, *Praying the Lord's Prayer*, Regal, Ventura, CA, 1997.

Trans Student Educational Resources, www.reachout.com

https://www.unfpa.org/gender-biased-sex-selection

https://usiaht.org/about-us/

USA Today, October 8, 2019.

https://www.vanityfair.com/hollywood/2015/06/caitlyn-jenner-bruce-cover-annie-leibovitz

Robert VerBruggen, *How the Sexual Revolution Unfolded,* The National Review, December 3, 2017.

Jerry Vines, *Vines – My Life and Ministry*, B & H Publishing, Nashville, TN, 2014.

Hannah Yasharoff, *USA Today*, December 27, 2018.

Washington Examiner, *Coronavirus Exposes Planned Parenthood's Biggest Lie*, April 2, 2020.

https://www.washingtonexaminer.com/opinion/coronavirus-exposes-planned-parenthoods-biggest-lie?utm

Washington Post, August 14, 2019.

Stu Weber, *Four Pillars of a Man's Heart*, Multnomah Books, Colorado Springs, CO, 1997.

Raquel Welch, CNN opinion article, *It's Sex O'clock in America*, May 8, 2010. https://www.cnn.com/2010/ OPINION/05/07/welch.sex.pill/index.html

Glenna Whitley, *The Second Coming of Billy Weber*, D Magazine, July 1989.

Jeanna Wise, *"Please don't misgener me": Reported Calls Pa. health secretary 'sir' multiple times during interview*, Pennsylvania Real-Time News, May 13, 2020.

Andrew Wolfson, Judge Rejects Louisville Mayor's claim he was 'suggesting' Drive-through Services were Banned, Louisville Courier Journal, April 14, 2020.

Ravi Zacharias, *Can Man Live Without God*, Word Publishing, Dallas, TX, 1994.

Other Books Available

by
Minister-at-Large Jerry D. Locke
LWBC Publications
4020 Caribou Trail
Fort Worth TX 76135
jdlocke@lakeworthbaptist.org
817-825-8991
www.lakeworthbaptist.org

STILL a Baptist...neither angry nor ashamed of it
History of New Testament churches & Baptists distinctives
10 chapters, 318 pages

Does God Care? 3 Stewardship Truths God wants you to know and live by
4 chapters 144 pages

NO DOUBT About It...for those who struggle with assurance of salvation
8 chapters, 103 pages

Nine Holy Habits...shaping, strengthening and sustaining our daily walk with God
10 chapters, 163 pages

What Kind of Love is This?...an honest evaluation of our love for God
10 chapters, 162 pages

Believers in Babylon...a biblical strategy for surviving in an anti-Christian America
10 chapters, 153 pages

What's Next?...a layman's guide for 21st century Bible prophecy
14 chapters, 215 pages

Pardon Me...Please...being forgiven and forgiving
13 chapters, 191 pages

The Gospel Truth...exposing 18 false gospels
22 chapters, 332 pages

Cross Examination...24 investigations of the greatest event in human history
24 chapter, 268 pages

Now That You've Believed...A Discipleship Guide for Spiritual Growth
13 chapters 65-page booklet